- The
Power of
Human Needs in
World Society

– The Power of Human Needs in World Society

edited by
Roger A. Coate
and
Jerel A. Rosati

Lynne Rienner Publishers • Boulder & London

To our families and friends

Published in the United States of America in 1988 by
Lynne Rienner Publishers, Inc.
948 North Street, Boulder, Colorado 80302

and in the United Kingdom by
Lynne Rienner Publishers, Inc.
3 Henrietta Street, Covent Garden, London WC2E 8LU

Library of Congress Cataloging-in-Publication Data

The Power of human needs in world society.

   Includes index
    1. Basic needs. 2. International relations.
I. Coate, Roger A.   II. Rosati, Jerel A., 1953-
HC79.B38P68 1988   338.9   88-11650
ISBN 1-55587-091-0 (alk. paper)

British Library Cataloguing in Publication Data
A Cataloguing in Publication record for this book
is available from the British Library.

Printed and bound in the United States of America

The paper used in this publication meets the requirements of the
American National Standard for Permanence of Paper
for Printed Library Materials Z39.48-1984. ∞

Contents

Foreword

This is a landmark book. Historically, "power politics" has dominated thought and policies; military and economic power have been held to be the main determinants of political relationships. Yet protest movements, reflecting deeply held feelings, have brought societies out of conditions of feudalism, slavery, and colonialism; there have been movements for racial and sexual equality; Vietnam protests; and fundamentalist revolutions—each evidence of a power greater than institutional power. But despite these realities, political philosophers and political scientists have clung to their power definition of "political realism."

Now we have in this book recognition not only that the power of human needs has been the dominating influence in politics over the longer term, but that now, in an age in which communications telescope time, it is the determining factor in the shorter term as well (and the shorter term is contracting). Institutions and policies that conflict with deeply ingrained human developmental needs, such as the need for recognition, are failing to achieve even immediate goals.

We now recognize that while material interests are negotiable, there is human behavior that cannot be coerced, and values and needs that are not negotiable. This means that for the first time we have a reliable basis for prediction, and therefore, for policy formation. Many consequences must be faced, especially by powerful nations. For example, adversarial negotiation must give place to problem solving so that nonnegotiable issues can be accommodated; this means that symptoms of problems, such as gang warfare and ethnic conflicts, must be recognized as symptoms and treated at their source, not just suppressed.

There is much yet to be explored. Just as the particles of the atom are known to exist even though their character is not yet clear, so we do not yet have a language to describe needs, or even any clear identification of what they are. Nonetheless, this book will stimulate further thinking about the concept of needs and its impact on politics.

The academic community is greatly indebted to Roger A. Coate and Jerel A. Rosati of the University of South Carolina, who have sponsored, edited, and written for this book. They provide important insights with which to assess domestic and foreign policies.

The community of policymakers also owes a great deal to these two scholars. At a time when policies of containment are failing, when repressive regimes imposed on countries by greater powers are requiring more and more costly support, when terrorism and other forms of protest are widespread, and when ethnic majorities seek unsuccessfully to impose majority government on minorities, this book makes a major contribution.

John W. Burton

Preface

The theme of this book is simple and yet has important consequences for understanding the world around us. As the title suggests, human needs are a powerful source of explanation of human behavior and social interaction in international relations. It is the existence of individual needs that makes society possible and necessary: human beings must interact in order to satisfy their needs. All politics, then, including global politics, are inextricably tied to processes and outcomes related to the satisfaction or deprivation of human needs. Thus, it is the interaction of people in the pursuit of needs in social settings that underlies and gives meaning to politics.

All individuals have needs that they strive to satisfy, either by using the system and working within the norms of mainstream society, or by socially deviant behavior in the form of withdrawal, acting on the fringes (e.g., criminal behavior), or acting as a reformist or revolutionary (e.g., mass movement behavior). Given this condition, social (including international) systems must be responsive to individual needs—or be subject to instability and forced change (possibly through violence or conflict). Therefore, it is the interaction of individuals and groups, who are attempting to prevent deprivation and promote the satisfaction of their needs in a social context, that provides the foundation for international politics.

The purpose of this book is to build on the interest and work that have already been generated in a number of disciplines to demonstrate how needs theory can improve our understanding of the general field of international relations. In focusing on human needs, the book deals with a concept that is consistent with much of the theoretical and empirical work currently being conducted in international relations. Realist, liberal, and Marxist approaches all share some crucial underlying assumptions about the nature and power of

ix

human needs, but these typically go unexamined. This book attempts to correct this deficiency by demonstrating explicitly the power of human needs in explaining human and international behavior.

The book aims at improving understanding of international relations in two main ways. *First*, a human needs perspective helps us understand the growing complexity that exists in an increasingly interdependent, pluralistic, and technologically advanced world society. People in one part of the world are increasingly affected by decisions and events in other parts—politically, economically, culturally. The rise of anti-colonialism, nationalism, and competing ideologies and religions has resulted in greater diversity of global thought. Third World states have become more prominent, as have non-state actors such as international organizations, transnational corporations, liberation movements, and terrorist groups.

This complexity is reflected in new issues on global agendas—hunger, poverty, terrorism, human rights, trade, resource allocation, dependency, financial indebtedness, pollution, ecological decay—issues that now accompany traditional policy concerns. But traditional approaches to the study of international relations, especially realism, do not address or explain many of them. A human needs approach can show the link between human needs satisfaction/deprivation and the emergence of problems and issues on the global agenda.

Second, the book endeavors to enhance our interdisciplinary understanding of the world around us. This is done by drawing on a concept that transcends a number of intellectual fields and applying it explicitly to the study of international relations. The concept of human needs (and human nature) has always been of importance in the human sciences—most intellectual traditions have been based implicitly on fundamental assumptions of human needs. More recently, scholars have begun to use this concept explicitly to explain human behavior (e.g., Maslow's work in psychology on a hierarchy of needs), and is beginning to be reflected in the area of politics and international relations, although most of the work has been limited to political philosophy and international development (e.g., Ross Fitzgerald, ed., *Human Needs and Politics,* Pergamon, 1977; Katrin Lederer, ed., *Human Needs,* Oelgeschlager, Gunn & Hain, 1980; Johan Galtung, *The True Worlds,* Free Press, 1980; Patricia Springborg, *The Problem of Human Needs and the Critique of Civilization,* Allen & Unwin, 1981; Han S. Park, *Human Needs and Political Development,* Schenkman, 1984; David Braybrooke, *Meeting Needs,* Princeton University, 1987). This work is intended to give additional impetus to a human needs approach to the study of international affairs.

The book represents a collective effort originating in a transnational study group that germinated at the University of South Carolina (USC) in 1983. The group was initially composed of three people: Roger Coate and

Jerel Rosati from USC, and John Burton, who was the International Studies Association Visiting Scholar at USC from the University of Kent. The group was subsequently broadened by the addition of Chadwick Alger from Ohio State University and Craig Murphy from Wellesley College. The group has met a number of times over the last several years to discuss needs theory and has presented panels and papers on the topic at professional conferences.

The Power of Human Needs in World Society is primarily based on original contributions by the study group members, but it also contains previously published work by other selected authors. Unlike the case in many edited volumes, which lack a coherent theme or framework, the interaction and contributions of the members of this transnational study group provide a fundamental coherence to the entire volume. Indeed, the planning of the book has been a group effort and reflects its multidisciplinary orientation (political science, international studies, sociology, political philosophy, political psychology) and multinational background (U.S., Australian/British, Canadian, Norwegian, Indian).

In addition to those mentioned above, there is a large number of people who played an important role in making this book possible. John Creed, Rick Haeuber, Steve Hook, Bill Kreml, Bobby Phillips, Dan Sabia, and Kurt Will provided valuable comments and assistance. Charles Kegley, Earl Black, Bill Mishler, and Don Puchala were kind enough to provide critical support in helping the project along. We thank them, and also the Department of Government and International Studies (GINT) and the Institute of International Studies of the University of South Carolina. Dave Carroll was instrumental in improving the overall direction and quality of the book, as well as bringing it to fruition. Sandra Hall, Lori Joy, and the GINT staff were most helpful in completing the manuscript. We would also like to acknowledge the role our students played, both at the undergraduate and graduate level, in getting us to think and rethink the concept of human needs and its application to the study of international relations. Finally, we would like to thank Pat and Jessica Coate, and Jo, Kristen, and David Rosati for their constant support and unending patience.

Roger A. Coate
Jerel A. Rosati

CHAPTER ONE

Human Needs in World Society

ROGER A. COATE and JEREL A. ROSATI

In introducing this volume, Roger Coate and Jerel Rosati provide an overview of a human needs approach and its relevance to the study of international affairs. The authors emphasize the importance of a human needs approach for explaining and understanding the complexities of the world today. They provide an overview of the interdisciplinary development of needs theory, describing its explicit use in political philosophy and international development and its implicit use in the study of international relations. They then review work by Paul Sites and John Burton that directly accounts for social and political behavior through the power of human needs. The argument is a simple, yet important, one. Individuals, interacting with other individuals in groups, attempt to pursue and fulfill their needs. However, if societies and social structures are unresponsive to human needs, they become increasingly unstable over time and suffer from a crisis of legitimacy. Thus, it is the interaction of networks of individuals and groups that results in the dynamic and complex phenomenon of international politics. The authors conclude by laying out a number of important questions that remain to be addressed in order to fully develop a human needs approach to the study of international relations. This book represents an initial search for answers that contributes to improved understanding.

Coate and Rosati are both Associate Professors of Political Science at the University of South Carolina. Coate's work focuses on the theory and practice of international organization. Most recently, he is the author of Unilateralism, Ideology and American Foreign Policy: The U.S. In and Out of UNESCO. *Rosati's work focuses on the theory and practice of foreign policy, with an emphasis on political psychology and U.S. foreign policy. He is the author of* The Carter Administration's Quest for Global Community: Beliefs and Their Impact on Behavior.

Changes in international relations during the twentieth century have brought to the attention of North American practitioners and social scientists alike an underlying complexity which had until recently been generally ignored. An exclusive focus on major power rivalry, interstate war, and other military and diplomatic affairs of state, which characterizes much traditional international relations scholarship, no longer seems adequate for confronting many emerging research problems and global issues. Such traditional concerns now share center stage on global agendas with other persistent issues. Hunger, poverty, terrorism, human rights, trade, financial indebtedness, pollution, and a myriad of other issues do not fit neatly into traditional conceptions of the proper domain of the field of study. These issues not only refuse to go away, but play increasingly important roles on global agendas.

Also, new and diverse participants have emerged as important actors on the global stage. The rise of anti-colonialism and nationalism has led to a proliferation of states. In addition, formal alliances, international organizations, transnational corporations, financial institutions, liberation movements, religious orders, ethnic movements, terrorist groups, and other entities increasingly interact alongside national state units. Assumptions limited to rational state actors, pursuing power and other national interests, seem somehow less relevant for explaining much of what is of interest in contemporary international affairs.

The study of international relations needs to develop and work from an orientation that is based on assumptions that reflect more realistically the complexity and flexibility of human interactions inherent in international relations. Such assumptions must be empirically grounded, flexible, and broad-based. A new "realism," which will embrace yet extend far beyond the old, is needed for addressing international issues in a world of greater interdependence, pluralism, and complexity. In this chapter and in those that follow, we will explore a human needs approach that attempts to capture such realism.

This approach proceeds from the belief that individual and collective pursuit of needs and values form the underlying core of social and international behavior and must be explicitly incorporated into our basic assumptions about human behavior and international relations. It is argued that a human needs approach can provide an adequate foundation for the development of empirical, as well as normative, theory relevant for understanding certain previously elusive aspects of international relations.

A HUMAN NEEDS APPROACH

While there is no universal agreement concerning the exact nature of these needs and their relationship to values and interests, there is a growing understanding that, however defined, needs must serve as a primary element of social science research. According to Christian Bay:

"Need" shall refer to any requirement for a person's survival, health, or *basic* liberties; basically meaning that, to the extent that they are inadequately met, mental or physical health is impaired. Thus, "need" refers to necessities for not only biological survival but also for the health and development (physical and mental growth) of persons as human beings.[1]

There is a developed body of literature (both experimental and documentary) in the social sciences that clearly demonstrates that individuals have fundamental human needs and that if they are deprived of those needs, especially in their early years of development, they will suffer physically and psychologically.[2] Human needs do exist and can provide the basis for empirical theories of politics.

A human needs perspective certainly is not new in the study of social relations. There has been a convergence across a variety of disciplines in this regard. A number of anthropologists, philosophers, political scientists, psychologists, sociologists, sociobiologists, and other scientists have focused on the importance of the concept of human needs in understanding human behavior. For example, scholars have recognized that the development and stability of individual beliefs are heavily dependent on the human needs that beliefs fulfill. This position was initially popularized by psychoanalytic theorists such as Sigmund Freud, Harold Lasswell, and Eric Fromm, culminating in *The Authoritarian Personality*, which argued that beliefs were dependent on ego-defensive needs. Developmental psychologists and other scholars such as Jean Piaget, Eric Erikson, and Abraham Maslow have emphasized that beliefs also fulfill more positive human needs of individuals.[3]

Not only is there growing support for the assumption that there exist specific and relatively enduring human needs, certain scholars have argued that individuals will inevitably strive to satisfy their needs, even at the cost of social disruption and personal disorientation.[4] In any event, social processes and outcomes related to the satisfaction or deprivation of such needs are very much political phenomena.

Two intellectual traditions have explicitly adopted a human needs approach to understand political phenomena. First, the concept of human needs has received considerable attention in the area of political theory. All political theories, whether conservative, liberal, Marxist, or derived from some other set of values—western or non-western—are based on assumptions of human needs. Patricia Springborg, for example, in *The Problem of Human Needs and the Critique of Civilization,* has demonstrated that human needs has been a central concept in the language of Stoicism, classical tragedy, Augustinian Christianity, Enlightenment discourse, and

Marxism.[5] Although much of political theory has been implicit in its assumptions about human needs, many theorists have been more explicit. The emphasis has been on the delineation of the "true needs" of individuals and an analysis of different polities in terms of their levels of individual fulfillment or deprivation.[6]

The second intellectual tradition which has explicitly adopted a human needs approach has been in the area of development. Studies of Third World, regional, and global development have been heavily influenced by the concept of "basic human needs." The work has been based on both empirical and normative efforts to identify minimal standards of basic human needs, to determine levels of human needs deprivation, and to recommend how such needs can be satisfied.[7]

In fact, most intellectual traditions developed by social scientists and philosophers have been based on some fundamental assumptions of human nature and needs. "Contemporary experience and the history of political thought confirm the existence of many different, and conflicting, models of man. And different models of man and conceptions of human ends, goals or purposes will generate different catalogues of 'needs'."[8] According to Stanley Renshon:

> Many examinations of political phenomena rely, either implicitly or explicitly, on assumptions about human motives. These range from concepts of the politically ideal from Aristotle to Wolin, to assumptions of maximisation and utility in mathematical decisionmaking models. Yet the role of psychological explanation in general, and personality theories in particular, remains controversial and not infrequently neglected. Given the ubiquity of psychological assumptions in political explanation more focused attention might have been expected: but then, what's assumed is rarely examined.[9]

In other words, the study of human behavior always rests on assumptions— whether explicit or implicit—about the nature of human beings.

Unexamined assumptions about basic human nature and needs have provided the foundation for the major competing theoretical paradigms in the study of international relations, including power politics realism, liberal idealism, and Marxism.   In power politics realism, it is assumed that individuals are primarily motivated by their need for security, power, and prestige. These needs are personified to the state and consequently give rise to the anarchical interstate system and power politics. Liberal idealists, on the other hand, tend to support the quest for global peace and prosperity through the promotion of interdependence, international law, and organizations, which are based on the individual pursuit of rationality, freedom, and enlightenment. Marxists perceive a dominant capitalist world system based on private ownership and the maximization of profit which results in the alienation, exploitation, and dehumanization of the individual.

Therefore, they argue for the necessity of a global transformation to world socialism that would be responsive to and satisfy the individual needs of rationality, freedom, labor, and community.[10]

Although the power politics realist, liberal idealist, and Marxist paradigms all are based on fundamental assumptions about human nature and needs, most writers have not been explicit in identifying the link between human needs and political processes.[11] Furthermore, the three paradigms have been selective in identifying only a few needs of individuals as the foundation for the development of their theory. In order to provide a fuller understanding, it is necessary to be more explicit and comprehensive about the importance of human needs as a fundamental source of human motivation and behavior.

The preceding analyses indicate that the concept of human needs might well serve as a solid foundation for the development of empirical theory to explain the evolution and dynamics of human social relations in world society more generally. In this light, *international politics* can be defined as those social processes, based on individual interaction in pursuit of needs satisfaction, through which resources and values are allocated in an authoritative manner—that is, in such a way as to exercise controlling or determining influence over the distribution of valued outcomes. Thus, the individual pursuit of human needs appears to be a fundamental dynamic force underlying political and international relations.

THE POWER OF HUMAN NEEDS

A number of scholars have explicitly attempted to integrate the concept of human needs into the study of political processes. Davies utilizes the needs conceptualization of Maslow as the foundation for explaining the evolutionary stages of political development.[12] Sites discusses the role of needs as explicitly or implicitly incorporated in the the writings of Maslow, Thomas, Fromm, Durkheim, Parsons, and Homans in order to explain the roots of social order and change.[13] Furthermore, Burton focuses on the concept of human needs as discussed by Sites in order to explain the evolution of national and global political processes.[14]

Although Davies, Sites, and Burton recognize important differences among the various conceptualizations of needs, they all conclude that the concept of needs is of critical importance for the development of social theory. "The point we wish to make here is that basic needs do exist and that they are more universal, and less specifically cultural, than some behavioral scientists would have us believe."[15]

Sites identifies the following eight human needs: consistency of response; stimulation; security; recognition; justice; meaning; rationality;

and control. He argues that the second four emerge out of the dynamics of the socialization process. Suggesting that "the last four needs emerge because the first four . . . are not and cannot be immediately and consistently satisfied," he allows that the need for justice, the need for meaning, the need to be seen as rational, and the need to control might more accurately be treated as "desires." However, he continues to refer to them as needs, arguing that "in practice the motivational dynamics involved tend to be similar or the same as those of the first four needs."[16]

Furthermore, Sites argues that the existence of needs makes society necessary. Human beings must interact in order to fulfill such needs and they need to control those aspects of the environment which are essential for needs satisfaction.[17] Thus, individuals enter into social relationships with others. The need for such control also gives rise to the possibility of being controlled by others. Therefore, the resulting need to promote and sustain valued relationships makes society possible and affects the evolution of society.[18]

For Sites, the satisfaction and deprivation of individual human needs is the key source of societal order and change.

> The influence of individual needs is many times stronger than the influence of the social forces which play upon man. That is, the individual is willing to go outside the socially acceptable way of behaving in order to seek gratification for more basic needs. He is willing to violate what, from a social point of view, might be considered his own good in order to obtain gratification for his basic needs.[19]

Although an individual is born a part of a larger society with its various cultural values and norms, the individual's interactions with others within society (e.g., parents, peers, the state) will determine whether the needs of the individual will be fulfilled and, thus, will determine whether or not the behavior of the individual will remain within the bounds of societal norms or pursue a deviant path. In other words, when individual needs are not fulfilled within the dominant values and institutions of society, deviant behavior becomes a necessity. "Society, then, never completely conquers the individual. It conquers him only to the degree that his needs are met or to the extent that he sees the possibility of meeting his needs within its context."[20]

John Burton has been a leading force in integrating a human needs orientation into the science of international relations.[21] He argues that human needs should serve as navigation points guiding our research and practice, since the degree to which they are fulfilled is the underlying force determining social order and social change.

> The human individual has particular capabilities, certain limitations in response, and, therefore, certain needs to be secured within the environment if he/she is to survive. Obvious needs are food and water. However, an

important part of survival is growth and development. The new-born can survive only if it develops. . . . The survival-growth mechanism requires an environment that is consistent: without consistent responses there can be no learning. A sense of identity of self is required so that the individual can experience separation of self from the environment. It requires a measure of physical security for there to be consistency in response. It must have, therefore, some capability to control the environment for these purposes. . . . Thus we can deduce that the human organism and human societies have certain needs which must be fulfilled that are social in character, and, in terms of species survival, that are at least as important as the so-called 'basic' needs of food and water.[22]

Burton further argues that the assumptions of the traditional (or orthodox) approaches used to study society—which he terms power theory—do not hold over time. Power theory assumes an integrated society which is ordered and based on shared values obtained through the processes of socialization and the use of coercion (e.g., law and order). However, Burton suggests that the net result of social practices and theories which are based on societal needs and values—yet are unresponsive to or ignorant of individual needs—is the maintenance of the status quo. Such a result, he argues, eventually leads to societal instability and conflict. "Structures and institutions that have evolved over time, as a result of differentiation of power and socialization, do not necessarily, either in the short or the long-term, reflect . . . [individual] needs and desires and frequently frustrate them."[23]

The power of human needs is such that individuals will strive to satisfy needs, even at the cost of personal disorientation and social disruption. Burton contends that individuals whose needs are not being met within a given social order will express deviant behavior through withdrawal, activity on the fringes of legality, or reformist and revolutionary activities within and outside the law. Therefore, "the attempt to impose integration in a given territory, either by coercion or by socialization processes that are designed to promote shared values, is likely to be counterproductive."[24]

Burton goes even further in suggesting that the concept of deviance as commonly used is actually a misnomer. An individual is never really deviant, he argues, because over the long term "he is needs-oriented, he is not capable of deviating from the pursuit of 'needs'."[25] While it seems overly rigid to assume that all human action is best understood as needs fulfillment behavior, it does appear to be reasonable to assume that societal stability and change are actually dependent on the satisfaction of individual human needs. Therefore, social institutions and policies which frustrate needs satisfaction for large numbers of individuals can be viewed themselves as deviant elements of social life.

At the heart of Burton's thesis of societal evolution is the concept of *legitimacy*. "Conventional thinking appears not to make any clear distinction between that which is 'legal' and that which is 'legitimized'."[26] The test of legitimacy, says Burton, "is performance in satisfying needs rather than the processes by which authorities are selected or self-selected."[27] Therefore, most societies suffer from a crisis of legitimacy:

> The needs factor creates a major dilemma in contemporary times in relation to political and economic structures. Socialism can create distributive justice, but it is likely to deny identity, control, and stimulus. Capitalism provides opportunities for some for recognition, control, and stimulus and in doing so creates distributive injustices. . . . The historical process is a search, not for a structural 'ism,' but for one that concentrates on processes by which structures can change and evolve in the quest for human needs.[28]

As explained by Burton, "the 'historic process' is the end result, over time, of the conflict between institutional values and human needs, between the structures and norms created and supported by powerful elites and the human needs that must be met at the individual level if societies are to be functionally efficient and harmonious."[29] It is this historical dialectic of societal needs versus human needs which gives rise and form to human evolution within the world arena.

Societies and social institutions must generally be responsive to the needs of their members, otherwise they will unwillingly yet inevitably undergo change due to efforts by people to fulfill needs which are being deprived.

> It is the politically realistic observation that, unless there is development and fulfillment of needs of individuals and groups, unless problems are solved and the need for coercion avoided, a social and political order may not be stable and harmonious, no matter what the levels of coercion. Protest movements, violence at all social levels, terrorism, communal conflicts, dissident behaviour, strikes, revolts, revolutions and wars are observable symptoms of unobservable motivations and needs.[30]

The deprivation of human needs has been a major source of social and political change around the globe. This perspective should help us understand such crises of legitimacy as revolutionary movements in Iran and throughout Central America, the overthrow of the Marcos regime in the Philippines, Palestinian terrorism, the Lebanese morass, the Afghan resistance, and the growing resistance to apartheid in South Africa, as well as the continual crises of leadership in the industrialized societies.

GROUPS, VALUES, AND SOCIAL NETWORKS

Although needs satisfaction is only one source of social change, needs-based approaches to political analysis enable us to see a side of social processes and history which power politics realism cannot. We acquire the flexibility to be able to include, as integral parts of any relevant system of action, all of the significant actors and participants involved. One of the major limitations of traditional international relations scholarship has been the focus on nation-states as the basic conceptual units. A needs conceptualization encourages the international relations analyst to focus explicitly on individual and group interaction within larger social arenas—thus returning a lost element of realism to our analyses.

A focus on needs as a basis for the scientific study of international relations must be linked ultimately to the individual as a human being. As argued by Richard Bernstein, it is necessary to reorient theory toward integrating roles of the individual into our understanding of human relations:

> If we are to understand what human beings are, then we must uncover those models, interpretative schemes, and tacit understandings that penetrate human thought and action. Any conception of what is 'strictly speaking' empirical or observable that excludes this dimension of human life, or simply relegates it to a realm of subjective opinions, is emasculated and epistemologically unwarranted. . . . There has been a persistent tendency in mainstream social science to neglect, suppress, or underestimate this essential feature of social and political practices. What is taken for granted as the starting point for empirical research, as the realm of 'brute fact' that presumably grounds such research, is itself the product of complex processes of interpretation which have historical origins.[31]

As Singer argued nearly two decades ago, we need to begin "some systematic research which can simultaneously 'think big' and 'think small,' and which embraces in a rigorous synthesis both the lone individual and all of mankind."[32]

In order to do so we need, at least initially, to make a clean break with the state power politics paradigm and return to basics. As Rosenau has argued, the key to making such a break "lies in the readiness to treat all collectivities as susceptible either to aggregative processes that transform them into larger wholes or to disaggregative processes that transform them from wholes to parts."[33] Neither the nation-state nor any other conceptual unit of analysis, including the human individual, should be treated as an a priori given and, thus, held beyond the bounds of scientific scrutiny.

A human needs approach, however, must confront a major problem—the link between the micro (that is, the individual) level and the macro (that is, societal—world and national) level. In order to understand the dynamics of world affairs we must bridge a substantial and persistent conceptual gap between what have been viewed conventionally as discrete and separable spheres of reality. This can be done by examining the interaction of three factors or concepts: groups, social networks, and values. Together, these three concepts can provide the core of understanding, since the interaction of different networks of relationships through which the needs and values of individuals and groups are fulfilled or deprived is what politics is all about.

The focus on the individual pursuit of human needs through groups, values, and social networks provides the foundation upon which to explore the "dynamic or set of dynamics whereby individual actions are summed and thereby converted into collectivities and then, at subsequent points in time, converted over and over again into more or less encompassing collectivities."[34]   A focus on the pursuit of individual human needs and values and the network of group relationships between individuals allows one to study how people become mobilized to form social aggregations and how and why such systems of action become disaggregated.[35]

Human needs satisfaction cannot be considered adequately in isolation from the social context in which the relevant parties are interacting. In other words, individuals need to be viewed as social beings. In the language of social control theorists, like Sites and Burton, individuals enter into relationships with each other to form groups—local, national, and global—in an attempt to establish at least some control over elements of the environment which are essential for needs satisfaction. Individuals may identify simultaneously with a wide variety of social groupings—"identity groups," such as religious, labor, business, civic, and ethnic groups, as well as political parties and national states. Such identity groups may be specific to a local community or may be organized on a world scale. Individuals and groups may be participants in a seemingly infinite array of identity groups at any particular point in time.

The primary focus of analysis, then, is the network of relationships that develop between and among various individuals and groups in pursuit of fulfilling needs. It is the activities and consequences of social networks, which result from the interaction of groups of individuals in a global setting, that comprise international relations.

In this regard, it should be noted that individuals and groups do not attempt to exert control over the environment in terms of specific needs, but rather in a more general and diffuse sense. According to Sites, "values form the blueprint which orders the individual's world, and makes sense of it from a need-gratification point of view."[36]   Any given behavior or social relationship will not necessarily be traceable to specific needs. Therefore, although all individuals identify with groups and are motivated to fulfill their needs, the environment will be interpreted differently and represent quite different "realities" to different individuals and groups. Such differences in values and perceptions arise from diversities in human personalities, group dynamics, culture, and the relative location of the individuals and groups in social time and space.

Since values are not universally similar, different interpretations and recommendations arise by different participants within social networks.

Such differences, for example, exist concerning the global political economy. Many individuals and groups prefer the maintenance of a capitalist world order; others see structural inequalities of wealth and dependency and call for a New International Economic Order; others want to transform the capitalist world system into a global socialist order; yet others call for protectionism in order to promote self-reliance and economic nationalism; and others have a much more limited focus, primarily concerned with their daily labor and day-to-day standard of living. Yet all are attempting to fulfill their human needs. Given that different individuals and groups within networks may perceive, and thus respond to, human needs and environmental conditions in different ways, we must be able to capture and deal with such diversity.

Furthermore, some participants, whose needs are either directly or indirectly affected by such processes, might not perceive that they are linked into and are part of such processes. Regardless of whether people such as peasants, villagers, industrial workers, or managers perceive or even conceive of an international political economy, the allocational processes of the global political economy have significant impacts on their lives. In turn, these individuals, acting either by themselves or collectively, have the potential to impact on other participants with whom they are linked. Such social processes are effectively authoritative in character and are thus fundamentally political. Therefore, social scientists would be remiss if they failed to treat such individuals as participants in the global process.

If the preceding discussion seems remotely familiar, it is probably because various international integration and international regime theorists have been making compatible arguments for years. Keohane's functional theory of international regimes is based on compatible assumptions about needs satisfaction, even though epistemological blinders seem to limit his ability to view regimes as human social institutions.[37] Other regime theorists, such as Hopkins and Puchala and Young, have been more receptive to the human foundations of such global institutions.[38] These analysts are perceptive in their view of international regimes as logical outgrowths of social systems composed of groups of individuals more generally. They acknowledge that the emergence and continuation of such institutional arrangements do not depend necessarily on the purposive behavior of state units. Regimes emerge out of patterned behaviors among a diversity of types of participants and are maintained in order that such valued relationships might be sustained. The resulting social structures "exist primarily as participants' understandings, expectations or convictions about legitimate, appropriate or moral behavior."[39]

Yet, while such orientations are compatible with certain characteristics of a needs approach, they stop short of making the deductive links necessary to make a clean break from the state power politics paradigm. International regimes are part of world society and world society results from the interaction of networks of individuals and groups as they go about attempting to satisfy needs and values in complex social environments. We need to view international relations as a function of processes of legitimization and delegitimization in world society, which result from individuals and groups pursuing needs and values, rather than as being reducible to state power politics. Such a process can be illustrated as follows:

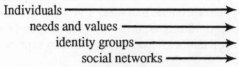

Individuals ⟶
    needs and values ⟶
        identity groups ⟶
            social networks ⟶
                individual need satisfaction/deprivation

A needs-oriented conceptualization should provide a firmer foundation for understanding the social changes and the global complexity of the twentieth century. Furthermore, a human needs approach will assist in analyzing and solving global problems by identifying the changes that are required in institutions and policies to ensure the legitimization of authorities and the satisfaction of human needs.

SUMMARY AND CONCLUSIONS

We have attempted to suggest a way in which the study of international relations can be enhanced by placing it in the wider context of interdisciplinary studies of human behavior. Our position is that world society or world affairs is composed of the interaction of social networks of group relationships based on the individual pursuit of human needs and values. A summary of our working propositions derived from a human needs approach is stated explicitly in Table 1.1.

This volume represents an effort to explore and construct a human needs paradigm in order to understand better the complex world around us. We have attempted to demonstrate the power of human needs as the basis for the study of international relations. In accordance with Thomas Kuhn, we believe that many of the unsolved international problems and questions are not likely to be solved within existing systems of thought, or "normal science."[40] Their solution requires the reexamination and reformulation of concepts and assumptions. A human needs approach is offered in order to provide a foundation for the development of empirical theory that provides an understanding of political and global phenomena.

Although the concept of human needs has been ignored by most scholars, this should not deter us from exploring and developing its potential for greater understanding of human behavior. Nor should we be deterred because of the lack of consensus over the concept of human needs. As Burton has argued:

> The deduced hypothesis that there are needs provides a reference point, even though their precise nature might not be known. That they relate to stimulus, recognition, security, identity is not in doubt: the disagreements occur when these broad terms are operationally defined for purposes of policy-making. This is not a reason for not using needs as a reference point: there will not be agreed operational definitions until there is wide experience in their use. . . . The important scientific requirement is that the policies so tested are based on interpretations of needs and not on ideologies and belief systems that have no foundations other than prejudice, personal interest, and [particularistic] value systems.[41]

A similar lack of consensus has confounded realists with regard to defining and using the concept of "power"; yet such difficulty has not prevented the development of a large body of thought and practice. If the needs concept has potential for allowing us to understand and explain much of international activity, in particular many of the new issues on the global agenda, then we should work with it and attempt to develop it further. We believe that the needs concept has such potential, which complements yet

Table 1.1 Propositions

1. All individuals have relatively enduring needs that must be fulfilled for them to grow and develop and for societies to function harmoniously.
    1a. While values and interests are culturally and/or situationally determined, needs are much more universal.
    1b. Individuals will strive to satisfy these needs.
2. Individuals will identify and associate with other individuals in pursuit of these needs.
    2a. Individuals pursue their needs through association with and participation in groups (e.g., political, class, ethnic, religious, national state, economic, language, and other groups).
    2b. Individuals and groups occupy differing locations in social time and space. Thus, they will vary in their level of political participation and will employ differing tactics to pursue their needs as seem to be called for by environmental circumstances.
3. Societies and other social collectivities depend on socialization and coercion for their maintenance in the short term, but ultimately are influenced by the satisfaction or deprivation of needs.
    3a. The values attached to these relationships in fulfilling human needs are more significant in the long run in determining the nature and outcomes of social relations than socialization, deterrence, or coercion.
    3b. In order for societies and other social collectivites to function harmoniously over time, individual needs must be satisfied.
    3c. Social collectivities and their leaders are legitimized only to the extent that they fulfill the needs upon which such relationships are based. The final locus of power is not the state but individuals in group relationships.
4. World society is the interaction of networks of individuals and groups as they go about attempting to satisfy needs and values throughout the global environment.
    4a. International relations are not a function of state power polities but of the processes of legitimization and delegitimization due to individual and group pursuit of needs.
    4b. Global problems will be resolved only by identifying the changes that are required in institutions and policies so as to ensure the legitimization of authorities and the satisfaction of needs.

differs from more traditional paradigms in the field.

If a human needs approach is to serve as a fruitful avenue of study, such an approach should contribute to an explanation and understanding of international phenomena. There are four general areas in which a human needs approach has the greatest promise of contributing to the study of international relations. *First*, a human needs approach should allow for the clear identification of the underlying determinants of human behavior and international relations: individuals and their pursuit of human needs. Most intellectual traditions and theories of human behavior are based on fundamental assumptions of human nature and needs. However, most of the literature in the social sciences has not been explicit in stating basic assumptions. The human needs approach outlined in these pages attempts to clarify the nature and power of individual human needs.

Second, a human needs approach should allow us to address the micro-macro problem by focusing on the aggregation of individuals into groups and social networks, thus accounting for global actors and structural relationships, while at the same time allowing for the disagreggation of local, societal, regional, and global relationships back to the individual level. Most of the work in the social sciences and the study of international relations has concentrated on different levels of analysis, usually focusing on one level to the exclusion of others. A human needs approach allows for the integration of different levels of analysis and produces the theoretical underpinning for examining and understanding the creation, development, and breakdown of aggregate units. In this way, the micro-macro problem is squarely addressed and the potential for developing synthetic theory is maximized.

Third, a human needs approach should allow us to examine the implications and impact of international institutional arrangements on individuals and groups. Most of the work in the study of international relations has focused on large aggregate "actors" at the national and global level, such as nation-states and international organizations. A human needs approach, however, makes it clear that international relations affect individuals and groups of individuals. Furthermore, it allows us to study the impact of such global relationships on "passive" participants who might be unaware of their roles within larger environmental contexts. It also should facilitate greater self-understanding by such individuals regarding the implications for the self-realization of needs that flow from their participation in various global relationships.

Finally, a human needs approach is dynamic and should allow us to explain international relationships and their consequences over time, thereby providing a foundation for understanding continuity and change. The key to the dynamics and evolution of world society is the satisfaction of needs and the associated legitimization of social (read "political") institutions. It thus allows us the opportunity to understand the global problems and issues that have developed and that are developing. The power of human needs will become increasingly apparent as the world enters the twenty-first century— for the future will be a time of greater challenges to, as well as opportunities for, the fulfillment of individual human needs. A human needs approach should further the study of the complex and changing world around us.

OVERVIEW OF BOOK

A number of important research questions need to be addressed in order to develop fully a human needs approach. This volume is devoted to beginning such a task. For example, is a consensus possible concerning the definition of human needs? Are they fundamentally physiological, psychological, ontological, or are they a complex mix? What are the basic needs that motivate individual behavior? Are human needs universal or relative?[42] That is, is there a common set of basic human needs across the globe or do these needs vary according to different contexts?

What is the relationship between human needs and the desires or wants held by individuals? According to Galtung, "a need should be distinguished from a want, a wish, a desire, a demand. The latter are subjectively felt and articulated: they may express needs, but they also may not; and there may be needs that are not thus expressed."[43] Therefore, how are the concepts of values and beliefs derived from the human needs of individuals? Furthermore, what is the role of ideology in fostering or inhibiting human consciousness as it relates to the pursuit of individual human needs?

How are human needs related to the explanation of political behavior? Although individuals are driven to pursue their human needs, different segments of society are active or passive at different times. Are human needs always active or are they also latent? What "triggers" certain needs at certain times to serve as primary sources of behavior? Furthermore, we need to address the concepts of "human need deprivation" and "human need fulfillment." How do we recognize when and why needs are satisfied or deprived? How do these concepts explain political passivity and trigger political activation? How does this affect the evolution of group behavior, social movements, and social networks? What are the implications of the fulfillment or deprivation of human needs for political legitimacy?

In order to address these philosophical and empirical questions, a consideration of epistemology and methodology is warranted.[44] What are the appropriate methods for identifying needs and examining their relationship to human and political behavior? According to Bay, "needs can only be inferred, not observed directly, except possibly the need for such biological basics as food, water, air, or sleep, etc. Wants, on the other hand, are facts, readily observable and measureable."[45] Needs are theoretical constructs. Therefore, "this means that the existence of an individual's needs, or, stronger, the 'truth' of those needs, cannot be proven in a direct, physical way. At best, the existence of a need can be concluded indirectly either from the respective satisfiers that the person uses or strives for or from symptoms of frustration caused by any kind of nonsatisfaction."[46]

Rather than emphasize an inductive approach by empirically inferring the nature of human needs and linking them directly to human behavior, the concept of human needs can be used as a set of assumptions for the development of theories of human behavior. In other words, one can take a deductive approach by building theory and empirically applying it to the study of international relations based on assumptions of individual human needs. The deductive approach raises questions about the overall validity of the assumptions (about human needs, or likewise, for realists, about power), but allows for the potential development of powerful explanatory theory. Obviously, the maximization of knowledge and understanding requires both inductive and deductive analysis. Nevertheless, it is important to make a distinction between inductive and deductive approaches to knowledge and ask: What is the best strategy for developing a needs theoretical understanding of international relations?

This volume is devoted to an initial search for answers to such questions. It has been divided into three parts. Part 1 provides a broad and diverse overview of the concept of human needs, discussing its general importance for individual and social behavior. Although there is no universal agreement concerning the exact nature of these needs, there is growing support in a variety of disciplines that specific and relatively enduring human needs exist and that individuals will attempt to satisfy these needs even at the cost of personal disorientation and social disruption. Chapter 2 reviews the empirical literature, demonstrating the existence of individual human needs. Chapter 3 discusses the contradiction between individual needs and societal needs, maintaining that political elites and social systems must be responsive to the needs of individuals if they are to maintain stability and survive over time. Chapter 4 examines the philosophical foundations and implications of human needs as the concept has been used in three streams of thought: liberalism, Marxism, and Gandhism. Chapter 5 discusses the concept of human needs as the basis for the existence and the importance of human rights for individuals and societies.

In Part 2, a human needs approach is applied in a number of areas in order to contribute to an understanding of international relations, including: local participation and local communities, international development, foreign policy, international conflict, international organizations, and international regimes. Chapter 6 examines the importance of a human needs approach on individual activation and local participation, and its impact on the thought and practice of international relations. The importance of a basic human needs approach to the theory and practice of international development is described in Chapter 7. Chapter 8 discusses the evolution of foreign policy as a function of human needs, with specific application to the explanation of U.S. foreign policy since World War II. The foundation of international conflict and conflict resolution from a human needs perspective is analyzed in Chapter 9. Chapter 10 examines the role of international organizations in meeting the needs of individuals with respect to international conflict and other non-security issues areas. Chapter 11 discusses the implications of a human needs approach for the study of international regimes and global networks of individuals and organizations.

The final section, Part 3, provides a critical review of human needs analysis and suggests a research agenda for the future. In Chapter 12, a self-critical assessment of a human needs approach to the study of international relations, in general and as presented by the contributors, is conducted. A series of questions are addressed: What are the major weaknesses and limitations of a basic human needs approach? What are its strengths and promises? What major research tasks need to be confronted? What appears to be the most profitable path to pursue in the future? Thus, a critical assessment is made of the power of a human needs approach in contributing to an understanding of international relations.

The editors have provided brief overviews before each chapter which introduce the chapters and tie them together. Short sketches of the scholars and their work are also provided in order to place each piece in perspective.

NOTES

1. Christian Bay, Chapter 5, emphasis added.

2. James Davies, *Human Nature in Politics: The Dynamics of Political Behavior* (Greenwood, 1978); and Otto Klineberg, "Human Needs: A Social-Psychological Approach," in Katrin Lederer, ed., *Human Needs* (Oelgeschlager, Gunn & Hain, 1980), pp. 19–35.

3. See Sigmund Freud, *Civilization and Its Discontents* (Hogarth Press, 1930); Harold Lasswell, *Psychopathology and Politics* (University of Chicago Press, 1930); Eric Fromm, *Escape From Freedom* (Holt, Rinehart, 1941); Adorno, Frenkel-Brunswick, Levinson, and Sanford, *The Authoritarian Personality* (Harper, 1950); Jean Piaget, *The Moral Judgement of the Child* (Free Press, 1932); Eric Erikson, *Childhood and Society* (Norton, 1950); and Abraham Maslow, *Motivation and Personality* (Harper & Row, 1954).

4. John Burton, *Deviance, Terrorism and War: The Process of Solving Unsolved Social and Political Problems* (Martin Robertson, 1979), p. 64.

5. (Allen & Unwin, 1981). See also Michael Ignatieff, *The Needs of Strangers* (Hogarth Press, 1984), and Ramashray Roy, Chapter 4.

6. See, for example, David Braybrooke, *Meeting Needs* (Princeton, 1987);

Ross Fitzgerald, ed., *Human Needs and Politics* (Pergamon Press, 1977); and Alkis Kontos, "Through a Glass Darkly: Ontology and False Needs," *Canadian Journal of Political and Social Theory* 3 (Winter 1979): 25–45.

7. See Johan Galtung, chapter 7 and "The New International Economic Order and the Basic Needs Approach," *Alternatives* 4 (1978–79): 455–476; Lederer, *Human Needs*; Han S. Park, *Needs and Political Development* (Schenkman, 1984); and United Nations University, *Human Development in Micro to Macro Perspective* (November 1982).

8. Ross Fitzgerald, "The Ambiguity and Rhetoric of 'Need'," in Fitzgerald, p. 204.

9. Stanley Renshon, "Human Needs and Political Analysis: An Examination of a Framework," in Fitzgerald, *Human Needs and Politics*, p. 52.

10. Hans J. Morgenthau, *Scientific Man Vs. Power Politics* (University of Chicago Press, 1946); Keith L. Nelson, and Spencer C. Olin, Jr. *Why War? Ideology, Theory, History* (University of California Press, 1979); Reinhold Niebuhr, *The Children of Light and the Children of Darkness* (Charles Scribner's Sons, 1944); Roy, chapter 4; and Miriam Steiner, "Human Nature and Truth as World Order Issues," *International Organization* 34 (Summer 1980), 335–353.

11. This is especially true of the literature in the last two decades. Many of the more classical works in international relations paid attention to the concept of human needs. As suggested by Peter Corning in discussing human nature, "for two generations the very concept was officiously, if not officially, pronounced dead by many social scientists—with significant consequences for our social practices, and for the practice of social science." Peter A. Corning, "Human Nature Redivivus," in J. Roland Pennock and John W. Chapman, eds., *Human Nature in Politics* (New York University Press, 1977), p. 19.

12. James Davies, *Human Nature in Politics*; and Abraham Maslow, "A Theory of Human Motivation," *Psychological Review* 50 (1943):370–396. Other scholars who have utilized Maslow's hierarchy of needs in order to explain political behavior include Knutson, Lane, and Renshon. Ted Gurr explains that the key cause of rebellion is the perception of relative deprivation of human desires and wants. Although certainly consistent with a human needs approach, Gurr's emphasis is on perception and psychological desires rather than on psychophysiological needs. Ted Robert Gurr, *Why Men Rebel* (Princeton University Press, 1970); Jeanne Knutson, *The Human Basis of the Polity* (Aldine-Atherton, 1972); Robert E. Lane, *Political Thinking and Consciousness: The Private Life of the Political Mind* (Markham, 1969); and Stanley A. Renshon, *Psychological Needs and Political Behavior* (Free Press, 1974).

13. Emile Durkheim, *Suicide: A Study in Sociology* (Free Press of Glencoe, 1951); Erich Fromm, *The Sane Society* (Rinehart and Company, 1955); George Homans, *Social Behavior: Its Elementary Forms* (Harcourt, Brace and World, 1961); Abraham Maslow, *Motivation and Personality* (Harper & Brothers, 1954); Talcott Parsons, *The Social System* (Free Press of Glencoe, 1951); Paul Sites, *Control: The Basis of Social Order* (Dunellen, 1973); and W.I. Thomas, *The Unadjusted Girl* (Little, Brown, 1923).

14. John Burton, *Deviance, Terrorism and War* and *Global Conflict: The Domestic Sources of International Crisis* (Wheatsheaf, 1984).

15. Paul Sites, *Control*, p. 7.

16. Ibid., p. 43.

17. Ibid., p. 10.

18. See Steven Box, *Deviance, Reality and Society* (Holt, Rinehart and Winston, 1971) and Renshon, *Psychological Needs*.

19. Sites, *Control*, p. 9.

20. Ibid., p. 11.

21. See, for example, Burton's *Deviance, Terrorism and War* and *Global Conflict*.

22. John Burton, "World Society and Human Needs: The Problem of Conflict Resolution," (University of Maryland, 1984, Mimeo.), pp. 10–11.

23. Burton, *Deviance, Terrorism and War*, pp. 64–65.

24. Ibid., p. 53.

25. Ibid., p. 183.

26. Ibid., p. 130.

27. Ibid.

28. Ibid., pp. 64–65.

29. Ibid., pp. 83–84.

30. Burton, *Global Conflict*, pp. 12–13.

31. Richard Bernstein, *The Restructuring of Social and Political Theory* (University of Pennsylvania Press, 1976), p. 230.

32. J. David Singer, "Individual Values, National Interests and Political Development in the International System," *Studies in Comparative International Development*, Vol. 6, No. 9 (1970):230.

33. James N. Rosenau, "Muddling, Meddling, and Modeling: Alternative Approaches to the Study of World Politics," in Rosenau, ed., *The Scientific Study of Foreign Policy* (Nichols, 1980), p. 543.

34. Ibid.

35. Thus, individuals should be analyzed in terms of the roles they occupy and the status they have attained as a result of their participation in varying networks of group relationships. Rosenau is insightful in this regard:

This is not to argue for a mechanistic view of people or otherwise to dismiss the values associated with the human spirit. Nor is it to say that people do not experience themselves and the feeling of being unique. Rather, conceiving of them as role composites provides an analytical context in which theorizing about world politics can systematically and meaningfully build in micro units expressive of needs, wants, orientations, and actions at the individual level.

James N. Rosenau, "A Pre-Theory Revisited: World Politics in an Era of Cascading Interdependence," *International Studies Quarterly*, Vol. 28, No. 3 (September 1984):267–268.

36. Sites, *Control*, p. 13. See also, Milton Rokeach, *The Nature of Human Values* (Free Press, 1973), p. 20.

37. Robert Keohane, *After Hegemony: Cooperation and Discord in the World Political Economy* (Priceton University Press, 1984).

38. Donald Puchala and Raymond Hopkins, "International Regimes: Lessons from Inductive Analysis," in Stephen Krasner, ed., *International Regimes* (Cornell

University Press, 1983), pp. 61–92; and Oran Young, "Regime Dynamics: The Rise and Fall of International Regimes," in Krasner, *International Regimes*, pp. 1–22.

39. Puchala and Hopkins, "International Regimes," p. 62.

40. Thomas Kuhn, *The Structure of Scientific Revolutions* (University of Chicago Press, 1970).

41. Burton, *Deviance, Terrorism and War*, p. 198. Likewise, for Peter Corning "human nature is proving to be far more complicated and subtle, and hard knowledge of the subject far less certain in many specific details, than has ever been dreamt of in our philosophy. As a scientific concept, we would do well at this juncture to treat human nature not as a set of dogmatic conclusions, but rather as a legitimate object of empirical research. It should only be at the conclusion of research and not at this intermediate stage that we might hope for a fully satisfactory understanding of the subject." And as suggested by Steiner, "no epistemology is politically neutral. Every method for acquiring knowledge about human nature and appropriate institutional forms necessarily embodies prior assumptions about them. At the very least, commitment to a particular epistemology requires acceptance of the assumption that we are so constituted as to be able to meet the demands of the epistemology." Corning, "Human Nature *Redivivus*, p. 21; and Steiner, "Human Nature and Truth as World Order Issues," p. 339.

42. Katrin Lederer, "Introduction," in Lederer, ed., *Human Needs*, pp. 1–14.

43. Johan Galtung, "The Basic Needs Approach," in Lederer, ed., *Human Needs*, p. 59.

44. See Lederer, *Human Needs*; and Steiner, "Human Nature and Truth as World Order Issues."

45. Bay, Chapter 5.

46. Lederer, "Introduction," p. 3.

PART ONE
THE CONCEPT OF HUMAN NEEDS

Part 1 focuses on the concept of human needs. Each of the four chapters provides a broad discussion of what is meant by human needs. Although the reader quickly becomes aware that there is no consensus concerning a definition or the nature of human needs, it also becomes clear that all four authors agree that human needs are a fundamental source of human motivation and behavior. Burton, Roy, and Bay, in particular, emphasize the power of human needs on social change and political development.

The Existence of Human Needs

JAMES CHOWNING DAVIES

James Chowning Davies is a Professor of Political Science at the University of Oregon. He has been in the forefront of the development of political psychology as a field of endeavor, with wide-ranging research interests such as human needs, socialization, and revolution. He is the author of many works, his most important being Human Nature in Politics: The Dynamics of Political Behavior, *from which this chapter is an excerpt of an updated version.*

Many people see the concept of human needs as "pie in the sky" or "wishful thinking," rather then hard-headed reality. This chapter should help to address this typical, but erroneous, critique by introducing the concept of human needs, and providing the intellectual and empirical basis for their existence. Davies briefly reviews the importance of the human needs concept in the work of some of the great philosophers and thinkers over time, leading up to the theory of the "hierarchy of needs" developed by psychologist Abraham Maslow. He then revises Maslow's classification of needs into four basic sets of needs: physical needs, social-affectional or love needs, self-esteem or dignity or equality needs, and self-actualization needs. Whether or not one agrees with Maslow's and Davies's particular classification or hierarchy of needs, Davies provides intellectual and empirical support for the existence of individual human needs. He also discusses the impact of individual needs on human behavior, including individual and mass political behavior. For example, Davies points out that by recognizing the differences in human need priorities, a better

Chapter 2 text reprinted by permission of New York University Press from *Human Nature in Politics*: NOMOS; XVII edited by J. Rolland Pennock and John W. Chapman. Copyright © by New York University.

understanding of what is often superficially considered "irrational" behavior can be gained. The section reprinted here represents the initial part of a larger piece in which Davies describes a theory of political development, consisting of five stages, based on the development of human beings in terms of the satisfaction of their needs.

Everyone, everyday, everywhere can readily verify the priority of some of the basic needs over all others. These most basic needs are the physical ones, which are shared with all animals and which many natural and social scientists regard as the only basic needs. All an individual has to do to verify the priority of physical needs over all others is to stop breathing. If he can go for more than a very few minutes without becoming totally concerned with breathing, then he has empirically refuted the priority of physical needs. If he goes without food for a few weeks, he has refuted the priority. And if he is injured or gets ill and pays no heed to his pain or ache, he has refuted the priority. Virtually no one who can intellectually contemplate the priority of human needs is preoccupied with meeting any of his physical needs. Unfortunately, the substantial majority of mankind, late in the twentieth century, still is preoccupied mostly with satisfying physical needs. For members of the middle class in advanced societies, satisfaction of the physical needs is only a mealtime and bedtime concern. For most of the rest of humanity, satisfaction of the basic but nonphysical needs is still, during most of their waking hours, a thing of the future.

The topmost priority of the physical needs has nevertheless been recognized by some writers and others who have experienced life in more fully human terms. In the Grand Inquisitor scene in *The Brothers Karamazov*, Dostoevsky has mankind say to the Church: "Make us your slaves, but feed us." In *Uncle Tom's Cabin,* Harriet Beecher Stowe has the slave Uncle Tom tell his master that he can control his body, but his soul belongs to God. There is a German saying: First comes food, then morality.

The retrogression in behavior that occurs when people are extremely deprived has been repeatedly observed. In the winter of 1846-47, among a group of California-bound pioneers, the Donner Party, while they were stuck by storm on the east of the High Sierra, some cannibalism occurred.[1] One woman ate parts of her dead husband; some children were fed parts of their dead father. In the Ukraine, as Khrushchev vividly reports, cannibalism broke out in the wake of the devastation of the Second World War.[2] In 1972, following an air crash high in the Andes on the 13th of October, sixteen survivors, who weeks before had been in the modern, civilized world, ate some flesh of the 29 men who had died before the final rescue on the 22nd of December.[3] In such circumstances, when hunger is strong, the social ties, let alone morality, are weak.

There has long been recognition that human beings have not only physical but also other innate needs, and there has long been more or less explicit recognition of the priority of physical needs over all others. Twenty-three hundred years ago, Aristotle regarded the family as the first social unit, noting that it is formed to satisfy minimally the "daily" physical needs of humans to eat ("as meal-tub fellows") and to procreate.[4] Man is thus by his nature a social animal[5]—and, Aristotle added, only in the political association can man pursue his highest good,[6] which is happiness. Two thousand years ago Jesus said that man does not live by bread alone, and he urged people to identify with each other in non-status, that is, in human or what Aristotle might call natural terms.

A hundred years ago Karl Marx hurled thunderbolts against the capitalist system as the cause of the inhuman reduction of poor people to mere appendages of machines. Because of this emphasis on the socioeconomic system in his *Capital* (1867, 1873), Marx's earlier and basic theoretical orientation has been neglected. In 1843 he wrote that "the root is man," adding that "theory is only realized in a people so far as it fulfills the needs of the people."[7] In 1846 he and Engels wrote that "life involves, before everything else, eating and drinking, a habitation, clothing, and many other things" and "that as soon as a need is satisfied. . . , new needs are made." The first new need is establishment of the family, the first social relationship, which itself later becomes subordinate to new social relations and new needs.[8]

It would be absurd to conclude that Aristotle, Jesus, and Marx agreed in their views of human beings, but it would also be absurd to fail to note the similarity in their starting points. Not being psychologists, none of these three ever elaborated on men's nature in ways that are now possible. Defining human nature as those tendencies to behave that are common to all human beings, we can note the growing acceptance of the existence of such common tendencies, one set of which consists of basic needs.

Building on a psychological tradition that includes William James,[9] William McDougall,[10] and Henry Alexander Murray,[11] Abraham Maslow hypothesized a hierarchy of needs. He made clearly explicit what was indefinitely explicit in such observations about human nature as those we have noted. He rank-ordered five needs, in descending priority, in his now well-known list: the physical, security, social-affectional, self-esteem, and self-actualization needs.[12] Since at least the 1950s, this hierarchy has begun to serve in political analysis. As far as I know, its first recognition was in my own doctoral dissertation in 1952 and its first basic theoretical integration in my *Human Nature in Politics* in 1963.[13] Others who have mentioned the hierarchy are Christian Bay and Robert Lane.[14] Some research based on it is mentioned below. . . .

THE PRIORITY OF HUMAN NEEDS

A behavioral theory is supposed to conform to the way people actually behave, and not vice versa. The arrangement of the priority of basic human needs that appears to have the best fit with the way people actually behave is as follows:

- *First*, the physical needs
- *Second*, the social-affectional or love needs
- *Third*, the self-esteem or dignity or equality needs
- *Fourth*, the self-actualization needs

While these categories are not definitive, they appear to include all the substantive needs common to all human beings, including of course those people whose major concern is with only their physical needs and the most elementary form of social needs. The substantive needs are those pursued primarily because they are inherently gratifying and only secondarily because they relate to some other, instrumental, desire. The instrumental needs are pursued in the process of satisfying a substantive need, to which their relationship is one of mode or means.

One minor note as to usage. The term "basic" is often used as though it meant "physical." On grounds that it is better to call all needs basic that are theoretically common to all human beings—whether these needs exist in actual or potential form—all four of the substantive needs I have listed are here deemed basic, . . . The consistent assumption is that all these basic needs are organically, genetically programmed predispositions.

Let me briefly spell out the argument for establishing priority among the four categories of substantive need. In this chapter it is impossible to do much more than illustrate the relationships. A wide range of experimental and other evidence relating to the priority of needs is presented in my *Human Nature in Politics*, particularly the first two chapters.

The nearly self-evident fact is that most people who eat and sleep regularly and are in good health are not preoccupied with satisfying the physical needs. For this reason and perhaps because it is deemed too banal or embarrassing or frightening to discuss physical needs, these needs tend to be overlooked. Nevertheless, . . . the physical needs remain of enormous importance in both political theory and political life, because mild physical deprivation weakens and severe physical deprivation often severs the most basic social ties, even within the family. This deprivation, whether as the consequence of never progressing beyond concern with their satisfaction or as the consequence of retrogressing to their concern, tends to produce anarchy in the struggle of each against all to survive. And this tends to maintain or produce tyranny.

In a provocative study of the effects of physical deprivation, Aronoff found striking differences on a Caribbean island between the life style and social interactions of physically more deprived cane cutters and physically more gratified fishermen. The physically insecure cane cutters led a fragmented, conflictful life of preoccupation with subsistence, more or less in isolation and social conflict—the Hobbesian war of each against all. The physically more secure fishermen were able to concern themselves fairly successfully with pursuit of the love and self-esteem needs.[15]

The social-affectional or love needs, which appear at or shortly after birth, are also rather often neglected or taken for granted by people who have experienced fairly stable emotional lives and thus are able productively to concern themselves most of the time with other things. Variously composed of quasiphysical (sexual) and nonphysical ingredients, the love needs form a continuously traveled bridge between a human being's most elemental physical needs and his/her more distinctly human needs as a unique individual. A person's demands for everything from food to recognition of his/her unique creativity are all transacted with other human beings. Aristotle was indeed understating it when he called man a social animal. Those who can calmly read or write about the need which, after survival, is the most basic do indeed take it for granted.

The deprivation of love needs helps demonstrate their high priority. Consider the mental condition of an individual who has become chronically preoccupied with love, as a consequence of either traumatizing childhood neglect or the capricious on-and-off concern of his/her parents or the breakup of a love attachment to girl or boy, betrothed, or spouse. At worst he/she will be continuously and neurotically preoccupied with his/her love life and social life, forever seeking affectionate interaction with others on an intense or casual basis. At best, when he/she does turn his/her mind to more distinctly human needs, he/she is likely to feel chronically insecure, because of the unstable emotional foundations on which he/she tries to build his/her life. (The awkward "he/she" pairing is used to emphasize that the innate desire for food, love, and any other thing is not a genetic endowment shared by only half the human race.)

Harry Harlow and his associates have extensively studied this need in its most elemental manifestation. They observed the effects of depriving infant monkeys of contact with their mothers and other monkeys. In some cases, the contact-deprived monkeys adopted a continuous catatonic crouch; in others they became incapable of defending themselves against the aggressive play of their nondeprived peers. In still other cases, when as adults they were involuntarily impregnated on what Harlow called a "rape rack," and had offspring, some tried to kill their infants and others merely ground their infants' heads against the floor.[16]

There are two more directly political studies relating to the deprivation of various needs, including the physical ones, affection, and status as it relates to the social-affectional needs. In a survey analysis using the need hierarchy as the theoretical basis, Knutson found, inter alia, that those higher on her indexes of political participation and of leadership were much less likely to mention deprivation of physical and affection needs.[17]

In a six-nation study in Europe, Inglehart found striking relationships between socioeconomic status and attitudes toward European integration. The lower-status people were more opposed to integration and the higher-status people (those who can concern themselves with lower-priority needs) were more in favor of integration. Similarly and perhaps more significantly, Inglehart noted an intergenerational difference, with the younger, postwar generation being less oriented toward acquisitive values and more toward what he calls "post-bourgeois" values. He also found a shift, in Germany, from 1949 to 1963, in which concern for "freedom from want" diminished in importance and concern for "freedom of speech" increased. This is precisely what a theory of the priority of needs would predict. Germans after the war were moving beyond their first concern, which was to get adequate food, clothing, and shelter. Inglehart offers a comparable explanation for the response of Frenchmen of various classes to the May 1968 student-worker rebellion.[18]

The self-esteem needs are those most directly related to political analysis, for which they can more appropriately be labeled the recognition or equality or dignity needs. They include the expectation of being accorded equal worth and therefore equal right to participate in social and political life. They are the kind that begin to surface when individuals try to establish their equal independence from others while retaining their ties of affection to them. When dignity needs are prominent, individuals wish both to be apart and to be a part. They cannot establish their independence, and thereby their self-esteem, as equals to others, if they are too close. But they require interaction with others in order to establish and confirm their equal and independent worth. What Erik Erikson called the adolescent identity crisis has much to do with self-esteem needs.[19]

This set of needs manifests itself in interactions ranging from the child demanding recognition from its parents and the spouse demanding equal treatment by spouse to the citizen demanding equal political rights and equal justice under law. But the esteem needs are typically overridden by the physical and social-affectional needs. A poor man who is hungry enough will take humiliation by someone who tosses him a coin and laughs when he scrambles for it—because the poor and hungry man can get food with the money. An individual who is deprived or threatened with deprivation of his/her social-affectional needs will sometimes crawl abjectly to someone who, along with contempt, will give him/her a morsel of love. Many women stay married despite even physical abuse by their spouses and other actions by which their husbands depreciate and degrade them. Many men do likewise, to avoid the ache of solitude.

However, when people gain sufficient security, in the steady satisfaction of their physical and love needs, they begin to demand recognition as individuals meriting respect and dignification. Most recently, blacks in America and women in many countries have begun to demand equality, in a host of ways. They became able to do so when they reached a level of material self-sufficiency (nondependence) and of social integration that substantially freed them from subordination to whites and to men, respectively. The blacks and women who are not particularly concerned with asserting their dignity, for whom the esteem needs are not salient, fall on both sides of the esteem level in the hierarchy. Poor and isolated blacks and women, those who have not yet achieved relatively symmetrical interdependence in the process of satisfying their physical and affectional needs with whites and men, are not yet ready to assert their equal dignity. Prosperous, socially integrated, respected, and career-oriented blacks and women often prefer to forget that they have moved out and beyond those blacks and women whom they have left behind.

The self-actualization needs are those that are fulfilled when an individual becomes absorbed and proficient in—both lost and found in—work or a hobby that he/she enjoys, quite apart from its utility as a means of earning a living or as surcease from toil. A person loses his/her self when the boundaries dissolve between the self and some aspects of the environment, in activity that is inherently pleasurable as an end in itself. The aspects of the environment may include people. A person finds his/her self in the discovery that this interaction *is* pleasurable, is profoundly gratifying for its own sake and not just as a means of satisfying the need for food, sex, companionship, or dignity. Such activity is self-actualizing, *is* her or him. A person may actualize her/himself in the practice of medicine, machine-tool design, camping, collecting old bottles or new automobiles, writing, painting, composing, or just reminiscing about the good old days. Many people (but still only a small minority) find much inherent pleasure in their work—even as wives and mothers. For most, their work—including housework—remains toil.

The self-actualization needs first become manifest among children when, for example, they become totally absorbed in building a sandcastle, riding a bicycle, or writing down the words they have hitherto understood only orally. The self-actualization needs continue from their earliest childhood beginnings down to the end of old age. But only when the physical, social, and self-esteem needs are routinely met can the self-actualization needs become the central concern. Let an individual begin to doubt the significance, the importance, of what he/she does, and he/she will seek the recognition and approval of others, whether these others be other physicians (or patients), toolmakers, collectors, or even occasionally spouses.

He/she needs others' approval of his/her self-actualizing activity in order to bolster self-esteem, a sense of worth. Let the person become lonesome after long hours in any actualizing activity, and he/she will seek the company of others. Self-actualization must not forever isolate him/her socially. Let him/her get sufficiently fatigued, and he/she will eat and sleep. His/her self-actualization must let him/her rest.

Three observations, peripheral to what has been said above, merit central emphasis at this point. The first is the often apparent reversal of priorities. Some people paint when they are hungry. Politicians have extraordinary stamina, particularly when campaigning. A composer may go without sleep for a night or so when in the midst of a symphony. A martyr, in the course of actualizing her/himself at the stake, may undergo everything from degradation (as people jeer and spit at her/him), to separation from all loved ones, to all-encompassing pain before the flames have seared her/him into unconsciousness.

People vary widely in their ability to stand hunger, pain, solitude, and degradation in the course of fulfilling themselves. Some individuals have enormous capacity to endure deprivation of higher-priority needs. But these reversals of the need hierarchy probably are very unusual in frequency and brief in duration. They are most readily explicable as the extraordinary behavior of extraordinarily strong individuals. Few—perhaps no—political purgees subjected to brainwashing have been able to withstand indefinitely the intense pain, isolation, and abuse of their inquisitors.[20] They are physically and mentally broken by their tormentors and then they either are killed or commit suicide. And even in his final agony on the cross, Jesus said: "My Lord, my Lord, why hast thou forsaken me?" Few people in the most nurturant environments are so single-mindedly absorbed, dissolved, in musical composition as Beethoven because of his deafness. For every Jesus Christ and Joan of Arc, there are hundreds of millions who prefer almost anything to deliberate martyrdom.

The second observation is that there is no clean-cut layering of overt acts such that any one of them can be categorized as satisfying only the physical, only the social-affectional, only the dignity, or only the self-actualization needs. The infant who is being breast-fed is also getting a healthy dose of affection. The adolescent who for the first time falls in love is experiencing not only love but also gratification of his/her need for recognition, esteem, and dignification, because another person makes him/her the object of attention, regard, and worth. Some people actualize themselves in love, gaining their most profound pleasure not only in sex but in the intense love of one other person. And some people actualize themselves as leaders in minority groups that have been denied dignification by the large society. Such people are fulfilling also their esteem needs, in the course of intensively seeking the social and political recognition of those with whom they identify—those whom they love as a group of people —as fellow members of a rejected, degraded minority. In their work such leaders combine the satisfaction of their social-affectional, dignity, and self-actualization needs. Any theory or any research is fundamentally defective if it develops without a recognition that virtually all overt acts of all people are motivated by more than one basic need.

The third is that there is a retrogression from advanced to primitive modes of living whenever any individual or social group (including a nation) loses the satisfaction of a higher-priority need. The behavior of a seriously ill or injured musician is hard to distinguish from that of a seriously ill or injured workingman. An individual who has a self-actualizing life as a successful tool-maker or musician will act like a hungry child if he loses his job. Some prime political examples are the mental states in Germany of both the unemployed of the 1930s and those whom the Nazi government placed in concentration camps. Both unemployed and internees behaved primarily in response to their hunger. Civilization can neither emerge nor continue on a basis of physical deprivation. It disappears when people are compelled by dire circumstances to regress to a primary concern with physical survival.

The fundamental value of using the priority of needs in political analysis is that it explains what is superficially called "irrational" behavior: it explains why people seem to behave "like animals" when their normal daily life is interrupted by concerns whose force can be explained only by indicating that these concerns relate to the orderly priority of needs. What would be irrational for a self-actualizing person is to let himself die rather than eat or go to the doctor. What is irrational in political analysis is to pretend that hungry people do or can behave politically like those who are well fed, socially accepted, dignified, self-actualizing upper-middle-class members of the establishment. It is unnatural, irrational not to respond first of all to hunger.

And the priority of needs helps explain political behavior that is not hunger motivated. It helps explain why young men who are threatened with military service are responding to at least two basic needs when they demonstrate against a small war overseas. The highest priority need affected is the desire to live, to which the possibility of combat duty is a real threat. In addition, military service interrupts the expectations of such young men to be able to pursue a career that will actualize them. Opposition to the Vietnam conflict would have continued on the same high moral tone it had for many years among university students in America, if it were not for the fact that ending the draft ended the threat to them of various fundamental deprivations.

Similarly, an individual who feels isolated socially and ineffectual personally may join a totalitarian political party if it not only diminishes his isolation and gives him self-respect but also gives him something serious to do in a time of widespread social despair. The "appeals of communism" to American and other intellectuals during the 1930s depression ran this gamut of basic needs.[21] Physical hunger was not a major concern for most of these intellectuals.

NOTES

It has been no easy task to try to integrate the ideas joined together here. Preparing this latest but not final statement on the theoretical problems was much facilitated by the very substantial help of James W. Clarke, Robert S. Frank, Seymour Martin Lipset, Darien A. McWhirter III, J. Roland Pennock, and the participants in a panel of the Western Political Science Association in San Diego, California, on 5 April 1973.

1. George R. Stewart, *Ordeal by Hunger* (1936) (New York: Ace Books, 1960), ch. 16, "The Will to Live," esp. p. 123; Bernard de Voto, *The Year of Decision: 1846* (1942) (Boston: Little, Brown, 1943), p. 421.

2. Edward Crankshaw and Strobe Talbott, eds, *Khrushchev Remembers* (Boston: Little, Brown, 1970), pp. 234–235.

3. *Facts on File*, Sunday, 24 December to Sunday, 31 December 1972, p. 1073.

4. Aristotle, *Politics* I. i. 4–7, H. Rackham, transl. (Cambridge: Harvard University Press, 1932), pp. 5–7.

5. Aristotle, *Politics*, p. 9, Rackham's translation of *politikon zoon* is the literal one, "political animal," but by this term Aristotle is deemed to mean that man is a member of the city community, including the political community. The Greek word *polis* did not distinguish the polity from the general society.

6. Aristotle, *Politics*, p. 8, and Aristotle, *Nicomachean Ethics* I. ii. 7, H. Rackham, trans. 1926, (Cambridge: Harvard University Press, 1934), pp. 5–7.

7. Marx wrote this in his 1843 critique of Hegel's *Philosophy of Right*. Citation is to Robert C. Tucker, ed., *The Marx-Engels Reader* (New York: W. W. Norton, 1972), pp. 18–19.

8. Quoted from *The German Ideology* (1846). Citation is to Lewis W. Feuer, ed., *Marx and Engels: Basic Writings on Politics and Philosophy* (Garden City: Doubleday Anchor Books, 1959), pp. 249–250.

9. See William James, *The Principles of Psychology* (1890) (New York: Dover Publications, 1950), vol. 2, ch. 24, "Instinct." And for an extended discussion of the evolution of some politically relevant psychology, see J. C. Davies, "Where From and Where To?" ch. 1 of Jeanne N. Knutson, ed., *Handbook of Political Psychology* (San Francisco: Jossey-Bass, 1973), pp. 1–27.

10. See William McDougall, *An Introduction to Social Psychology* (1908) (Boston: John W. Luce, 1918), pp. 51–92.

11. See Henry Alexander Murray, *Explorations in Personality* (New York: Oxford University Press, 1938), pp. 77–83.

12. Abraham H. Maslow, "A Theory of Human Motivation," *Psychological Review*, 50 (1943), pp. 370–396.

13. The full citations are: J. C. Davies, *The Political Implications of Psychoanalytic and Academic Psychology*, Ph.D. dissertation (Berkeley: University

of California, 1952), pp. 123–124; and *Human Nature in Politics* (New York: John Wiley & Sons, 1963).

14. Christian Bay, *The Structure of Freedom* (1958) (New York: Atheneum, 1965), pp. 11–12, 327–328; Robert E. Lane, *Political Life: Why People Get Involved in Politics* (Glencoe, Ill.: The Free Press, 1959), ch. 8, esp. pp. 102, 105–108; and Lane, *Political Thinking and Consciousness* (Chicago: Markham Publishing Co., 1969), pp. 26–27, 31–47.

15. Joel Aronoff, *Psychological Needs and Cultural Systems* (New York: Van Nostrand Reinhold Co., 1967), esp. ch. 4.

16. Harry F. Harlow and R. R. Zimmerman, "The Development of Affectional Responses in Infant Monkeys," *Proceedings of the American Philosophical Society*, 102 (1958), 501–509; H. F. and M. K. Harlow, "Social Deprivation in Monkeys," *Scientific American*, 207 (1962), 136–146; H. F. Harlow and S. J. Suomi, "Induced Psychopathology in Monkeys," *Engineering and Science* (California Institute of Technology), 33 (April 1970), 8–14.

17. Jeanne N. Knutson, *The Human Basis of the Polity* (Chicago: Aldine-Atherton, 1972), esp. chs. 2 and 4, and pp. 204–206, 341–342.

18. Ronald Inglehart, "The Silent Revolution in Europe: Intergenerational Change in Post-Industrial Societies," *American Political Science Review*, 65 (1971), 991–1017; and Inglehart, "Revolutionarisme Post-Bourgeois en France, en Allemagne et aux États-Unis," *Il Politico* (Università di Pavia, 36, 1971), 209–235.

19. Erik Erikson, *Childhood and Society* (1950) (New York: W. W. Norton & Co., 2nd ed., 1963), Part 4, "Youth and the Evolution of Identity."

20. Robert Jay Lifton's *Thought Reform and the Psychology of Totalism* (New York: W. W. Norton & Co., 1961) is a sensitive and somber appraisal of the brainwashing process in China in the 1950s.

21. Gabriel Almond, *The Appeals of Communism* (Princeton: Princeton University Press, 1954).

Human Needs Versus Societal Needs

JOHN W. BURTON

*John Burton takes the concept of human needs and discusses its significance
for social change. A distinguished Australian diplomat and scholar who
resided at the University of Kent in England for much of his academic
career, he is a Visiting Professor at the Center for Conflict Resolution at
George Mason University in Virginia. He is the author of numerous books
on conflict resolution, world society, and, most recently, a human needs
approach to world politics. His most important work is* Deviance, Terrorism,
and War: The Process of Solving Unsolved Social and Political Problems,
from which this chapter is excerpted.

*Burton examines the relationship between human needs and societal
needs. He argues that the widespread assumption that individual human
needs should be subordinated to societal needs requires reexamination.
According to Burton, there exists a set of individual human needs that are
universal and which serve as the basis of human behavior—that is,
individuals will strive to pursue those needs. However, societal needs as
reflected in social values and institutions are often inconsistent with
individual human needs. Social values and institutions are less oriented
toward satisfying individual human needs then with legitimizing the role of
elites and authority within the state. Therefore, the promotion of social
needs, through socialization and the use of coercion, results in deviant
behavior that, eventually over time, has destructive consequences for
society. Therefore, movement from a political philosophy based on "societal
needs" to one based on "individual human needs" is necessary for
organizing society and furthering social stability.*

Chapter 3 text reprinted by permission of the publisher from *Deviance, Terrorism,
and War* (In U.K., Oxford: Martin Robertson, 1979; in U.S. and Canada, New York:
St. Martin's Press, 1979).

Legal scholars and philosophers have asserted the primacy of social values ever since relations between citizens and the state were first considered. The justification for this view is that the interests of most citizens, over the long term, are best catered for by the preservation of social institutions and structures (including the institutions providing for change) even though in the short term, and in some particular cases, there may be some curb on individual freedom and development. On the face of it there can be no objection to this mode of thought. It is widespread: most regimes and authorities tend to take this view, as do usually those over whom they exercise their authority.

However, there is another assumption implied in the notion of an integrated social system that seems to destroy the validity of this mode of thought. It is that integrated social systems are possible as the result of shared values and some element of coercion: individual values can be subordinated to social values. This is an important assumption for coercion theory and for any value theory that admits the existence of non-normative behaviour which must be controlled. Both attribute deviance to imperfect socialization or to a failure of the system to impart and to enforce its values, to "role strain" resulting from a conflict between social and individual values and to ambiguities and inconsistencies in the social value system. Johnson comments: "These are extremely important sources of potential conflict, violence, and even revolt; and they are sufficient in themselves to warrant institutions of authority to enforce social behaviour."[1] The assumption is that enforcement is not merely desirable, but also possible.

Both of these assumptions, that individual values need, in the general interest, to be subordinated to social values and can be so subordinated, require examination. Neither may be valid, thus revealing possible sources of unsolved problems, for attempts to coerce that are unnecessary (in the sense that an integrated social system is unnecessary) or impossible are likely to stimulate hostile responses including deviant behaviour. Furthermore, even though both assumptions were justified by experience, even though the need for coercion were present and coercion were effective, it could be that the process of coercion, while achieving immediate compliance, is itself in the longer term a source of deviance and revolt. Asserting the need for coercion and its practical effectiveness without taking into account its consequences, may be merely defining social problems out of existence. Consequently there is a reformulation of this assumption that requires examination, that individual values can be subordinated to social values without the side-effects of destructive consequences for society and individual abnormalities in behaviour that threaten the system itself. A contrary proposition would be that, if an attempt is made to subordinate individual values to social values, then, because it is not possible to enforce social values that are inconsistent with individual values, there will be responses that are damaging both to the individual and, through him, to the social system.

Two questions come to mind. First, are there human values held by all people in all societies by reason of their being individuals living within social organizations that may be important and perhaps essential to individual social interactions, but which may be incompatible with some of the values of a society? For example, there may be a universal value attached to participation in decisionmaking, to a sense of control over one's own destiny, either generally or in relation to a particular environment. If social and political structures and values attached to them have their origins in the relative influence of competing interest groups, i.e., if roles and their occupants are the outcome of relative power positions, there is a strong presumption that these same structures and roles may impede growth and the full expression of personality of the majority by depriving them of this participatory experience. It is generally assumed that this is the case; but it also is held that such a sacrifice is part of the price the individual in society is expected to pay to be a member of a society and to benefit from the security and services it offers. However, a second question relates to this last observation. Assuming there are such human values, can they be frustrated by a socialization process or by some other means, without endangering, not just individual development, but the stability of the society which the socialization process seeks to establish? For example, can an ideal form of organization, with justice and equality built in, so overcome a desire for a sense of control as to guarantee social stability? May it not be that no process of socialization, no coercion, can suppress or sublimate certain universal human values that are not provided for within the value system of a society?

These are clearly fundamental questions; but they are capable of being answered both within a theoretical and an empirical framework. Indeed they have been answered in contemporary thought, at least to a degree that casts grave doubt on the assumption that individual values can be subordinated to institutional values and, therefore, doubt on the proposition that social systems can be made to cohere by coercion and by socialization into shared values.

THE DISTINCTION BETWEEN VALUES AND NEEDS

At the heart of the problem of social and individual values is the notion of values itself. If by values is meant only those superficial attitudes and behavioural patterns that are acquired because they are found to be useful in living within a particular society or civilization, i.e., cultural values, it is axiomatic that respect for institutions and the norms of society will take precedence over any merely idiosyncratic individual values. However, individual values may not be limited to those that are successfully internalized through the socialization process. There may be values which are held by individuals as individuals—human values. Some societies may not be conducive to their pursuit because of their size, their particular system or for some other reason. Further, there may be values required by society that are not and cannot be internalized, because they are incompatible with these human values.

The likelihood is that there are, in addition to cultural values, more basic and fundamental human drives, common to all humans and shared generally by developed organisms. There are systemic properties common to all living organisms, ranging from dependence on oxygen to repair and adaptive capabilities. These and basic physical requirements common to all members of the human species are acknowledged. We are presently concerned with individual needs that have a societal significance, i.e., those needs without which there cannot be on-going social relationships and harmonious organizations. It is a reasonable hypothesis that there are systemic needs of the individual that are operational at the level of social organization. They are the needs of individuals interacting within a social group and of social groups interacting within larger societies: they are relevant to all levels of behavioural relationships.

Classical and conventional thinking does not draw a distinction between (cultural) values and (universal) needs. On the contrary, they are all seen to be in a continuum. The more obvious needs of survival have been regarded as basic needs, e.g. shelter, food, sex and reproduction, the satisfaction of which leads to other needs such as participation and recognition. In this view it is reasonable to draw a line at some arbitrarily determined welfare standard, according to stages of development of society and the nature of political control, other needs being a luxury or non-essential increment that can be earned by, or that happens to be the lot of, some individuals and some nations. If, however, it were found that there are certain human needs that are universal in the sense that they are a systemic requirement of the individual and that no society can be harmonious or survive indefinitely unless they are satisfied, then the argument about freedom and organization takes on another complexion. For freedom we would need to read certain requirements of the individual which, if not met by society, makes the individual a malfunctioning unit, finally destroying the total system. If there are needs that must be satisfied before there is individual development and socialization, then the relegation of these to the category of values, some of which are mere luxuries to be experienced only after others are satisfied, would be a sufficient explanation of dissidence and of deviant behaviour.

There is a problem of language in this discussion about values and needs which must be dealt with before proceeding further. There is no generally accepted word that signifies human needs in the sense used here. We are familiar with "values" or "needs" signifying the basic requirements of the individual, such as food, shelter and others; but there is no agreed term that covers the basic needs of the individual as a social unit and which are, therefore, basic to social organization. Needs, values, wants, are all used in different senses by different writers, sometimes interchangeably. Whatever use is given implies a notion, a theory. Davies equates wants and needs, whereas Burns makes a clear distinction between the two.[2] For Burns, wants relate to those goods and services that one lacks; needs imply a more socialized phenomenon: needs are the more widely sanctioned wants. In this view it will obviously be the role of leadership to transform wants into needs.

"Needs" are being used here in quite a different sense to describe those conditions or opportunities that are essential to the individual if he is to be a functioning and cooperative member of society, conditions that are essential to his development and which, through him, are essential to the organization and survival of society. Again, this use of the term implies a theory: the efficient and harmonious functioning of society (as distinct from its integration) is not explained by coercion or by shared values, but by the development and functioning of its component parts, individuals and groups. These requirements are not "wants" or "values"; they are needs that are more fundamental than either. It would be useful to have some agreed vocabulary that would make thinking clearer and enable better communication, but in practice we have to use words in common speech and to give them a precise meaning in the particular context in which they are used. Spelling out the theory implied in the special use of the terms is one way in which this can be done: new theories, new insights, new perspectives lead to an enriched language and more precise employment of words. However, the reader cannot always divorce himself from the meaning he is accustomed to attach to these words. In this case he is probably saying to himself that these needs cannot be satisfied in every case until societies have developed further, until more pressing wants have been met. Such a response would lead to the point of the argument being lost. What we are referring to in this context are needs that are always present: individual needs that are as basic to harmonious social relationship as food and shelter are to the individual. They do not depend on stages of development. The argument is that without the satisfaction of these needs the individual will find the norms of the society in which he behaves—primitive, traditional or industrial—to be inappropriate because these norms cannot be used by him to secure his needs. He will invent his own norms and be labelled deviant, or disrupt himself as a person, rather than forego these needs.

The assertion of systemic needs, i.e., needs that are universal in the human species, is not inconsistent with the existence of cultural values. The relationship between needs and cultural values is that the latter include not only the local manifestations of needs, but also, like social norms, the tools used to pursue needs. In one culture property is a means to recognition; in another, the giving of property; in one, aggressive behaviour satisfies a need; and in another cooperative behaviour is the tool to satisfy the same need. In the same culture the deviant seeks recognition in one way, the businessman in another. As Maslow reports: "There is now sufficient anthropological evidence to indicate that the fundamental or ultimate desires of all human beings do not differ nearly as much as do their conscious everyday desires. . . . In one society, one obtains self-esteem by being a good hunter; in another, by being a great medicine man or a bold warrior or a very unemotional person, and so on."[3]

However, not all cultural values are manifestations of universal human needs. Some are clearly acquired and relate to interests. For example, there is evidence that some cultural norms and behavioural patterns relate to class, occupation and ideologies. They exist across national and ethnic groups. There is a student, a professional, a deviant, and a working class culture and associated values that cut across geographical boundaries.

One way of determining needs is to postulate that the expression of values in cultures over time reflects human needs and that attention can therefore be focused on cultural values.[4] The argument is that members of societies, each rational and in competition and cooperative with each other, evolve and inherit a set of values that, by a process like a fine market mechanism, maximize satisfactions. Individual choices and hierarchies of preference create the cultural values. As in a market mechanism, some values are sacrificed as a means of securing others. In the main, these are "shared" values. Nevertheless, even this approach does not necessarily assume that cultural values so arrived at reflect a consensus, since people occupying different locations and situations within the society have correspondingly different interests and performances, forming subcultures. Because of power relationships within the society and consequent market "imperfections," the recognized social values tend to express the values associated with higher status and elite role occupations. There is no reason to believe that cultural values so arrived at, even over long periods of time, reflect human needs. On the contrary, the probability is that past societies and civilizations failed to develop precisely because the "shared" or cultural values were skewed in favour of particular elites and powerful authorities, were not adaptive to altering conditions and demands and were destructive of the whole society.

Kelman has argued that universal values are reflected in "all major ethical systems and acknowledged in as many national constitutions. They are even formalized in international agreements, such as the Universal Declaration of Human Rights. . . . The existing consensus can at least serve as a starting point for continuing transnational exploration and specification of criteria that would have universal validity."[5]   However, even these international declarations reflect a special value system, that of authorities, and furthermore, authorities in only some cultures and political systems. They are not necessarily a reflection of any universally held values. . . .

Whether or not there are such attributes as universal needs and behavioural patterns that are universal as a consequence, it has long been assumed that this is the case, even though there has been little attempt to be specific as to what they are. Take, for example, general works such as that of Gurr and the reader edited by Davies.[6] The authors are prepared to generalize universally about the consequences of deprivation, the coercive balance between values and constraints, the relationship between frustration and aggression and many other aspects of human relationships. In other areas the same general assumption of universal patterns of behaviour and means of control are in evidence, as for example in the reader edited by Thomas and Bennis.[7]

HUMAN NEEDS AS A NAVIGATION POINT

Before turning to define and to be specific about human needs, there is one other proposition to examine. Traditional scientific thought has argued that there can be no objectivity about human goals and, therefore, no objectivity about policies. There can be a purely scientific approach only to description—conditions of life as they exist, degrees of relative poverty, altering levels of crime, the incidence of war and such matters. This is a description of "reality." In this view there cannot be any scientific determination of goals: it cannot be argued scientifically that wealth is more important than freedom or stability more important than progress. Hence we are led to "scientific value relativism." There are hypotheses that a goal of societies (and of political science) is, for example, the greatest happiness for the greatest number. In short, it has been argued that there are no scientific navigation points, no references by which value priorities can be determined, no guides to policy that are outside and above ideology, class or cultural prejudice. Western political science and governments have been content to rest on a vague consensus, that defies precise interpretation in any practical situation:

> that government should be based on respect for the dignity of man and on freedom of conscience; that there should be independent judges, equality before the law, no slaves, no torture, no cruel punishment; that the principles of habeas corpus should give every arrested person the right to be heard by a judge who could, if detention was not warranted under the law, free him with or without bail; and that science, art, and press must be uncensored.[8]

In this conventional view, human needs and social values are asserted as part of religion, ideology and class or cultural philosophy. Different assertions lead to different structures and policies. Changes in governments lead to changes in policies. Different value orientations lead to quite opposite conclusions in academic discussions. Left-right, hard-soft debates dominate discussion about the handling of situations. As a result problems are not approached as such with a view to a solution.

We are asserting that if there were to be discovered a definite set of human needs on the basis of which societies could be harmonious, major methodological problems in behavioural sciences and in policy-making would be avoided. If there were agreement as to human needs then there would be a scientific basis for determining goals. Institutional forms and social values could be assessed in relation to known needs and the efficacy of public policies and processes could be judged by reference to them. There would then be a shared value system; we would know what was and was not adaptive behaviour by authorities for it would be assessed by reference to human needs; we would have some means of judging the relevance of social norms and conventions; we would have valuable knowledge about what causes frustrations and, therefore, about some conflict situations; and we could examine particular problem areas—industry, education, kinship, law and order—and be quite precise about policy orientations that would reliably achieve these known and agreed needs. We could analyze the human condition, how people and social organizations behave and will behave, on the basis of what is, not what ought to be, what will inexorably evolve, not what is thought to be desirable.

Normative and culturally oriented lists of human needs imply that social and political structures and cultures evolve over time, guided by and reflecting human needs. This reinforces the idea that what evolves is "natural," even ordained, justifying the classical emphasis on the preservation of institutions and structures that have evolved over time. An empirically based list of human needs, on the other hand, could reveal marked discrepancies between evolved structures and human needs. For example, there could be a differentiation of power or some elite leadership influences, that over time created structures that frustrated the fulfillment of human needs, even though satisfying in the shorter term the special interests of elites. There could be non-adaptive behaviour from the point of view of the society generally, while there appeared to be satisfaction of norms and interests as articulated by elites.

This is not to say, however, that a list of culturally or ideologically based human needs would not overlap an empirically based one. On the contrary, religion and ideology are vehicles by which experience and conventional wisdom are transmitted. The connecting link in the history of thought between ideological viewpoints and empirically determined ones are the observations and insights of observers, especially in conditions of change that stimulate observation and constant revision of ideas.

A social system is made up of units that are themselves entities. Each of these units enacts many roles in the complex society of which it is a member. The quality of social interaction, the adaptive and problem-solving potential of the total society, bears a direct relationship to the quality of behavioural response of the units that comprise it. Personalities are the guardians of the accumulation of knowledge and experience in societies and of the process of change.[9] The satisfaction of human needs and desires is, consequently, of systemic interest. The patterns of response of units within a system are the basis of observed systemic properties. For this reason, it can be deduced that systems and subsystems will have behavioural properties in common. Recognition, control and security are human needs in the sense that individuals require them; but no less do small and large groups. In these cases the display of these needs are described as "independence struggles," "nationalism" and "freedom." In this sense human needs are the navigation or reference points, not only for psychologists, but no less for sociologists, and students of politics and international politics.

The selection of a particular unit of analysis has a significant effect on interpretation of data. The psychologist, taking the individual as the unit, defines a situation in one way—e.g., some form of maladjustment—the sociologist, taking the group as a unit, defines the same situation in another—e.g., some structural condition leading to deviant behaviour. Thus, the definition of a problem becomes confused. If "system" is adopted as the unit of analysis, a different perspective occurs for it is a notion of interaction that is general. In a system "authority" is not the relevant or all-important center of attention as it is when relationships in some particular social structure are being analyzed. There are some systems, e.g., the international system, in which it is difficult to find the locus of authority or even to determine whether an authority exists.[10] It could be that in social analysis that focuses on individual or group behaviour the existence of authorities is assumed and given a locus, even though they do not exercise influence. What is relevant are the patterns of behaviour and frequently these will show regularities despite different authorities and different cultures. It is the existence of human needs and interests or the denial of them, that is the basis of the regularities in patterns of behaviour. Take, for example, the problems of identity. Worldwide there are tribal, religious and language difficulties, in addition to class and cultural clashes. The strong tendency to identify with ethnic and other such groups, even with football teams, is self-evident. The need to identify is experienced by everyone when threatened or insecure. It is a phenomenom that can probably be explained in terms of security and recognition. So with legitimization, role behaviour and other forms of relationships, including deviant behaviour.

If we could postulate and find empirical evidence of fundamental or universal needs and desires, rather than changing cultural values, we would have a firm basis on which to judge whether knowledge and policy were being applied to human development—or merely to some speculative notion of it. In a discussion of the authority problem this is clearly important. It is authorities that articulate values and create institutional frameworks. Their legitimized status can be assessed only by reference to the degree that they promote adaptive behaviour. Adaptive behaviour can be defined only by reference to human needs and desires—whatever they prove to be. In the meantime, in the absence of any certain knowledge of human motivations and drives, we can operate deductively. This could be the better methodological course in any event. We arrive at a list of needs which is the best we can do at the moment, then we seek to test it by asking whether on such a basis, we can arrive at definitions of problems and at policies that more reliably achieve their stated purposes. Can we give more meaning to conceptual notions about which as yet there is little agreement or clarity, can we predict social developments? Modifications of the notion of human needs and desires will undoubtedly be required as we proceed: but methodologically we will have taken an important step in moving from induction to deduction, from analysis and classification to testing by falsifying.

This position is now widely recognized. Indeed, it will be difficult to be credible in the future without taking into account the influence of needs, which Sites argues "is many times stronger than the influence of the social forces which play upon man."[11] Those concerned with law and order will still continue to argue on the basis of social norms and their enforcement and many politicians will find it expedient also to adopt this approach; but sociological and political analysis is without any sure foundations without this conceptual notion of needs. This is not the occasion on which to review contemporary writings and to demonstrate the prevalence of a needs approach. Sites has already done this, concluding: "The point we wish to make here is that basic needs do exist and that they are more universal, and thus less specifically cultural, than some behavioural scientists would have us believe."[12] In elaboration, he points out:

> In using the need concept we must ever be conscious that we are operating at an abstract conceptual level and that in the last analysis the actual basis of the need is tied up with certain psychophysiological processes which are in interaction with the environment and which are not at this point in our scientific development directly observable. The fact that these processes are not directly observable, however, should not prevent us from working with the need concept if it allows us better to understand and to explain human activity. (The atom was conceptualized long before it was "observed.") That is, if we observe certain kinds of activity (or lack of

activity) in behaviour which we need to account for, and can do so with the use of certain concepts which do not do violence to other things we know and which are consistent with other data which cause us to think in the same direction, there is no reason why we should not do so. We can always admit we are wrong.

To be more specific, if we find that men have certain anxieties and perhaps engage in bizarre activity under conditions of insecurity, we might fruitfully posit the need for security and see where it leads us. If we find or observe the same thing when individuals are alienated or seem to lose their identity, we might talk about a need for identity; and if we observe that people suffer from boredom, we might talk about a need for stimulation.[13]

Burns consciously employs needs as his navigation point: he is interested in the nature of leadership and observes that we lack a general theory of political leadership. Yet the phenomenon is clearly universal. He, therefore, seeks a central variable, rather than to be content with yet another description of leadership behaviour.

Such a variable conceptually would have to cut across a wide range of cultures and classes and politics, for it is a general theory of leadership in social causation that we are pursuing. . . . Where do we start? . . . The primal sources of political leadership lie in the vast pools of human energy known as wants, needs, aspirations and expectations.

Later:

Wants and needs and the elements into which they may be transformed may all be considered examples of motivation, a blanket term that has come to mean all variables from innate biological drives to the most refined and developed attitudes. It is these motivations, whether in their more individual or collective manifestations, that the leaders tap on the basis of their own motivations as well.[14]

So, too, in other fields of behavioural inquiry. This reference point, this goal of human endeavour that can be checked empirically within social and biological behaviour, takes the place of personal value systems and ideological orientations. It should provide the basis of a science of behaviour, thus overcoming the methodological problems and ideological debates that have characterized thought and politics.

HUMAN SOCIETAL NEEDS

What then, are human needs, these universal drives that influence all social behaviour in all societies?

There has been an endeavour over the years by philosophers and political sociologists to tackle the problem of conflict between social and individual values. The early political sociologists were less concerned with needs and their definition than in the forms of social and political structures that would, according to their own personal value systems, meet the requirements both of societies and its members. The idealistic literature of the fifties and sixties was characterized by condemnations of capitalism and faith in socialism; but it showed no clear understanding or knowledge of human needs. The concern was with structure: not directly with people. For example, Heilbronner traced the transformation of capitalism to socialism; Fromm was interested in the international system from the same point of view; and Niebuhr dwelled on the morality of political institutions, a theme developed by him in the thirties.[15] Human needs were applied as being the reason for these interests, but they were not articulated. Consequently, the implied and stated prescriptions were suspect: too much faith was placed in an ideal "socialism" without sufficient consideration of the needs that had to be met.

A little more than a decade later a different emphasis was reflected in the writings of Nisbet. For him, the issue was not capitalism or socialism, but "the identification of functions, processes, and membership which do not belong to the state and whose protection from the state and its bureaucracy should be a first order of business."[16] He invited consideration of private and not public organization, human and not institutional needs and aspirations.

This shift from institutional to human concerns was a significant one. It was stimulated by developments in the totality of world society, in relationships at all levels, the family, industrial, national and interstate: i.e., a more conspicuous, less ambiguous and positive assertion of human needs. What was noted was that human needs were not generated by events: they were a constant. Altered conditions gave rise to their expression.

While there have always been assertions of human needs—described broadly by reference to "rights," "independence," "participation," "dignity," etc.—in recent years very large numbers of situations scattered over wide areas have drawn attention to them. Behind this development has been the postwar breakdown of former authority systems, feudalism, colonialism, etc., and, more importantly, an explosion in education and in communication that ensures that the assertion of needs anywhere is noted everywhere.

In this political and social climate it is not surprising that many writers are basing their thinking on a list of needs, either implied or specifically mentioned. These are needs that are significant, not for the individual primarily, but through him for society. While Gurr was greatly concerned with relative deprivation, he saw the necessity of defining this in terms of needs. "In psychological terms, values are the goal objects of human motivation, presumably attributable to or derived from basic 'needs,' or 'instincts'." He employs a three-fold categorization that includes welfare values, power values and interpersonal values.[17]

Implicit in the thinking of most political and social scientists has been a hunch that there are some fundamental human needs that must be fulfilled if social institutions are to be functional. For example, the literature on industrial relations abounds in implied assumptions regarding the needs and motivations of workers: participation, justice, self-respect, etc.[18] In the field of deviance, many writers imply that a causal factor is a denial of needs such as identity relationships, opportunities and expectations.[19]   Indeed, a characteristic of twentieth-century thinking on social problems is this concern with individual fulfillment as a source of conflict: yet the particular needs are not often articulated. Galtung developed the notion of "structural violence" by which he meant the gap between the actual and potential of individual development. He was implying some drive, urge or potential that was being frustrated by social and political conditions, particularly those that led to rank disequilibrium. His notion of structural violence could have had meaning only if he could have hypothesized certain basic conditions of life that required fulfillment.[20]

Most social scientists deal with human needs as a by-product of their interest areas. Burns is concerned with them in order to determine the nature of leadership and its purposes. Nisbet, whose concern is the freedom of the individual, refers to the need for stimulation to offset boredom and its consequences, the need for kinship and a sense of belonging, and the need for security, amongst others. Rokeach argues the need for a belief system about both self and the total environment. Enloe is particularly concerned with development and points to ethnicity as a vehicle for need satisfaction.[21]

Not surprisingly, some of the earliest attention to human needs from the point of view of society was given by social workers. They work within a political environment that accepts an integrated or coherent society as a goal and are, therefore, confronted by the conflict between the demands of the social environment and human needs. A book by Charlotte Towle, commissioned by the United States Bureau of Public Assistance, had the title *Common Human Needs*. It set out to be a guide to those engaged in public social services and dealt with those problem areas that fall within the field of social work, the needs of children, the aged, the sick and disabled. It dwelt on security (through love and valued relationships), the opportunity for creativity and the attainment of skills. The National Association of American Social Workers dealt with "human needs common to each person" and asserted the recognition of such human needs as one of its six philosophical concepts on which to base the practice of social work. In the particular area of child welfare, Mia Pringle of the (British) National Children's Bureau, asserted certain specific needs of children: love and security, new experiences, praise and recognition and responsibility.[22]

This concern with human needs calls attention to the conflict between institutional and human needs that pervades not merely social work, but many areas of law, sociology and politics. Social work—along with law—is plagued by such a conflict: it is the everyday experience of social workers that their duty to their clients and their duty to authorities and to society are frequently at variance. The more thought and attention given to human needs, the greater precision in defining them, the greater and not the less this conflict becomes. The established view is based on the general proposition that the primary purpose of socialization is "to provide individuals who will not only conform to socially prescribed rules (and roles) of conduct but will, as members of society, accept them as their own values."[23] In this view, the role of the social worker is to assist those individuals who have failed to come to terms with these rules or who have failed to use them sufficiently to their own advantage. It is not to change the rules or to encourage clients to change the rules. Consequently in the established view, the role of the social worker is to help the individual who cannot cope in his society. It is concerned with people "at risk" who without assistance have little prospect of adequate welfare or normal behaviour. However, social work also reflects the same behavioural pressures experienced by all behavioural studies and has persistently moved in a problem-solving-needs direction. In 1958 it was argued by Boehm that social work has a problem-solving function; that it is an art with a scientific foundation; that it seeks to meet human needs and aspirations; that while the goals sought should not be incompatible with the values held by society, these values are often conflicting and social work is based on a selection of these; and that social work often adopts unpopular positions as it serves as the conscience of society.[24] She argued, furthermore, that basic philosophical propositions include that an essential attribute of a democratic society is the realization of the full potential of each individual and the assumption of his social responsibilities through active participation in society and society has a responsibility to provide ways and means in which obstacles to this self-realization can be overcome and prevented. . . .

Those working directly with people and social problems are the most responsive to the behavioural environment. . . . The school of control theorists has given attention to needs, both what they are and what are the consequences of their not being met. Sites postulates eight, all of which require fulfillment and, therefore, none of which is necessarily more important than others.[25]

The first is a need for response and, furthermore, consistency in response. It is only by consistent response that there can be learning and consistency in behaviour. Response is reaction to the actor's behaviour— whether it be an individual or a group. Second, the other side of the coin, is stimulation, i.e., an input into the actor, no less required in learning, for example, of language, customs and skills. The learning process requires a third need, security: without it there is withdrawal from both response and stimulus. The fourth need is recognition. It is by recognition that the actor receives confirmation that reactions to stimulation are relevant and approved:

recognition provides the encouragement factor in learning, whereas responses can be positive or negative.

Out of these four needs others develop which make a qualitative difference to development, though learning may be possible in their absence. The fifth is distributive justice, i.e., not merely a consistency in response, but an appropriate response or reward in terms of experience and expectations. Sixth, there is a need to appear rational and to develop rationality. This follows from the need for consistency of response. However, the separate mention of rationality draws attention to the fact that the need is for consistent behaviour in others: rationality is a function of the behaviour of others. Inconsistent responses bring deviant and inconsistent behaviour— irrationality. Seventh, there is a need for meaning to be deduced from consistent response. Unless the response is meaningful to the actor it is interpreted as an inconsistent response. Even consistent responses can be interpreted falsely, and, therefore, lack meaning. This need is stated to direct attention to problems of communication and perception in social relations. Eighth, there is the need for a sense of control. Control is a defence mechanism: if other needs are fully met then there is no need for control. But this is never the case: an ability to control rather than merely to react in the social environment is consequently a need.

All of these lists of needs are made from the point of view of the "inferior" in relationships: attention is directed to the individual's struggle for security, control, identity, etc. Perhaps they could all be grouped together within the conceptual notion of "role": the individual attempts to secure a role and to preserve a role by which he acquires and maintains his recognition, security and stimulation.

This thought directs attention to those who already have achieved roles, who have achieved a satisfactory measure of these needs and who act to preserve their role, i.e., the "superiors." If there are needs that are universal they must be experienced by elites, authorities and the privileged in a society as much as by anyone else. The whites in Africa have needs to satisfy and to be preserved, no less than others, particularly security and recognition. The para-militaries in Northern Ireland could contemplate a cease-fire and a peaceful solution to their majority-minority dispute only at the sacrifice of roles that cater for needs such as those which Sites lists. Consequently, we must add to the Sites list and to those mentioned by others, "role defence," or the protection of needs once they have been acquired.

Whether or not we happen to be in sympathy with those defending roles, such as in South Africa, is besides the point. No explanation of a conflictual situation or the behaviour of individuals, groups and authorities is complete without consideration of role defence as an important need. It is a need for which biological evidence is available, for it explains the behaviour of dominant members of packs and the main fighting within species that takes place. Without the notion of role defence there cannot be a complete explanation of industrial conflict, the behaviour of management in preserving we-they relationships, of union leaders in seeking to maintain their own positions by reacting against management. Nor can we explain continuing communal conflict, the excesses in behaviour of some dictatorial leaders who in practice have a monopoly of violence or the behaviour of politicians who indulge in forms of corruption to maintain themselves in office. Family, matrimonial, pupil-teacher conflicts all invite the inclusion of the role dimension in their analysis.

Adding this dimension helps to focus attention on prescriptions that are more realistic than those suggested by coercion and value theories. Processes are necessary that allow the costs and consequences of role defence to be considered. . . .

If there are human societal needs that are universal and necessary to the existence of societies, then it could be expected that some evidence would be found of them in all species that form societies or functional wholes. The sociobiologists have been examining biological evidence from this point of view.

Wilson has taken a first step, by empirical studies, toward a theory of sociobiological human motivations. In his view, purely sociological studies of human behaviour have been intuitive and concerned only with social structures and non-genetic factors. In his view, "much of what passes for theory in sociology today is really labelling of phenomena and concepts. . . ."[26] Certainly, when one looks at some current treatments of man and his social problems, there is evidence that this is so. For example, the table of contents of Zawodny's important book is confined to labels: "Frustration— anxiety; Fear and anger; Hostility; Aggression; Conflict; Behaviour under stress; Social maladaptation."[27] Wilson believes that human needs can be determined by taking into account evolutionary influences. He is impressed, for example, with the functional similarity of the social systems properties of termites and monkeys.

> Both are formed into cooperative groups that occupy territories. The group members communicate hunger, alarm, hostility, caste status or rank, and reproductive status amongst themselves by means of something in the order of ten to a hundred nonsyntactical signals. Individuals are intensely aware of the distinction between groupmates and nonmembers. Kinship plays an important role in group structure and probably served as a chief generative force of society in the first place. In both kinds of society there is a well-marked division of labour, although in the insect there is a much stronger reproductive component. . . . This comparison may seem facile, but it is out of such deliberate over-simplification that the beginnings of a general theory are made.[28]

Overall, Wilson's findings give strong support to the list of needs and desires put forward by Sites, with its emphasis on identity, recognition, security, rationality and control. There are the sociopsychological and sociobiological needs that finally underpin, modify or destroy institutions. They are the needs institutions ideally help to promote: group integrity, identity, freedom from "structural violence," legitimized relationships and others that some writers now choose to place under the heading "liberation"[29] and which are described by creative writers who endeavour to depict the lives and drives of peoples and social groups living within institutional frameworks.

While Wilson may have written the most comprehensive review of the biological literature, others have come to similar conclusions. For example, Ardrey points to "territory" as evidence of the need for security and identity; Eibl-Eibesfeldt to the need for positive relationships that contribute to respect; Nance to evidence that security through isolation eliminates aggressive behaviour.[30] It is an inconclusive yet developing literature that could reveal in detail that which is as yet only conceptually known.

For the purposes of this study it is not necessary to enter into any argument whether such needs are genetic or environmentally induced. A theory could be developed that such universal needs are universal for neither biological nor environmental reasons. They could be systemic and occur merely as a result of the individual in society being a unit in a social organization. In this study universal human needs, such as Sites lists, that have a societal significance, are asserted as a hypothesis; in Popper's terms, this is a personal as distinct from a scientific assertion.[31] The testing of hypothesis, how it helps to explain unsolved problems, and whether it is a reliable base from which to predict is the scientific interest.

THE UNCONTROLLABLE NATURE OF NEEDS

An empirically based list of needs would not alter analysis or advance policy if it were still assumed that their satisfaction were controlled by environmental and normative conditions. Such a list would have limited practical significance unless accompanied by empirical evidence that such needs cannot be suppressed and will inexorably be pursued. It has always been agreed that there are human needs, even though what precisely they are has not been agreed. It has also been accepted in traditional thought that needs can be achieved or satisfied only to the extent that conditions allow: if not so satisfied they are required to be suppressed by self-control, by acceptance of law and custom and by moral obligation. However, implicit in the hypothesis that there are certain human needs and desires that are universal is the view that they will be satisfied. Altered environmental conditions, changed political and social relationships and altered differentiation of power, give opportunities for the overt expression and pursuit of needs. As a consequence there was an explosion of latent drives toward independence and participation in the decades after 1945. However, even without such environmental changes, needs are satisfied either by deviant or pathological behaviour when other means prove futile. In the view of Sites, social norms are used as a means of satisfying needs. Many, if not most members of societies, find some or most norms useful to them. However, norms will not be observed if they are not found useful. They are tools and useful only to the extent that they accomplish what is sought. The individual in society—any society—will engage in deviant behaviour despite the possible consequences, if needs and desires can be satisfied only by these means. "Society, then never completely conquers the individual."[32]

This represents a significant change in approach to the study of behaviour and, consequently, to social policies. The emphasis is no longer on the ability and necessity for the individual to adapt to his social and political environment, to be socialized, to conform; but on his ability to use the system for his own purposes. If this is a valid interpretation of behaviour, there are some significant implications for education and other means of socialization. It could be that societies are endeavouring to guide and to control behaviour by means and along lines that cannot succeed, toward goals that are behaviourally irrelevant. There are similar implications for the fields of crime and deviance generally: no amount of deterrence and "retraining" permanently alters behaviour while conditions prevail that continue to frustrate needs. Herein lies the irrelevance and invalidity of traditional coercion theories and the notions of integrated societies.

Furthermore, such a theory offers an explanation of the "inhuman," "mindless" behaviour associated with communal murders, mugging or other forms of violence. "If acting in accordance with one's beliefs does not produce sufficient control, the individual will typically change his behaviour even though his new behaviour goes against his own beliefs at that particular moment."[33]

This is a sufficient explanation of why deterrence by threat is a weak control of behaviour. It justifies the conclusions reached by Niemeyer and more recent international and civil law scholars. "International order, in the proper sense of the term, cannot be established by organizing an agency of power over and above the separate states, or through any other collective accumulation of force. . . . The effectiveness of international law rests fundamentally on its own merits, not on the assumption of some pressure behind it."[34] In the domestic field, in cases where the socialization process has failed: "The harder we try to induce conformity to the law where conformity does not exist, the more we seem to fail."[35]

It is of political significance that universal needs are not treated as such. Even where it is generally accepted that the need for participation in decisionmaking or the need for recognition is a "right," the exercise of this right by others is none the less often resisted within and between groups. Other values or institutional norms of behaviour are invoked, such as values associated with particular forms of law and order. They are held to be overriding and to justify the suppression of these social-psychological needs. The drives and motivations of people are thus suppressed by institutional and cultural values. The reason for this conflict between human needs and institutional norms is not hard to find. Specialization in social exchange leads to loss of independence and to relations based on bargaining and power.[36] Institutionalized norms then serve to legitimize and preserve the resultant social structures. Normative sanctions emerge as the means of controlling power relationships. In these circumstances the motivations and responses of others—even though they are identical with one's own—come to be regarded as a threat to existing institutions and positions of privilege. Indeed they are: there is a latent conflict between needs and institutional norms so established. The pursuit of their needs by some actors is interpreted by others as ideology and even irrationality. In historical and political writings needs are sometimes treated as being among influences that should be curbed and against which institutions of restraint should be directed. The pressure to achieve, to be accorded recognition, to obtain security and control, result in a variety of behavioural patterns. There is rarely any mutual recognition that different patterns are evidence of the same motivation. The activities of professionals and others favourably placed to dodge tax, to use office facilities for private purposes, are held by some people to be acceptable patterns of behaviour, while petty thieving is held to be not merely beyond the law, but unacceptably antisocial. Similarly, the petty thief condemns the tax dodger and the maker of money by financial manipulation.

One reason for this ambivalent attitude to human societal needs is probably that while their existence is recognized in social investigation, it has not yet become a part of conventional wisdom. In 1964, a Nobel Prize winner for chemistry wrote:

> What are human goals? Basically man seeks freedom from hunger and want, adequate warmth and protection, and freedom from disease. Added to these he wants reasonable leisure and recreation and with these the freedom to seek an understanding of the workings of the universe in which he lives. These seem to me the main goals of humanity in 1964 as they were in 1864 or 1064; I have no reason to doubt that they will still be its goals in 1984 and they will still seem far off for many people.[37]

We arrive at the position that the individual in society will pursue his needs and desires (some of which may be programmed genetically and may include some elements of altruism) to the extent that he finds this possible within the confines of his environment, his experience and knowledge of options and all other capabilities and constraints; he will use the norms common within society and push against them to the extent necessary to ensure that they work in his interests: but if the norms of the society inhibit and frustrate to the degree that he decides they are no longer useful, then, subject to values he attaches to social relationships, he will employ methods outside the norms, outside the codes he would in other circumstances wish to apply to his behaviour. In so doing he will be labelled deviant by society; but this is the cost he is prepared to pay to fulfill his needs. He will act this way, pay this cost, because in terms of human behaviour there are not options. Threat of punishment, punishment itself, isolation from society will not control his behaviour: already there has been a loss of identity, of a sense of control and of other needs that led to the deviance and further loss will not constrain.

POLICY IMPLICATIONS OF NEEDS

The interest in human needs in the behaviour paradigm does not reflect an ideological or sentimental interest in the individual as is the case in the conventional system of thought. On the contrary, the pursuit of human needs and the sacrifice of the individual are not necessarily incompatible goals: altruistic behaviour, Wilson has argued, is genetically programmed.[38] The interest in human needs is an interest in properties of actors behaving in a social system, the recognition of which is required for system survival. The behavioural interest in human needs is not in making the individual happier, though this may be the outcome. It is in determining the conditions necessary for social organizations to survive harmoniously. Problem-solving at the social level—be it the small group, the nation-state or interactions between states—is possible only by processes that take the needs of the individual as the basis for analyzing and planning. Any settlement of a conflict or attempt to order society that places the interest of institutions or even of the total society before those of its individual members, must fail—unless, as rarely is the case, institutional values happen to coincide with human needs. The legitimized status and authority of institutions is finally derived from behaviour at this sociological-biological level.

Traditionally social problems have been tackled within the existing social structure and the general aim has been to preserve it. The emphasis has been on the need for the individual to adjust to social norms: society has been the unit of analysis and its norms the reference points in deciding whether behaviour is conforming or deviant. The problems posed have seemed to be how to persuade the units within the system—be it a society, an industry or a school—to cooperate in achieving its goals. The interest has been in the preservation of the system by minor adjustments in its structure and by persuading actors within it to adopt its goals. This approach assumes that human behaviour is or can be controlled by "will" or some such influence that can ensure social conformity. Certainly social-psychological values change with altering conditions and different environments; cultural, religious and ideological values are evidence of this. Social-biological needs have the same appearance of alteration or of emergence, but this is probably due to altering environmental conditions that allow them to find expression. It may be that we have mistakenly regarded these needs as evolving or being created over time instead of merely coming into evidence as social and political changes have permitted. Feudalism and slavery, even the "happy slave" phenomenom, do not demonstrate that needs for recognition and participation did not exist. Indeed, the collapse of these systems suggests they did.

We have had difficulty in explaining the widespread and apparently spontaneous nature of independence movements, political revolutions and social rebellions, that have been recorded in history. A hypothesis that there are social-biological needs that are fundamental particles, parts of the information content of biological organization, serves to explain the historically evident phenomenon of continuity of social and political change in certain directions, as for example, the continuing struggle for participation and freedom to develop personality within a social environment. Aggression and power drives may be no more than manifestations of frustrated needs and evidence of more basic drives. At a political level, such a hypothesis serves to explain the persistent demand for independence of nations and for identification of groups within states. These manifestations of nationalism have biological origins and protective functions.

There is a supposition here that, in the course of social evolution, basic drives and motivations have been suppressed by institutional restraint, initially of a purely social or communal character and later by those resulting from economic specialization and organization. In accordance with this supposition, the overt expression of needs that characterizes every level of contemporary society is a reaction against this institutional overlay. In other words, there is a supposition that social-institutional development includes an interaction between the expression of needs and their control. In relatively stable and satisfied political communities the processes of political socialization effectively channel and control social-biological drives. Where, however, there are ethnic communities that feel threatened, economic groups that feel prejudiced, or minorities that have no means of effective participation in political decisions, there is reduced political socialization. This applies as much, if not more, to highly developed industrial societies as to underdeveloped ones where the problem of alienation is also becoming acute.

It is ultimately an empirical question whether solutions to authority problems can be achieved on any basis other than that of human needs.

However, an answer to the question can be deduced from the proposition that needs will be pursued. The emphasis on human needs as the basis of analysis and problem-solving is oriented toward the stability and progress of societies: the human needs of the individual that enable him to operate as an efficient unit within a social system and without which no social organization can be harmonious.

The handling of social problems requires problem-solving techniques that take into account the total situation, including the goals and frustrations of the actors. However, the attempt has been made to make a puzzle out of serious and complex problems by positing social goals: law and order, control of inflation, new towns and re-housing, integration of communities and ethnic groups and others. The goals, thus stated, are pursued as social goals requiring the cooperation of people and units within society, apparently on the assumption that they have the same goals and the further assumption that the processes of attaining them are compatible with their interests. There is always an answer to a puzzle: given powers of coercion, finance and techniques, most social goals can be pursued to a conclusion. New towns can be built, ethnic groups can be bussed and mixed, inflation can be controlled, law and order must be enforced. The result is usually that these immediate social goals are achieved; but the social problems they were supposed to solve become more complicated, other problems are created and even the immediate goals are finally given up or changed.

The alternative is to take individual needs as social goals and adopt the relevant strategies— re-housing within altering kinship groups and without threatening ethnic identity, using instruments other than unemployment to control the money supply, tackling deviant behaviour in its social context and not merely by the coercive application of social norms: in short, applying the tests of recognition, security, stimulation, distributive justice and others to the strategies adopted in solving social problems.

There appears to be a linear trend in the relations between institutional and human needs. There are many continuous trends in the development or growth of societies. For example, there appears to be a persistent tendency for labour to be concentrated initially in primary and extraction industries then for diversion into secondary industries, followed by the growth of tertiary industries and subsequently by diversions into welfare, research and environmental control as economic development proceeds. Some degree of prediction in development of societies is possible as a consequence. To take another example, there are trends in social mobility, in the declining power of central authorities after a certain peak, in the concentration of populations in cities, in the increased use of energy, in the growth of communications and in the availability of education and welfare services. We have postulated a continuing conflict between human and institutional values. If this is valid then there should be evidence of a continuing trend in the evolving forms of social structures and in authority relationships. Evidence of pressures for independence, participation and other human needs should appear in institutional changes over a period of time. It is more likely that each is part of a continuum which would include also current we-they attitudes in industrial relations, class and cultural barriers to end inequality of opportunities. The increase in the last thirty years of the number of states following the success of independence movements may well be part of this trend toward greater political participation and greater opportunities for identification with language and cultural groups.

The problem we are investigating—deviant behaviour generally—relates to such a linear trend: it is part of a continuing erosion of coercive authority. It could be that the longer-term trends and the immediate deviance problems societies face have some common origins and causes. Demands on authorities and society have extended from immediate working and economic areas to political and to aesthetic areas where freedom of expression is more and more demanded.

To the present day we have perceived each point in this linear trend—the challenges to slavery and colonialism—as a challenge to social stability and as a problem of law and order. We have failed to ask why it has occurred, just as we today are more concerned with preventing terrorism than investigating and dealing with its cause. The emphasis has been on preservation, law and order, defence of institutions, the promotion of morality in terms of the observance of social norms. Educational curricula, legal systems, religions and rewards for achievement have been directed toward the preservation of institutions and the observance of norms, commendable in itself, save to the extent that the development of the individual is sacrificed. The linear trend has now reached the stage at which the emphasis is on individual development, even at the cost of institutions and of respect for authorities.

For these reasons we must conclude that if an attempt is made to subordinate individual values to social values, then, because it is not possible to enforce social values that are inconsistent with human needs, there will be responses that are damaging both to the individual and, through him, to the social system.

Once we move from the integration of society to the satisfaction of human needs as the goal of social organization and of authorities, we can give some meaning to the otherwise emotive phrase "historic processes". . . . The "historic process" is the end result, over time, of the conflict between institutional values and human needs, between the structures and norms created and supported by powerful elites and the human needs that must be met at the individual level if societies are to be functionally efficient and harmonious. This definition of the historical process, in turn, points to the significance over time of role defence, being an important reason for the lag that exists between human aspirations and their achievement.

NOTES

1. Chalmers Johnson, *Revolutionary Change*, (Little, Brown and Company, 1966), p. 33.

2. J.C. Davies, *Human Nature in Politics*, (Wiley, 1963). James MacGregor Burns, "Wellsprings of Political Leadership," *The American Political Science Review*, LXXI, March 1977.

3. A.H. Maslow, *Motivation and Personality*, (Harper Brothers, 1954), p. 67.

4. A. de Reuck and M. de Reuck, "Value Systems and Value Change," *Science and Absolute Values*, Vol. 1 (1974), 429.

5. H.C. Kelman, "The Conditions, Criteria and Dialects of Human Dignity," *International Studies Quarterly*, Vol. 21, No. 3, 1977.

6. T.R. Gurr, *Why Men Rebel*, (Princeton, 1970). J.C. Davies, *When Men Revolt and Why*, (The Free Press, 1971).

7. J.M. Thomas and W.G. Bennis (eds.), *Management of Change and Conflict*, (Penguin, 1972).

8. Arnold Brecht, *Political Theory*, (Princeton, 1967), p. 6.

9. For a similar view, see Talcott Parsons, "The Relations between the Small Group and the Larger Social Systems," in R.R. Grinker (ed.), *Towards a Unified Theory of Human Behaviour*, (Basic Books, 1956).

10. For further discussion, see M. Barkun, *Law Without Sanctions*, (Yale, 1968), p. 28.

11. Paul Sites, *Control, the Basis of Social Order*, (Dunellen Publishers, 1973), p. 9.

12. Ibid., p. 7.

13. Ibid., pp. 7–8.

14. Burns, "Wellsprings of Political Leadership."

15. R.L. Heilbronner, *The Future As History*, (Grove Press, 1959). E. Fromm, *May Man Prevail?*, (Doubleday, 1961). R. Niebuhr, *Moral Man and Immoral Society*, (SCM Press, 1961).

16. R. Nisbet, *Twilight of Authority*, (Heinemann, 1976), p. 242.

17. Gurr, *Why Men Rebel*, p. 25.

18. For example, see R. R. Blake, et al., *Managing Intergroup Conflict in Industry*, (Gulf Publishing Co., 1964).

19. See, for example, S. Box, *Deviance, Reality and Society*, (Holt, Rinehart and Winston, 1971).

20. Johan Galtung, "Violence, Peace, and Peace Research," *Journal of Peace Research*, No. 3, 1969, pp. 167–91.

21. Burns, "Wellsprings of Political Leadership." Nisbet, *Twilight of Authority*. M. Rokeach, *Beliefs, Attitudes and Values*, (Jossey-Bass, 1976). Cynthia Enloe, *Ethnic Conflict and Political Development*, (Little, Brown and Company, 1973).

22. Charlotte Towle, *Common Human Needs*, E. Younghusband (ed.), (Allen and Unwin, 1973). National Association of American Social Workers, *Social Work*, 1958. Mia Pringle, *The Needs of Children*, (Hutchinson, 1974).

23. E. E. Maccoby, "The Development of Moral Values and Behaviour in Childhood," in J. Clausen (ed.) *Socialization and Society,* (Little, Brown and Company, 1968).

24. W. W. Boehm, "The Nature of Social Work," *Social Work,* 1958.

25. Sites, "Control," ch. 2.

26. E. O. Wilson, *Sociobiology: A New Synthesis,* (Harvard, 1973), p. 574.

27. J. K. Zawodny, *Man and International Relations,* (Chandler Publishing Company, 1966).

28. Wilson, pp. 4–5.

29. See Denis Goulet, *The Cruel Choice,* (Atheneum, 1973).

30. Robert Ardrey, *The Territorial Imperative,* (Dell, 1966). Iraneus Eibl-Eibesfeldt, *Love and Hate, the Natural History of Behaviour Problems,* (Holt, Rinehart and Winston, 1971). John Nance, *The Gentle Tasaday,* (Harcourt Brace, 1975).

31. Karl Popper, "Normal Science and its Dangers," in Imre Lakatos and Alan Musgrave (eds.), *Criticism and the Growth of Knowledge,* (Cambridge University Press, 1974).

32. Sites, "Control," p. 11.

33. Sites, "Control," p. 21.

34. G. Niemeyer, *Law Without Force,* (Princeton, 1941), p. 21.

35. H. E. Pepinsky, *Crime and Conflict,* (Law in Society Series, Martin Robertson, 1976), p. 2.

36. P. M. Blau, *Exchange and Power in Social Life,* (Wiley, 1964).

37. A. R. Todd, "Working with What We Know," in N. Calder, *The World in 1984,* Volume 1, (Pelican, 1965), p. 9.

38. Wilson, "Sociobiology: A New Synthesis."

CHAPTER FOUR

Three Visions of Needs and the Future: Liberalism, Marxism, and Gandhism

RAMASHRAY ROY

The fact that virtually all philosophical traditions have some underlying perspective on human needs is illustrated in this selection by Indian political scientist, Ramashray Roy, director of the Center for the Study of Developing Societies in New Delhi. In fact, he carries on in the same vein as John Burton, examining the potential for establishing harmony between man and society and nature. Roy's areas of research include international development, international political economy, and South Asia. He is the author of The Uncertain Verdict: A Study of the 1969 Elections in Four Indian States.

Roy distinguishes among three philosophies—liberalism, Marxism, and Gandhism—in terms of, first, their perception of human needs (implicit or explicit), and second, their implications for the interaction of man, society, and nature. He begins by addressing the ambiguity and disagreement over the concept of human needs, reviewing the interpretations offered by the three "streams of thought." He then evaluates to what extent each philosophical orientation promotes individual freedom, social justice, and ecological balance—the key to achieving a link between man, society, and nature. Roy makes a strong case for the superiority of Gandhian philosophy, and appeals for "self-restraint" and the "reform of man himself," as the key to establishing harmony between man, society, and nature. While the reader may obviously agree or disagree with Roy's analysis, some of the crucial points underpinning his logic are worthy of special note. For example, Roy argues that both liberals and Marxists do not recognize that industrialization and technological advance produce a

Chapter 4 text reprinted by permission of the publisher from "Human Needs and Freedom: Three Contrasting Perceptions and Perspectives," *Alternatives* 5 (1979-1980), pp. 195-212.

conflict between the fulfillment of individual human needs with society and nature, thereby impeding the achievement of the all-important harmony. Thus, Roy demonstrates the importance of the concept of human needs to each of the three philosophical traditions and the implications of each for the future.

Discussions on human needs assume, even when not explicitly stated, certain ontological, historical and anthropological perspectives, and they often represent a mix of normative and empirical elements. Moreover, such discussions often ignore or sidetrack the linkages of need-satisfaction with larger issues such as freedom, social justice . . . and ecological balance. These linkages point to the necessity of establishing harmony between man, society and nature. This paper deals with how these linkages have been perceived in three streams of thinking, Liberalism, Marxism and Gandhism. Believing in the idea of linear progress, the liberals (excepting J. S. Mill) and Marx did not recognize that unrestrained proliferation of needs was subject to limits to growth, depletion of natural resources and degradation of natural environment. Marx believed that the process of need-satisfaction mediating between Man as subject and Nature as object releases the dormant creative capacities of human beings. Marx therefore stood for large-scale industrial production as necessary for human need-satisfaction. He saw dehumanization and alienation as the consequence, not of industrialization, but of a disjunction between the forces of production and the relations of production, which is the characteristic of capitalism and which will disappear in socialism. Neither the liberals nor Marx saw that industrialization itself entails centralization, degradation of human values and spoliation of nature. Gandhi, on the other hand, saw in need proliferation the root cause of human predicament and in industrialization its exacerbation. He did not accept the proposition that by changing social forms, man will shed his covetousness, self-aggrandizing tendency, etc. He therefore called for self-restraint and limitation of wants, which would obviate the necessity of large-scale industrialization. He clearly saw that man himself has created the civilizational predicament through his own activities, and therefore emphasized that the reform of the system must begin with the reform of man through non-attachment, non-violence and quest for truth.

INTRODUCTION

The current interest in human needs springs from two major sources. One symbolizes the return to a valuing social science that answers the "need for relevance, significance and action"[1] from the tendency, under the influence of the behavioural movement, to eschew a normative approach to social inquiry. The second, specially in the economically backward part of the world, arises from the failure to achieve economic growth with social justice to solve the problem of persistent poverty, penury and illiteracy.

However, the concept of human needs bristles with difficulties. First, while the notion of need involves imperatives, it must also be rooted in common sense and empirical reality. This amalgam of the normative and the empirical produces a tendency to slide from the actual to the desirable. More often the desirable itself is derived from the actual, creating a confusion of perspectives and making it difficult to say categorically whether need is an empirical and factual necessity, a logical or analytical necessity, or a normative necessity.[2]

Second, since the specification of needs cannot be wholly independent of ontological considerations, some concept of human nature becomes unavoidable. The distinction between "true" and "false", "good" and "bad" needs is made on the basis of one set of assumptions about human nature. Those who object to such a distinction on the ground that no individual, or group of individuals, has the right, or the competence, to decide what is a need for others proceed from a different set of assumptions. They argue that all wants or needs are equal.[3]

Then there are those who posit a hierarchy or rank order of wants or needs, ranging from those which must be satisfied first, for the mere sustenance of life, through those which, though not essential for mere life, are essential for a fully human life. The Maslovian categories of human needs is one instance of this approach; the distinction between basic, material and non-material needs is another.

Implicit in all these are particular views of the human essence, which makes it difficult to arrive at a consensus.

Third, the concept of needs has little meaning apart from organized social existence. To satisfy his needs, man not only consumes or uses what is provided by nature; he also transforms nature to meet his needs, creating, in this process, new needs. Thus, needs are not fixed for all societies, nor for all times in the same society. This is so because the technology used to sustain economic progress determines what needs are created and how they change or multiply over time. On this view, no a priori definition of needs is possible. It can only be an empirical question, depending upon the nature of technology used, the stage of economic development, and the concomitant socio-cultural formations. Thus, the concept of needs is basically historical and therefore relative.

Implicit in the historical conception of needs is the idea of progress. The notion of progress comprises two elements: the development of human potentialities more and more fully, and the simultaneous development of the individuals's potentialities to the full. It is assumed that as mankind develops human potentialities, it makes it possible for individuals to develop their own powers. The development of potentialities, collective or individual, is usually equated with the enrichment of economic life which, in turn, is supposed to enrich spiritual or cultural life.

While the interconnection between collective and individual enrichment must be recognized, it needs to be examined, in the light of empirical experience, whether the one always and necessarily leads to the other, or whether the two are always and necessarily compatible. It is true that human capacities cannot develop except through social interaction. It is also in this process that certain social and cultural structures evolve that are instrumental in directing, stabilizing and controlling social intercourse. But these very structures may, at a later stage, begin to constrict individual development.

The equating of progress with the satisfaction of ever-spiralling and ever-complexifying material needs (believed to be synonymous with well-being) gives rise to three crucial questions: the question of individual freedom or autonomy, the question of social equity or justice, and the question of ecological balance.

Freedom: Although economic development assuredly creates a vast and increasing variety of occupations, it severely restricts the choice of most people, condemning them to occupations that are repetitive, monotonous and dull. But freedom is curbed in other ways, too.

Social justice: The process of need-satisfaction creates the relations of production, i.e. a form of social organization which governs the exercise of power and control over resources. This puts a few in a position of dominance over the many.

Ecological balance: The use of rapacious technology for inducing, maintaining and extending economic growth has forcefully brought to attention the fact that the defiling and degradation of nature has been carried to the point of endangering human existence itself. Hence the recent concern with limits to growth.[4]

This paper examines three streams of thought—in terms of the concept of needs and the underlying relationship in each between man, society and nature.

THE CLASSICAL LIBERAL SCHOOL

The classical liberal thinkers erected the structure of their thought on a particular view of wants and needs.[5] Hume, for example, distinguishes man from animal in that man has innumerable and insatiable desires, wants and necessities as well as a natural inability to satisfy them without the assistance of others. Man is endowed with abilities proportionate to his wants in order to overcome "the unnatural conjunction of infirmity and necessity." It is, however, only in society that his infirmities are overcome. For Hume, the articulation and expression of self-interest, however, leads, in due course, to a sense of moral obligation and promotes a sense of common interest.

If the sense of common interest does not always succeed in inhibiting the pursuit of self-interest to a point where unbridled pursuit of self-interest comes into clash with the general good, it is for two reasons. First, man's passions are generally directed towards particular objects rather than towards his total good. Second, man has a tendency to be influenced more by the immediate than remote values. Moreover, man's "calm passions" of prudence and good will, although very real, are not sufficiently constant or intense to act as effective restraints upon man's other passions.

The main social vices, according to Hume, are thus "purposelessness" and "factions." As the civil society lacks the sanction of "physical reprisals," the state emerges to establish laws and impose restraints upon its members. The primary function of the state, then, is to supply man with motives and habits to counteract those ineradicable weaknesses that would otherwise destroy him. The main function of the state is thus to prevent or remove evil rather than to institute positive good.

Hume considers rights and obligations artificial in the sense that they presuppose a system of rules, which is a product of society rather than of the individual will. He believes that individual interest does not create rights, nor does the pristine nature of man alone determine his obligations. Rights are functions partly of individual interest and partly of the opportunity which society affords or will permit. Similarly, obligations are functions partly of man's interests and partly of the conditions which society imposes as the price of their satisfaction.

Hume, while recognizing the importance of self-interest and the desirability of its pursuit, recognizes the essentiality of the preservation of social order, without which individuals will slip back into the solitary and savage condition of the state of nature. The good of the individual is, however, not always the same as the good of all. That is why individual drives for the maximization of wants and needs must be restrained if they conflict with the realization of the common good.

Bentham, another philosopher of the Liberal school, also believes that every individual by nature seeks to maximize his pleasure without limits. Each want satisfied produces a new want, and in this process "the horizon elevates itself as we advance, and each new want, attended on the one hand by pain, on the other by pleasure, becomes a new principle of action."[6] Recognizing the primacy of self-interested pursuit of pleasure and avoidance of pain, Bentham feels that such a principle provides the basis of ever newer action to ensure the "greatest good of the greatest number." He does posit the goal of the common good, but he believes that natural harmonization of interest produces this result automatically in many situations. And yet, he concedes, conflicts between the individual good and the common good cannot always be ruled out. Thus the political problem for Bentham is to ensure that individual appetites, which must be recognized and must not be condemned, never become so strong as to tear society apart. For the muting of conflicts, he relied on the psychological principle of avoiding pain and, in the event of its failure, on mild reforms to evolve certain checking and elevating devices. Bentham was not much concerned with the quality of human wants; he even denied that any one was intrinsically superior to others. Wants, in his view, were to be judged by the consequences of their satisfaction. Nor was he concerned with the manner in which different commodities produced to satisfy human needs were distributed among the members of society, nor with whether a particular manner of distribution was conducive to human happiness in the widest sense and on the most extended scale.

By the time J.S. Mill arrived on the scene, these two questions had assumed great relevance. Mill took note of the basic fact of man's improvidence and the niggardliness of nature; but he thought that technologically induced economic growth would be instrumental in overcoming both man's improvidence and nature's niggardliness—though within certain limits. However, with resources more or less fixed but man's power of reproduction limitless, poverty, ignorance and social conflict were the natural outcome.[7]

To Mill, then, the adverse ratio between resources and population was the main cause of poverty, ignorance and social disharmony. He had no fault to find with the existing social arrangements or technological innovations, although he strongly condemned the industrial market society for its values and for the passivity and self-enclosed existence of the bulk of the population. He hated the life dominated by the commercial spirit, selfishness, and ascendancy of mere wealth. While the Industrial Revolution had made it possible to maintain a greatly increased population, providing an excellent example of human intelligence improving nature, it had also produced acquisitive entrepreneurs who took the accumulation of wealth to be the sole object of human existence. Mill also deplored the drudgery and narrowness of the lives of the industrial labourers, subjected to the division of labour:

> The insignificant detail which forms their whole occupation—the infinitely minute wheel they help to turn in the machinery of society—does not arouse or gratify any feeling of public spirit or unity with their fellow men. Their work is a mere tribute to physical necessity, not the glad performance of a social office.[8]

Mill was also alive to the danger of the acquisitive spirit unleashed by industrialization leading to the defilement and despoliation of nature:

There is not much satisfaction in contemplating the world with nothing left to the spontaneous activity of nature; with every rood of land brought into cultivation, which is capable of growing food for human beings; every flowery waste or natural pasture ploughed up, all quadrupeds or birds which are not domesticated for man's use exterminated as his rivals for food, every hedgerow or superfluous tree rooted out, and scarcely a place left where a wild shrub or flower could grow without being eradicated as a weed in the name of improved agriculture. If the earth must lose the great portion of its pleasantness which it owes to things that the unlimited increase of wealth and population would extirpate from it, for the mere purpose of enabling it to support a larger, but not a better or a happier population, I sincerely hope, for the sake of posterity, that they will be content to be stationary, long before necessity compels them to it.[9]

In Mill's view, then, the malaise of the industrial society lay neither in unjust social order nor in technological progress but in the pursuit of "sinister interests," caused, on the one hand, by acquisitive spirit (aggravated by the adverse ratio between population and resources) and, on the other, by the rise of "collective mediocrity," made possible by the absence of a unitary body of principles.

Unlike Bentham, Mill made a distinction between cruder wants and needs. He rejected the postulate that every want was as good as every other. He held that wants might, and should, change in quality, away from material desires and the desire to have more than the next man to intellectual, moral and aesthetic wants.[10] As far as material needs are concerned, Mill was convinced that "the natural law of the progress of wealth" promised to satisfy the material needs of all without a transformation of the economic system. The two impediments to this—pressure of population and asymmetry in distribution—could be taken care of—the first by self-discipline or, failing that, by external discipline on reproduction, and the other by suitable changes in the law so that economic rewards were not wholly determined by pre-existing advantages. Mill advocated the kind of social policy which, without affecting the institution of private property, would, in the words of Cowling:

break down inequalities of wealth . . . destroy the greater inherited disparities and ensure that the middle rank of society—the rank of educated people—will have that 'moderate' financial independence on which mental cultivation sometimes depends, whilst being neither too far distant, nor too greatly alienated, from an improved proletariat.[11]

Since the cultivation of mind cannot be sustained by financial independence alone, Mill turned to education. The education of his conception is the process of infusing that general culture which enables professional and vocational activities to be informed by certain general principles—not habit, particularly when it is influenced by "the despotism of custom," nor moral and political questioning, which, though essential to social health, may, if unrestrained by principles, lead to anarchy or, even if principled, erode consensus which is the bedrock of society. Since education will be open to most, if not all, men, they will be able to arrive at ethical and social purposes through the process of reflection. They will also be able to replace their deference to arbitrarily established authority by a rational commitment to elevated intellect and agree among themselves on the means of deciding what actions and institutions are right.

Mill, then, calls for self-conscious critical examination of the reason for all actions and all institutions. Such an examination must be free of coercion, deference to arbitrarily established authority or obedience to custom. No opinion need be accepted because tradition sanctions it or the majority agrees on it. Truth may well be found in the judgement of an individual, even an eccentric individual, defying the collective judgement of society. This, however, does not mean the assertion of total individual freedom. Mill believes that men who have been properly educated will ultimately agree in their view of the grounds on which, and the extent to which, individual freedom should be limited.

Mill's notion of self-conscious critical rationality is linked with his idea of happiness. What he argues for is not just the happiness of the individual, but the greatest amount of happiness altogether. It is not sufficient that an individual pursues his own happiness; it is incumbent upon him to increase the sum total of happiness. Where his preference for his own happiness conflicts with the happiness of the society as a whole, he has to rise above self-interest and act in a way that maximizes the happiness of society. He envisages a society where the pursuit of not just any sort of happiness but disinterested pursuit of the greatest amount of happiness is possible—that higher happiness, especially, which comes from moral altruism, on the one hand, and intellectual cultivation, on the other. Mill's concept of justice is grounded in this belief. In his view, justice inheres in the condition that guarantees the maximization of collective happiness and higher cultivation of the self.

Mill advocated democracy, particularly democracy at the grass-roots level, because of the superior merit of democracy as an instrument of higher cultivation, but also because it encourages diversity, which is essential for approximating to truth. Moreover, democracy, for Mill, is a "school of political capacity and general intelligence."

Mill thus believed in cultivating higher passions and controlling cruder ones. Committed to the ideal of social solidarity, he advocated the development of self-conscious critical rationality as a basis of social action and disinterested pursuit of elevated happiness in a way that contributed to, but did not conflict with, collective happiness. Education became in Mill's perspective a crucial institution, not only for the creation of the class of clerisy which would propagate the principles of right moral conduct, but also for the training of the mind of the common man.

For liberals, then, man is the pivot of the social order, man who is a bundle of passions, desires, wants and needs. The articulation, expression and fulfilment of these drives are possible only in society. Man is conceived as an agent conscious of his wants who, because he is rational, can learn from experience and pass on what he learns to succeeding generations.

Liberal thinkers, barring Mill, did not concern themselves either with the quality of wants or with the limits to growth. They recognized the possibility of a disjunction between private interest and public good, but believed that an increase in material resources would be an adequate answer to the problem. Progress connotes the passage of society from the existing level of development to the next higher level of development. The liberals, except for Mill, believed that this progress was to continue indefinitely. The two attendant problems—resources limitation and distributive justice—did not engage their attention. Mill recognized these problems, but refused to believe that there was anything wrong either with the free enterprise system or with technological innovations. Along with other liberals, he believed in incremental change consequent upon the modification of certain institutions fortified by cultural improvements.

MARX'S SOCIAL THEORY

Marx's major criticism of the Utilitarian philosophy, particularly of Bentham, was twofold. First, Marx objected to Bentham's attempt to determine human nature on the basis of some abstract principle, the principle of utility in this case. Pointing to Bentham's failure to "first deal with human nature in general, and then human nature as modified in each historical epoch," Marx accused him of taking the "modern shopkeeper, especially the English shopkeeper, as the natural man," and then positing the idea that "whatever is useful to this queer normal man, and to his world, is absolutely useful."[12]

The starting point of Marx's theory is the real, corporeal man—no abstraction or figment of the speculative imagination—as he goes about the business of producing and consuming. In the nature-imposed condition of human existence, man changes nature through tool-making purposive activity. And through this he changes himself and society. He develops new needs, new ways of satisfying these needs and, as a result, creates new social and cultural forms. Thus, life and society are essentially historical. Marx repudiated static conceptions of human nature, which confine human capacities arbitrarily.

Second, Marx took Bentham to task for accepting bourgeois values wholesale and uncritically and then trying to improve bourgeois society by petty reforms. He rebuked Bentham for not seeing that man was to a great extent also the victim of society because society inhibited his developing capacities. Marx saw in the capitalist social order the roots of man's alienation. Society, as a hindrance to the full development of man, brings into sharp focus the connection between man's wants and social formations.

Marx's concept of need is central to his theory of human nature. It brings together the different strands of his thought and provides a measuring rod for distinguishing between human activity proper and mere animal or alienated activity, between different societies, and between different stages of the same society.

Two distinct phases in Marx's concept of needs are clearly visible. In the first phase, when he was under the influence of Hegel and Feuerbach, Marx made needs the central piece in his account of the human essence and the actualization of man's dormant capacities in characteristically human society. Needs, for Marx, play the role of mediation between man as subject and nature as object. Marx also talks of nature as man's "inorganic body." In the next phase when he wrote *The German Ideology*, Marx had shed off the Hegelian influence and cast his conception of needs in material, anthropological mould. He argued that to satisfy needs man uses tools giving rise to a production system. He emphasized the constant proliferation of needs and the corresponding expansion of man's power with the application of developing technology to meet them.

Marx, thus, saw a dynamic relationship between needs, their satisfaction and the creation of new needs. His theory asserts the primary significance, within an organic system, of certain activities and forces—narrowly, technological, but, more broadly, economic—and the dynamic impact which they have on existing social forms, which are gradually but inexorably subverted. This makes possible the progression of society from primitivism to feudalism, to capitalism and, hopefully, to communism and even beyond.

Marx makes a distinction between biological and human needs. He argues that man is different from animals because, besides biological needs which he has in common with animals, man has other non-biological needs that can be satisfied only in society. But Marx insists that non-biological needs (cultural, spiritual, etc.) arise out of activities directed in the first place towards satisfying biological needs.

However, in the process of need satisfaction there develops a disjunction between the forces of production—the resources that man can command through his augumented powers—and the relations of production—the forms of social organization which govern the exercise of these powers and control of the resources. The disjunction is the genesis of dehumanization of needs and alienation.

In the capitalist society, where this disjunction becomes very acute, use value is transformed into exchange value. Money and private property emerge to create artificial needs. "Money is the pimp between man's need and the object, between his life and his means of life."[13] Money replaces the real object and dominates the subject. Needs and power coincide in an abstract way; only those needs are recognized as real needs that can be bought by money. Labour becomes a commodity and is bought and sold. The worker gets alienated from his own labour. When Marx speaks of alienation, he means, first, that the worker's product becomes alien to him because it is appropriated by his employer. Secondly, he means the consequences of this appropriation: labour becoming a commodity and capital becoming both a product of labour and a power over labour. Marx also means the "entire production system, and even the whole social order, considered as an effect of what men have done, an effect which they never intended, do not understand, and cannot control."[14]

Alienation in all the three forms, Marx believed, would cease with the end of capitalism and the ushering in of communism, when man will become himself and begin to satisfy all human needs.

For Marx, progress consists in the satisfaction of human needs. If man is a natural being with a multiplicity of needs, human fulfilment—the realization of human freedom—cannot be conceived as an abnegation or subjugation of these needs, but only as their properly human gratification. (In this sense, freedom is to be equated with necessity.)

Unlike the Liberals, Marx saw that human wants affect, and are affected by, man's conception of himself, of the social relations in which he stands, and of the world generally, and he made it part of his social analysis. He saw, too, that social man was both the product and the victim of his own activities; he felt frustrated or reduced to despair in a cultural world of his own making. Unlike the Liberals, Marx recognized that conflict and cultural disharmony as facts of life are themselves the effects of progress, of increasing knowledge, wealth and power.

But Marx did not, for this reason, reject the idea of progress. He did not subscribe to the necessity of curtailing wants or technologically induced economic growth. He believed that the coming of the rational state—the society of the equal and the free—was possible if man's understanding of his environment and his ability to control it continued to increase. He did, however, make a distinction between "artificial" and "human" needs and spoke of the necessity of eliminating the former in order to realize the latter. Once "artificial" needs are abandoned, work (through which man's creativity is expressed, but which is a mere means in the present social and economic relations) becomes an end in itself. Marx does not, however, suggest how this can be done.

When Marx speaks of the elimination of "artificial" needs, he has in mind the necessity of man transforming his own nature, even if partially. However, his main emphasis is on bringing about profound social and political changes for man to be free. This freedom consists in work, through which man transforms nature and himself—work that is directed towards the fulfilment of unlimited human needs. Marx thus sees in the equation of freedom with necessity a solution to civilizational ills.

For Marx, capitalist economy symbolizes a stage of development that promises, because of its enormous productive capacity, to make possible the realization of a higher type of society whose fundamental principle is the full and free development of each individual. While in the capitalist system the financier seeks after profit and, in this pursuit, "relentlessly drives human beings to production for production's sake," it also creates the material conditions that make the development of the individual possible. Capitalism, though it allows the worker to be exploited also produces wealth abundantly and provides for material wants more copiously than any economy did before. What it does not provide is the "full and free development of each individual."

This "full and free development of individual" is, in Marx's view, possible once workers come to control the means of production. He did not envisage any change in the industrial mode of production even in his ideal communist state. He overlooked the fact that the progressive enlargement of the scale of production, which industrial production inevitably leads to, is in fact a major cause of the ills he talks of. Even if, in consonance with the theory, workers in their collectivity own the entire means of production, each will still feel helpless and therefore alienated. There would be no way of ensuring that industrial democracy in such a mass production system was not as much of a "sham" as political democracy in bourgeois society.

Marx did not concern himself with these questions. He missed completely the fact that once technologically induced economic growth became the prime value, certain consequences were bound to follow, one of which was alienation about which Marx was so concerned. Since alienation is endemic in high industrialization, it would be inevitable no less in a communist than in a capitalist society.

GANDHI'S VIEW OF MODERN CIVILIZATION

This was the point of departure for Gandhi. And this is where his genius becomes manifest. He saw with rare perspicacity that proliferation of wants was the root cause of the ills of modern civilization. It is to this that he ascribed the inexorable drive towards ever more sophisticated technology, demanding ever expanding scale of production, and leading to centralization of wealth and power, inducing dependency relations.[15] Large-scale production also creates unemployment, he added.

The systemic consequences of industrialization are no less serious.

Industrialization stimulates a value system that emphasizes acquisitiveness, which, in turn, breeds inequality, exploitation and domination: "essentially, power over men: in its simplest sense, the power of obtaining for our own advantage the labour of servant, tradesmen and artist."[16]

Lastly, industrialization means, as is borne out by history, exploitation of and domination over, other countries and loss of man's dignity. Gandhi also saw in industrializaion, and deplored, the exploitation and degradation of nature.

For Marx, the civilizational malaise was created by the capitalist mode of production, or production relations of capitalism. For Gandhi, it was created by large-scale industrializaion itself, which both fuelled and was fuelled by unrestrained multiplication of wants. For Marx, the remedy lay in social revolution—violent, if necessary—effectuated under the leadership of the working class. For Gandhi, the remedy lay in man transforming himself and, through this transformation, founding a just social order. Gandhi argued that social transformation, no matter how profound, would be neither enough nor lasting if man himself was not transformed. He elaborated a strategy for such a transformation (but a discussion of this would take us beyond the scope of this paper). A part of this strategy was voluntary limitation of wants. Not that he grudged people a reasonable degree of physical well-being and comfort. But he made a clear distinction between needs and wants. He summed it up pithily in one sentence: "The earth provides enough to satisfy every man's needs, but not for every man's greed." He rejected the ideal of creating an unlimited number of wants and satisfying them as "a delusion and a snare", and argued that

> the satisfaction of one's physical needs, even the intellectual needs of one's narrow self, must meet at a certain point a dead stop, before it degenerates into voluptuousness. A man must arrange his physical and cultural circumstances so that they do not hinder him in his service of humanity.[17]

For Gandhi, man in the performance of physical functions—such as, eating, sleeping, etc.—is not different from the brute. "What distinguishes him from the brute is his ceaseless striving to rise above the brute on the moral plane"[18]—in one word, self-restraint. Real self-restraint is born of the realization that one has no right to have more than what the lowliest has, and forms, in the social sphere, the bedrock of economic equality. Economic equality does not mean that every one should eat the same amount of food, or wear the same amount of clothing. It simply means that everybody should have enough for his needs.

According to Gandhi, the principle of economic equality can be operative only if man realizes the dignity of labour and does his share of "bread labour." To use the labour of others for the satisfaction of one's needs is not only exploitation but also degrading for both the exploiter and the exploited.

Gandhi outlined the type of non-violent socio-politico-economic structure which would ensure a perfect balance between man, society and nature, human freedom and dignity, absence of man-man and man-nature exploitation, and equality (including economic equality). Truth and non-violence were to form the "foundation of the order of my conception"; it would be composed of small, largely self-sufficient communities. To dispel the misunderstanding that this was a plea for village autarchy and isolation, he clarified his concept thus:

> My idea of self-sufficiency is that villages must be self-sufficient in regard to food, cloth and other basic necessities. But even this can be overdone. . . . Self-sufficiency does not mean narrowness. To be self-sufficient is not to be altogether self-contained . . . we shall have to get from outside the village what we cannot produce in the village, we shall have to produce more of what we can in order thereby to obtain in exchange what we are unable to produce.[19]

The social order of Gandhi's conception is not a pyramid with impulses emanating from the apex and traveling down to the base. As he put it:

> In this structure composed of innumerable villages, there will be ever widening, never ascending circles. Life will not be a pyramid with the apex sustained by the bottom. But it will be an oceanic circle whose centre will be the individual always ready to perish for the village, the latter ready to perish for the circle of villages, till at last the whole becomes one life composed of individuals, never aggressive in their arrogance but ever humble, sharing the majesty of the oceanic circle of which they are integral units.
>
> Therefore, the outermost circumference will not wield power to crush the inner circle but will give strength to all within and derive its own strength from it.[20]

The emphasis on self-sufficiency means that a large part of the production system will consist of small-scale and household industrial activities requiring physical labour and, only in a few cases, the use of machinery. Gandhi is not against machinery. However, he insists that the use of technology that leads to centralization and exploitation and enslaves man must be shunned. For self-sufficiency to work, decentralization (that is, localization of production and consumption) becomes necessary. With it goes also political decentralization.

Gandhi attached the greatest value to individual freedom, but he was opposed to individualism; for, he said, "unrestricted individualism is the law of the beast of the jungle." Because the individual is but a part of society and lives on its "sufferance," he should use his talents, not for self only, but for society. Gandhi argues:

> If the individual ceases to count, what is left of society? Individual

freedom alone can make a man voluntarily surrender himself completely to the service of society. If it is wrested from him, he becomes an automaton and society is ruined. No society can possibly be built on a denial of individual freedom.[21]

Gandhi thus believes that the good of the individual is contained in the good of all. Man's freedom lies in the development of the self in conjunction with other selves and his preparedness to serve others.

CONCLUSION

This rather simplified outline of three distinct streams of thought illustrates the connection between human needs and social order. Man's needs take concrete shape in a social context; he takes the help of technology to meet his needs and, to this end, organizes the forces of production, giving rise to certain types of production relations, social institutions and cultural formations. In this process, new needs emerge which call for the use of new technologies. New technologies lead to new social formations. This dynamic interaction between human needs, technology and social order propels society from one level of development to the next higher one, as the believers in the idea of progress think.

It is interesting to note that, for all this progress, the individual feels frustrated in society, seeking in vain to satisfy needs which are born of social intercourse but which existing social formations cannot satisfy. It is in this context that the questions of freedom and justice rooted in the relationship between man and society, on the one hand, and of the limits to growth as inherent in the relationship between society and nature, on the other, become relevant. It is also in this context that the question of what constitutes need assumes a wider significance, going beyond the determination of needs merely on some objective, empirical or historical grounds. The question of needs is basically ontological, the nature of needs depending on how man views himself and the world surrounding him.

The talk of "basic needs," "material needs," etc. reflects an orientation that divorces the concept of needs from a wider constellation of ideas; it is no more than a sop to the guilty conscience of the affluent segments of society. The intermeshing of the material and cultural and the fact that the satisfaction of needs denotes something more than the satisfaction of material needs—prestige, status, power, etc.—indicate the difficulty of determining, from the point of view of an individual, what is need and what is not.

The categorization of some needs as basic implies that there are other needs which will have to be satisfied once basic needs have been taken care of. But the experience of the industrialized countries suggests that once basic material needs of the population have been attended to, intense competition for "positional goods" ensues, making a larger claim on societal resources and thereby raising the question of the limits to growth.

The liberals and Marx were firm believers in the idea of linear progress and did not visualize that there were limits to growth, that natural resources could be exhausted, and that natural environment could be polluted and degraded in the process of the satisfaction of ever proliferating wants and needs. While they recognize that human needs can be satisfied only in society, they also believe that the individual is prior to society, that society is created by individuals and that society exists to serve individual purposes. They believe that man is, therefore society is. This instrumental value of society easily leads to the position that if social forms do not satisfy individual needs, they must be changed.

This raises two important questions: What should change and how? It is here that profound differences exist between the liberals, Marx and Gandhi. Most liberals, excepting Mill, did not consider it necessary that man himself should change. For Bentham, the calculus of pleasure and pain was enough to restrain the individual from acting injudiciously. If a conflict occurred between individual interest and collective good, mild institutional reforms would take care of the conflict. Mill and Marx both spoke of the necessity of the satisfaction of higher, more refined needs. Mill put his faith in certain institutional devices, while Marx believed in the social dialectic to bring about profound social and political changes. Once these changes—incremental or revolutionary—took place, harmonious relations between man, society and nature would be established, giving the individual the fullest scope to develop his potentialities.

Gandhi saw clearly that man himself had created the civilizational predicament through his own activities. He also saw that the egoistic conception of man adhered to by the liberals and Marx was not only outmoded but also disastrous for man, society and nature. To Gandhi, accordingly, freedom did not lie in multiplying wants but in developing the self in harmony, not antagonism, to society and nature. He insisted that the quest for self-realization must begin with the individual himself. No amount of reforms, or even violent revolution, would succeed in eliminating conditions that enslave man as long as technologically induced economic growth remained the major instrument of need gratification. He, therefore, emphasized the transformation of man on the basis of non-attachment, non-violence and quest for truth.

Conflicts will, however, occur and so the means of conflict resolution must be found. Mill proposes consensus arrived at through self-conscious critical rationality. He does not indicate how this method can work if two antagonistic positions emerge. Liberal theory, as Bondurant observes, "has been concerned with mechanism, not with action, with form rather than performance, with instrument more than with technique. It has raised questions, less of how a people may struggle towards an end, than through what devices."[22]

Marx pinned his faith on the dialectical interaction between the social environment, on the one hand, and human needs, on the other. On the philosophical plane, he posits the structure of thesis and antithesis simultaneously operating in the process of growth and finding a resolution in synthesis. It assumes the predetermination "of the content of both thesis and antithesis—a development which, in Marx, defines class struggle and anticipates a synthesis in the realization of a classless society where, of course, the dialectical process must, for Marx, end."[23]

Here Gandhi disagrees with Marx:

> I do not agree [with Marx] that our ideologies, ethical standards and values are altogether a product of our material environment without any absolute basis outside it. On the contrary, as we are, so our environment becomes.
>
> We have to eradicate possessiveness and greed and lust and egotism from our own hearts. We have to carry war within ourselves to banish it from society. . . .[24]

The Gandhian Satyagraha is a technique characterized by constructive, peaceful action and infused with the determination to enlarge the area of agreement and to achieve resolution of conflict by persuasion. It is a process of "truth testing" in which a restructuring of the opposite elements takes place "to achieve a situation which is satisfactory to both the original opposing antagonists but in such a way as to present an entirely new total circumstance." Thus, Satyagraha is at once creative and constructive. It is, in the words of Erikson, "pervaded by a spirit of giving the opponent the courage to change even as the challenger remained ready to change with the events. . . . [It helps] others both to discard costly defenses and denials and to realize hidden potentials of good-will and energetic deed."[25]

For Gandhi, the quest for truth is the essence of human existence. The quest is directed towards articulating and strengthening conscience, a universalized conscience, a conscience that blends the self with the universe. It is only through this that the question of human motivation and the individual's relations with society (that is, economic and cultural forms) and with nature can be tackled. It is on the basis of this that a structure of justice can be erected.

NOTES

1. Ross Fitzgerald (ed.), *Human Needs and Politics* (Rushcutters Bay: Pergamon Press Australia Pvt. Ltd., 1977), Introduction, p. ix.

2. Fitzgerald, "The Ambiguity and Rhetoric of Need," in Fitzgerald (f.n. 1), p. 195.

3. See Agnes Heller, "Can 'True' and 'False' Needs Be Posited?," GPID Project Meeting, Berlin, May 1978, p. 2; see also, Antony G. N. Flew, "Wants or Needs, Choices or Commands?," in Fitzgerald (f.n. 1), p. 217.

4. Donella H. Meadows, et al., *The Limits to Growth: A Report for the Club of Rome's Project on the Predicament of Mankind* (New York: A Signet Paperback, 1972).

5. The term "want" is often used for appetites or desires (or even instincts), while the term "need" denotes what creatures of appetite and instinct require to keep themselves alive or healthy, or to attain or maintain some condition held to be desirable for them. The liberal tradition clearly distinguishes, or comes close to making a distinction, between wants and needs. Marx, however, used a single term "Bedurfnisse" for both wants and needs.

6. Bentham, quoted in C. B. Macpherson, "Needs and Wants: An Ontological or Historical Problem," in Fitzgerald (f.n. 1), p. 29.

7. J.S. Mill, *Principles of Political Economy,* (Ed.) Donald Winch (Harmondsworth: Penguin Books, 1970), p. 111.

8. J.S. Mill, *Auguste Comte and Positivism* (Ann Arbor, Michigan: The University of Michigan Press, 1961), p. 95.

9. J.S. Mill, *Principles of Political Economy* (Hammondsworth: Pelican Classics, 1970), Book IV, p. 116.

10. C.B. Macpherson, "Needs and Wants: An Ontological or Historical Problem," in Fitzgerald (f.n. 1), p. 31.

11. Maurice Cowling, *Mill and Liberalism* (Cambridge: Cambridge University Press, 1963), p. 11.

12. *Capital,* Vol. 1 (Harmondsworth: Penguin Books, 1976), (f.n. 51), pp. 758-759.

13. I. Meszaros, *Marx's Theory of Alienation* (London: Merlin Press, 1970), p. 179.

14. John Plamenatz, *Karl Marx's Philosophy of Man* (Oxford: Clarendon Press, 1977), pp. 139–140.

15. See, for example, V. B. Kher (ed.), *Economic and Industrial Life and Relations* (Ahmedabad: Navjivan Publishing House, 1957), p. 169.

16. *The Selected Works of Mahatma Gandhi,* Shriman Narayan (ed.), (Ahmedabad: Navjivan Publishing House, 1968), Vol. IV, p. 59.

17. *The Selected Works,* Vol. VI, p. 326.

18. *Harijan,* 7 April, 1947, p. 74.

19. *The Selected Works,* Vol. VI, pp. 349-350.

20. *The Selected Works,* Vol. VI, p. 449.

21. *Harijan,* 1 February, 1942.

22. Joan V. Bondurant, *Conquest of Violence: The Gandhian Philosophy of Conflict* (Berkeley: University of California Press, 1971), p. 217.

23. Ibid., (f.n. 22), pp. 191–192.

24. *The Selected Works,* Vol. VI, pp. 2422 and 45.

25. Erik H. Erikson, *Gandhi's Truth: On the Origin of Militant Nonviolence* (London: Faber and Faber Ltd., 1970), p. 435.

CHAPTER FIVE

Human Needs as Human Rights

CHRISTIAN BAY

Christian Bay, like John Burton and Ramashray Roy, discusses the contradiction between the pursuit of individual human needs and the existence of modern society. He offers a wide-ranging discussion of human needs as a general concept and as the foundation of universal human rights. Bay is a Professor in the Department of Political Science at the University of Toronto. A distinguished political philosopher who emphasizes the study of freedom, justice, citizenship, and political education, he is best known for his work Structure of Freedom *(Stanford, California: Stanford University Press, 1958).*

In this chapter, Christian Bay develops a linkage between "human needs" on the one hand, and the establishment of "human rights," as protected by political, legal and institutional supports, on the other hand. In a thoroughly reasoned and persuasive article, Bay outlines a prioritization of four basic human needs categories—survival needs, health protection needs, community solidarity needs, and individual freedom needs—which he argues must correspond to human, political, and legal rights enforced and protected by the state. Taking issue with John Rawls's view, which he summarizes, Bay argues that the right of self-esteem (which flows from, and corresponds with, the basic human need of community solidarity) is prior to, and therefore takes precedence over, the right of individual liberty. While defending a commitment to both of these needs as rights, Bay maintains that the state must ensure that the political supports for the right of self-esteem are provided for. Bay suggests, however, that

Chapter 5 text excerpted by permission of the publisher from "Self-Respect as a Human Right: Thoughts on the Dialectics of Wants and Needs in the Struggle for Human Community," *Human Rights Quarterly* (1982), pp. 53-75.

ultimately the state itself is an obstacle to the establishment of a peaceful and "authentic human community" supportive of all human rights, since its commitment to democratic principles—whether capitalist or socialist—is deceptive and manipulative, only serving as a veneer to obscure its oligarchical nature.

THREE ASSUMPTIONS

Self-respect is the positive side of the continuum between the extremes of high and low, or ambivalent, self-esteem. The term will be used in this article according to this definition. While every person is assumed to have self-esteem, whether positive, negative, or ambivalent—while everyone is assumed to esteem oneself, whether favorably, unfavorably, or ambivalently—not everyone respects himself or herself as a worthwhile human being.

How can it make sense to propose that there should be a right to self-respect, or even, as it is claimed in this essay, a human right (that is, a universal moral right)? It can make sense only if we first accept the following three propositions. (This is necessary, but not, as we shall see, sufficient.)

The first proposition is that every human being is or has a self, in a sense that includes an awareness of being a human individual, capable of making choices that affect one's life and that of others. In a recent discussion Morris Rosenberg cites the common view that of all animals, the human alone has self-consciousness. After discussing some of the complexities of the self-concept, he offers the following definition: "the totality of the individual's thought and feelings having reference to himself as an object."[1] Even to survive, physically and socially, every human being must give some thought to one's own identity and other characteristics.

The second proposition is that one accept as valid at least a rudimentary system of moral values and of moral discourse which permits and requires judgments of right and wrong, of good and evil. Such a system would apply, whether with consistency in application or not, to oneself and to others. There is in every human being a self in the sense of an individual identity, and a judge of motivations, acts, and behavior, including one's own.[2]

The third initial assumption is that self-respect, or a positive self-esteem, is a basic human need: it is a requirement for optimal human health. Conversely, a deficient self-respect is of necessity associated with pathologies of motivation or behavior. I follow Abraham Maslow in supposing that the universality of this need as an actual need is limited to persons whose even more basic physiological needs, personal security needs, and social belonging needs have been met at some minimum threshold.

Under jungle-like conditions of living, if one has experienced only those conditions, there is a self but not necessarily a craving for self-esteem. Under such conditions it would make little sense to refer to physical violence or treachery as pathological.

These three assumptions may seem extravagant. Nonetheless, I will not attempt to defend the first two, either in philosophical or psychological terms. My argument will proceed within the limits of assuming that there is in every person a self, a sense of being a human person, however inarticulate or underdeveloped or repressed it may be or seem to be. Moreover, there exists, in ours and probably in every civilization, to the extent that the jungle has been left behind,[3] a shared universe of elementary moral values and discourse.

The third assumption, however, that there is a basic human need to achieve a positive self-esteem, or a need to respect oneself and to feel worthy of self-respect, requires elaboration and justification before we can examine whether or in what sense we ought to speak of a possible human right to self-respect.

Milton Rokeach, one of the foremost modern students of human values and attitudes, cites William McDougall's classical assertion that "the master sentiment" is the sentiment of self-regard. In Rokeach's own empirical work, "all of a person's values are conceived to maintain and enhance the master sentiment of self-regard—by helping a person adjust to his society, defend his ego against threat, and test reality."[4]

Rokeach's theory and research on value and attitude change derive from his assumption that there is a basic need for self-respect in all his respondents; and some of his most remarkable findings would seem hard to account for on any other basis.[5] In his own words, this is the most general statement of the import of these findings: "Cognitive and behavioral change begins when a social comparison process ends in some identifiable state of self-dissatisfaction concerning (one's own) competence or morality."[6]

Rokeach does not develop the issue of the relative importance of competence aspects and morality aspects of individual self-respect under alternate contingencies. Perhaps the emphasis on morality may tend to outweigh the emphasis on competence in the more secure persons, and/or in the more "civilized" or "advanced" human communities.

Another, somewhat similar and yet distinct pair of concepts central to our understanding of self-respect is self-esteem and self-consistency as this distinction is articulated by Rosenberg.[7] A sense of self-consistency is necessary to achieve a sense of stable identity. It would be hard to plan at all unless one assumes a degree of consistency and permanence in personal-need priorities. However, the "master purpose" of our life-planning as individuals surely is to achieve, not consistencies in behavior as an end in itself, but effective ways of achieving physical and other need satisfactions without loss of self-respect. Our life-projects tend to seek whatever personal satisfactions we can achieve in ways compatible with preserving our self-respect to the fullest possible extent, our individual values and social circumstances and options duly considered. Presumably, this basic logic of choice operates even when we merely behave by habit or predisposition rather than act by conscious choice. Our discourse about ourselves and our self-attributions is profoundly influenced by our enduring concern with protecting and enhancing our self-respect. For example, as Rokeach points out, this is why most of us often prefer to talk about our (generalizable) values rather than our (self-oriented) needs: "Needs are cognitively transformed into values so that a person can end up smelling himself, and being smelled by others, like a rose."[8]

John Rawls concurs with McDougall, Rokeach, and a large number of psychologists when he asserts that "perhaps the most important primary good is that of self-respect." Like Rokeach, Rawls sees two basic aspects of self-respect: "it includes a person's sense of his own value, his secure conviction that his conception of his good, his plan of life, is worth carrying out. And second, self-respect implies confidence in one's ability, so far as it is within one's power, to fulfill one's intentions."[9]   So important is this particular primary good, that "the parties in the original position would wish to avoid at almost any cost the social conditions that undermine self-respect."[10]

In the same context, Rawls elaborates on the first aspect of self-respect, having a sense of one's own worth, as in turn depending on two kinds of circumstances: (a) having a rational plan of life that is conducive to draw on and develop the individual's talents and capacities; and (b) finding "our persons and deeds appreciated and confirmed by others who are likewise esteemed and their association enjoyed."[11]

So far as these statements go, Rawls occupies a ground that is psychologically firmly based, and philosophically defensible from liberal as well as humanist perspectives. The difficulties with Rawls's theory of self-respect, and of justice in relation to liberty, begin when we ask why it is that self-respect is to be considered only one of the most important primary goods, but not an essential aspect of liberty itself and a value that a just political order must make available to all, to the fullest possible extent.

SELF-RESPECT IN THE CONTEXT OF HUMAN NEED PRIORITIES

What is conspicuously missing in Rawls's theory, as in most liberal theorizing, is a conception of human need priorities; one that realistically acknowledges the biological and sociopsychological prerequisites of a meaningful access to, and exercise of, liberty. Paradoxically, many psychologists' discussions of self-concepts exhibit the same deficiency.

Rawls's theory of justice stipulates that a just regime must, above all else, offer to each person "an equal right to the most extensive total system of equal basic liberties compatible with a similar system of liberty for all."[12] At the same time, Rawls postulates an economic necessity for social and economic inequalities and, to be sure regretfully, accepts it as inevitable that members of some social classes will have considerably less access than others to that hypothetical "total system" of liberties. Rawls "cannot be said to have shown that his model is the most just," objects C.B. Macpherson, "since all models not run on principles of capitalist rationality are ruled out."[13]

However, the problem with Rawlsian liberalism does not end there, as Donald J.C. Carmichael has pointed out as a friendly critic. Carmichael credits Rawls with being the most advanced of liberal theorists in regard to tempering the commitment to liberty with a concern for equality and social justice. He observes that a human person to Rawls, as to other liberal writers, is a singularly atomistic animal, divorced from his or her social context and destined (doomed?) to a lonesome quest for personal, individual need-satisfactions which are distinct from, for example, the joys of sharing with others, or of partaking in a community. Rawls's human persons are seen as "agent-individuals," writes Carmichael; that is, as individualist maximizers. To Rawls, the range of primary social goods is restricted to "those which would be a value as much in isolation as in any social relations. Conversely, (excluded from the class of primary goods are) any values which are peculiar to social existence."[14]

Carmichael demonstrates the falseness of this common liberal conception, from Hobbes to Rawls, of the normal human person. This just isn't the way you and I and people we know and care for actually live, he writes; for, "conceived apart from others and relations with them, even the best self is but a diminished person." It makes no sense to construe the self so narrowly, he continues, for "the social relations which (for the liberal individualist) are merely the external environment of the separate self might instead be seen as the intrinsic dimensions of a man's significance as a person."[15]

The normal self is extended beyond the single individual. The subject of "ego-extensions" is discussed by Rosenberg, who takes his departure from the classical definition of William James: "In its widest possible sense, however, *a man's Self is the sum total of all that he CAN call his,* not only his body and his psychic powers, but his clothes and his house, his wife and children, his ancestors and friends, his reputation and works, his land and horses, and yacht and bank-account."[16] Could this not be extended to also include his or her country, for some? All of humanity, or all victims, for others? I have argued in another context that positive self-esteem is likely to be associated with self-expanding identification, a social extension of the self, while negative self-esteem tends to induce self-sacrificing identification, a kind of flight from the individual self.[17]

Only superficially or mechanistically viewed can the human self be seen as associated with one person only. One way to gain a rational perspective on this is to analyze the self in the context of human need priorities. Whether we follow Abraham Maslow, Karl Marx, or Herbert Marcuse, or any number of other need theorists, only the most basic physical needs, for sustenance and safety, are usually associated with the physical individual first of all, but along with the person's immediate family and friends. Even in the realm of physical self-perservation, I doubt that the Hobbesian-Rawlsian picture of the liberal individualist is realistic when we consider that many, perhaps most, human beings tend to be prepared for extremes of self-sacrifice for family, friends, comrades, or a cause.

Beyond self-perservation, Marx stressed the social nature of the human species-needs, and he analyzed the profound alienation inflicted on most people, especially on the working class, by the capitalist system.[18] Maslow emphasized the human need for community (love, belongingness) and for self-esteem, as prior to the need for individual self-actualization.[19] Marcuse spoke of "an instinctual foundation for solidarity among human beings" which, unfortunately, can be repressed in a class society and replaced by an artificial "second nature" which ties the individual "libidinally and aggressively to the commodity form."[20] William Leiss has in recent works elaborated on Marcuse's conception of capitalism's induced repressive needs, and has demonstrated how our fixation on commodities, programmed to make the market economic system prosper, impoverishes our selves, our social relations, and incidentally makes us plunder and poison our earth's natural resources, needlessly (in the sense of "need" to be developed in the following paragraphs).[21]

There is clearly a continuing contest, in the modern individual consciousness, between narrowly individualist and more broadly social self-concepts. While Carmichael is right to point to the liberal-individualist self as a caricature, it must be conceded that Marx's (and Maslow's and Marcuse's) broadly social self is still utopian: few of us, if any, have left entirely behind the primitive narrow self-concept that is so suitable to survival under jungle conditions and under social Darwinist capitalism. Alienation takes its toll in all social classes. However, with every new generation there are fresh resources of youthful ideals, moral generosity, and commitment to struggle for decent personal relations and for a better world. Symbolically speaking, the narrow self and broader selves are in continuing contest; perhaps it is only our need for self-consistency that keeps many of us from conceding victory one day to the narrow self, on given issues, and other days to a broader self, on the same issues.

Much is to be gained in self-understanding and in normative political insight, I will argue, if we can come to conceive of this kind of continuing struggle in dialectical terms, seeing the emerging and often unsteady self-product in the context of a realistic conception of more basic and less basic human needs, and of needs in competition with wants.

Leaving the wants-needs distinction for the next section, let me first discuss need priorities. The issue is all important, if we insist, as I do, that legitimate politics must serve human needs in the order of their importance to human life. A disciplined use of common sense provides us with a good point of departure, and one or two steps further, provided that we can extricate ourselves from the liberal rhetoric which asserts that liberty is the highest good:

Government, which is always coercive and by definition infringes on "natural" liberty, can only be justified to the extent that it serves to ensure, first of all, human survival. The worst evils, surely, are genocide, nuclear or other chemical warfare, and destruction of the life-sustaining habitat of our world.

Beyond the ultimate collective disaster, the worst individual human disaster is not loss of liberty, but loss of life itself. The second is the loss of one's health; third, the loss of all community ties; and only fourth, the loss of one's liberty. One can, to be sure, choose to sacrifice one's life for one's liberty, or indeed for other people's liberty, or well-being; but one cannot rightly choose to sacrifice other people's lives or health for one's own priorities of liberty. "Give me liberty or give me death!" is noble rhetoric. Less noble, but more often what is implicitly being said, is "Give me liberty or give other people death!"

This brings us back to the importance of seeing the human self, and the value of self-respect, in the context of human need priorities. First of all, the self is a representation of the individual, whose identity can be known only through his or her attributes, characteristics, qualities, or predilections. Each self is unique, and yet all human selves have something in common as humans. To me it matters not so much whether this "something" is analyzed in terms of shared basic attributes, or characteristics; it is important to avoid prejudging such issues by way of postulating "a human nature" that is immanent, perhaps biologically predetermined, and not subject to change. Also, I want to avoid the opposite kind of prejudgment, which assumes that human nature is extremely malleable, so that human attributes and characteristics are seen as all historically determined and anchored, or hardly at all, in human biology or psychology.[22]

Let us advance, then, by way of common sense observations about the most basic needs that we all have in common as human beings. Some are shared with all animals: first, the need to survive as a species, as a nation, or tribe, and as individuals. Second is the need to keep healthy; the need to avoid, when possible, physical and mental injury whether caused or threatened by violence, preventable disease, or deprivation (by way of maldistribution or destruction of resources essential to meet basic human needs).

Third, there is the need to belong to and be accepted in a (nonexploitive) human community so that our social species-needs may be met—if we use the Marxist idiom—or to have our need for love, belongingness, and self-esteem met—if we use Maslow's language. It is at the point of this third level of need that I concede I am moving beyond the obvious, or what is generally accepted as common sense. The conventional liberal wisdom tends, on the contrary, to affirm or imply a need for liberty ahead of a need for community. There is no hard empirical evidence either way, in this area of broad and loosely conceptualized generalizations.

My claim, then, that the need for community must take precedence is not at this point a verifiable psychological proposition; nor do I intend to advance it as an ontological claim. Rather, I intend it to be understood as a Rawlsian-type normative proposition: if this issue were open to choice in an "original position," I submit that every rational person would be bound to opt for a social order in which people would see their need for community-solidarity as prior to their need for individual liberty. Why? Because an optimal liberty not constrained by community-solidarity would doom us to preserve a capitalist-type social order, with permanent reward structures for enterprising individuals who choose to be free riders, exploiters, con artists, bullies, and the like. If some have this choice, and even are rewarded for making it, then, as Hobbes saw so clearly, this option will be forced on most others as well. Later liberals, Rawls included, have tended to miss the full significance of this point.

Once we have affirmed the prior need for community, we must also affirm the need for liberty, as an essential attribute of the self, and an attribute of particular relevance to self-respect. Each human being is a biological individual first, who must stay alive and healthy so that he or she can begin to develop his or her human needs and capabilities; these needs and capabilities are first of all social, but within the limits of a social consciousness they are also uniquely subjective in each person. Thus, the need for individual, or subjective, freedom of expression is the fourth priority need but still a basic human need.

In an alienating social order such as ours, individual self-respect is often diminished through the lack of human community, because so many social relations are hierarchical rather than fraternal; and contractual, reducing persons to commodities, objects of sale or barter, rather than communal, with whole persons relating to whole persons, treating one another as ends rather than means.

Much the same appears to be true in the so-called socialist societies, in spite of the Marxist procommunity rhetoric: individualist status and career motivations seem to outweigh, more often than not, the kinds of communist procommonweal motivation that Marx anticipated in his vision of the "society of producers."[23]

Compared to the individualist libertarianism in the so-called democratic societies of the West, those governed by Marxists tend to go to the other extreme when it come to recognizing individual subjectivity needs as essential to self-respect. While in the West it is a dogma of great benefit to the corporate strong that everyone should be free to control and dispose of one's properties as one sees fit, even at great injury to others or to the common good, in the East it tends to be a dogma that individualist critics and dissenters must be silenced, and even penalized, as a menace to social solidarity.

In my view the "cause of liberty" without a prior commitment to community is as unworthy of support as the "cause of socialism" without a corollary commitment to individual liberty of dissent. Moreover, the spectacle of the two "causes" edging toward a worldwide military confrontation is utterly obscene and outrageous. How can we turn the drift around? Where can we seek a basis for a less lethal, more rational dialectics of political confrontations? Is the new worldwide attention to human rights a source of hope?

NEEDS, WANTS, AND HUMAN RIGHTS: TOWARD A DIALECTIC OF CONFLICT RESOLUTION

Self-respect is a human need, I have argued. My further contention at this point is that it should be seen, not just as a primary good, as Rawls does; it should be seen as a human right. I shall argue that acknowledgment of basic human needs ipso facto establishes human rights; for example, the right to self-respect. Self-respect is a basic social need and also a basic individual need, in the sense that it is met only by a combination of adequate conditions of community and liberty.

Professor Maurice Cranston has defined human rights as individual moral entitlements that are 1) universal, 2) paramount, and 3) practical.[24] I think his third criterion is unduly limiting. To illustrate, he criticizes the UN Declaration's stipulation of "vacations with pay" as a human right as an overly ambitious claim. It is not "practical" today, to be sure, in many poor countries; but in my view that is all the more reason to insist that this is and must become recognized as a human right. "Practical" should be taken to mean "in principle possible," or "practical in the future, if appropriate political changes are achieved."

I would want to add two more criteria to Cranston's definition of human rights: 4) these are moral entitlements that should be given legal protection, as a highest-priority political goal; and 5) these rights should be enacted or adjudicated and enforced as legal rights, according to priorities of human need. I mean to imply, and this is crucial, that there can be no human right that does not meet, generally speaking, a human need (not necessarily at each specific moment, of course). Thus, corporations, associations, and states can have no human rights, although they may have legal rights. We humanists must struggle to make human rights universal and paramount as legal rights, too. Claims based on dire human needs must come to take precedence, legally as well as morally, over all sorts of other claims, including (other) legal rights.

This is where I part company with Rawls and the liberal tradition. Using Ronald Dworkin's phrase, I will argue that, once we have linked human rights to human needs, we must begin to "take rights seriously" as citizens, and also as lawyers and judges if we are called on to act in these roles.

Dworkin is a jurist committed to the view that moral theory must guide legal decisions, above all in "hard cases" in which conventional liberal-positivist jurisprudence attributes considerable discretion to judges. To Dworkin, a hard case differs from easier cases in its degree of complexity, or in the degree to which there is a dearth of relevant precedents to give clear guidance on the issue at hand. Nonetheless, he emphasizes that also in a hard case one has to deal justly with a situation of competing rights-claims, in which one claim in the final analysis is entitled to prevail over the other. He also asserts that in this determination the jurist must ultimately be guided by moral philosophy. He hails Rawls's *Theory of Justice* as a work that "no constitutional lawyer will be able to ignore."[25] Nor should any other lawyer or judge who is involved in difficult cases disregard it, he implies.

Dworkin's critique of Rawls is complex and cannot be analyzed here. I will briefly discuss only Dworkin's classification of types of moral philosophy, which assigns to Rawls a right-based position; and then consider Dworkin's view that Rawls's "deep theory" makes the right to "equal concern and respect" the most basic right, not the right to optimal liberty. I will dissent from certain views of each writer: from Dworkin with my argument that the right to life takes precedence over his right to "equal concern and respect," and with my view that Dworkin misconstrues Rawls on the point just referred to in Rawls's alleged "deep theory"; from Rawls I shall dissent more sharply, since I take him at his word on the priority of optimal liberty, and on self-respect as a primary good, not a right. For the remainder of this section I shall then define "needs" and "wants," and develop a dialectical position on the politics of needs and wants, as a way of locating a right to equal self-respect as a human right of a higher priority that the right to optimal liberty, or even of liberty up to the outer limits of freedom needs (beyond which there may be legal rights but no human rights, according to my conception of human rights); at the same time I will reiterate that the right to equal self-respect must be given less weight than the rights to life and health . . . .

Rights and Needs: Toward a Rational Order of Priorities

The importance of Dworkin's *Taking Rights Seriously* for my present purposes is not in the crucial value that he attributes to the right to be treated "with equal concern and respect." While this is an important advance over the Rawlsian primacy for individual liberty in the abstract, it stops short to the humanist commitment to life itself as the first priority concern of legitimate policies.

The greatest merit of Dworkin's argument, in my view, is in his articulation of the general perspective that the weightiest rights should be made to prevail in all legal contests; most certainly in all the "hard cases," to sweep aside traditional positivist "discretion," but apparently in many other relevant cases as well; even, when necessary, in defiance of precedent and legislation, to remedy grave right-violations. While he is less than clear on how far he would have human rights prevail over competing legal claims, Dworkin's position lends itself to extensions that would favor the process of turning the most basic human rights into legal rights in the United States, through the courts: "In our society a man does sometimes have the right, in the strong sense, to disobey a law. He has the right whenever the law wrongly invades his rights against the government . . . . If the government does not take rights seriously, then it does not take law seriously either."26

Burton Zwiebach affirms just as emphatically the position that laws in defiance of rights establish not only a right to commit civil disobedience but, in appropriate circumstances, an obligation to do so as well. Our political obligation is not owed primarily to the state, he writes: "our primary obligation is to our fellows. Our obligation to the state is prudential."27

Neither Dworkin nor Zwiebach goes beyond vague and general statements, however, when they argue for legal protection for a moral or legal right, or even a moral obligation, to disobey the law. While both writers commendably raise basic human rights, each stops short of tackling the question of when a human right may be, or even should be, asserted against the word of the law. Also, Zwiebach is silent on what to do when different human rights are in conflict. Dworkin discusses this issue under the topic of "hard cases" but does not offer any substantive criteria for weighing competing rights, except that he makes it clear that the right to "equal concern and respect" must prevail over supposed property rights.

I cannot address here the momentous issue of the scope and limits of substantive grounds for civil disobedience. I can only stress the prior importance of defining human rights in relation to more crucial and less crucial human needs. There is no persuasive rational scheme that I know of for assigning priorities among rights, as long as rights remain disconnected from the concept of needs. For example, how does one prioritize the many rights stipulated in the thirty articles of the 1949 United Nations Declaration of Human Rights? Among categories of needs, on the other hand, there are reasonably clear and plausible priorities. As a general formula, to serve as a point of departure, I propose the following universal order: survival needs, health protection needs, community solidarity needs, and individual freedom needs. I am not claiming "objective validity" for this order of need-categories, but I do claim that this is the most rational and realistic ordering available at this time, and that this order can serve as a rational basis for ordering priorities among human rights as well.[28]

The proposition that self-respect is a human right is supportable because self-respect is a basic human need; it is a need that requires human community and individual liberty, but a need secondary to survival needs and the need for health protection. It follows that appropriate acts of civil disobedience are legitimate, should be legal, and even should be deemed a matter of moral obligation at times. If someone is treated as a second-class person, not given equal concern and respect, for example, because he or she is in conflict with claims to property values, or is discriminated against on the ground of race or religion, acts of civil disobedience would be appropriate.

Needs and Wants

Much work remains to be done to develop the implications of the general priority rules. I will conclude this part of my discussion by defining "need" as distinct from "want." It is a crucial distinction when one holds, as I do, that needs establish human rights, while wants should be accommodated or frustrated according to the rules of democratic procedure, always yielding to basic human needs.

"Need" shall refer to any requirement for a person's survival, health, or basic liberties; basic meaning that, to the extent that they are inadequately met, mental or physical health is impaired. Thus, "need" refers to necessities for not only biological survival but also for the health and development (physical and mental growth) of persons as human beings.

Needs can only be inferred, not observed directly, except possibly the need for such biological basics as food, water, air, or sleep, etc. Wants, on the other hand, are facts, readily observable and measurable. "Want" here refers to any perceived need, any desire, any perceived short-term or long-term interest. A want may or may not reflect one or more "real" needs. Wants are measurable in many ways: personal wants can be measured by interviews or observations of behavior, for example, and collective wants by survey research or vote-counting.

Herbert Marcuse is right when he observes that many of the perceived needs of modern man are imposed from the outside, by way of ideology, advertising, propaganda, or alienating circumstances of life. "The so-called consumer economy and the politics of corporate capitalism have created a second nature of man which ties him libidinally and aggressively to the commodity form."[29] Yet, I take issue with Marcuse's language of "true" and "false" needs,[30] because it encourages oversimplification, and prejudgments to the effect that some people's perceived or felt needs can be treated without "equal concern and respect." It is by no means an easy task to distinguish immediately between needs that are "true needs" in Marcuse's sense, and needs, or wants, that do not so qualify.

What is required in order to address Marcuse's substantive concerns, which are important, is a dialectical development of needs and wants theory. Needs theory requires a continuing analysis of complex data and issues involving human health and pathologies (including attention to phenomena such as resort to drug use and actual drug addiction, suicide, homicide, child neglect, and violence in the family) while wants theory requires much empirical work on political and social behavior, including conventional survey research.

There is a familiar tendency among liberal writers, and among most analysts of so-called democratic political orders, to be interested in want-problematics only, for it is generally assumed that the primary if not the only task of a democratic government is to be responsive to "what people want." Under Marxist regimes there is an opposite tendency to prevent the accumulation, or at least the publication, of empirical evidence on what "public opinion" might want or demand, since the regime presumes to "know" what policies are in accord with what the public needs.

Both systems are unsatisfactory. The former encourages favoritism for privileged and articulate minorities, especially those that control great wealth. The latter encourages dogmatism and intolerance of dissent. How can we move toward a resolution of this crucial dilemma of our age?

Only a few preliminaries can be suggested here: a critical attitude to so-called democratic elections, and to "Free World" rhetoric; an insistence on "taking rights seriously" through carefully planned civil disobedience against right-violating laws and policies; vigorous political education efforts in the spirit of Paulo Freire;[31] and demands for regulations of mass media to ensure equal space or equal time in which to contest editorials and news reports that are disdainful of or even in violation of human rights.

To suggest such an "il-liberal" idea as this last one may well invite ridicule; or, alternatively, it might provoke some discussion of fundamentals of the so-called democratic order.[32] I concede that to implement any mass media reform of this kind without insisting on a continuing free and open discussion of such fundamentals would be to incur the risk of a slide toward near-totalitarian arbitrariness in public policy making. However, is unlimited liberty of the press a human right? I should think not. The human need is for exposure to, and a free and open choice within, a very broad spectrum of well-reasoned public policy views; there can be no human need to run a newspaper empire, or even a newspaper, for not many would be given a chance to do that.

In this essay, I can barely touch on the tangled but important issue of how to delimit liberty as a human need. Those limits should determine, as well, the other limits to liberty as a human right. A liberty to keep on discussing and contesting what those limits are, to ensure the continuing dialectics of needs- and wants-perspectives in the mass media, classrooms, and neighborhood meetings is a crucial liberty-right, well within those limits. Other liberty-claims should be judged to be beyond those limits: for example, the liberty of mass media editors to engage in war propaganda, without giving equal space to critics in the same columns; or the right to own or control properties in amounts or kinds that lead to power over other people's working lives.

I cannot here elaborate further on the outer limits of human rights or on the necessity of a continuing dialectics of need-claims and want-claims with their competing justifications, as a way of defining and constantly redefining these outer limits. In conclusion I will briefly return to the issue of justifying one category of human rights that is well within these limits: self-respect as a human right, in relation to the need for community.

SELF-RESPECT AND THE STRUGGLE FOR HUMAN COMMUNITY

The phrase "self-respect as a human right" may well be puzzling to some, in that I am referring to a psychological process, a process within the person. It may be objected that a "right" to self-respect is as impracticable as a "right" to be happy, or to be free from guilt or shame. All humans occasionally have thoughts or commit acts that are, or ought to be, hurtful to their self-respect. Moreover, even if my behavior were to approximate consistent saintliness, there could be no obligation or duty for specific other persons to sustain my self-respect by being appreciative, or even polite, if they happen not to like me; the notion of attempting to enforce such an obligation is absurd. Self-respect is hard to achieve without the genuine respect of others, at least some others.

On the other hand there are, or should be, certain limits to any overt show of disrespect and discrimination, directed at anyone. At the crucial states of infancy and young childhood there is not only a moral duty but a legal obligation for the parents to appreciate and love the child; the child can be taken away from the parent(s) in the event of child neglect.

Among adults, no one has the right to insist that I, or anyone else, be excluded from my neighborhood or community, except by way of temporary incarceration, if convicted of a grievous crime against other individuals, or against the commonweal. No one can rightfully demand that, on any other ground, any sane person be granted less than the same legal rights as anyone else. Expressing the same point in positive terms, the late Harold Lasswell spoke of democracy as a "commonwealth of mutual deference"; the democratic principle that he championed above all others was "regard for the dignity of man," equal dignity for all men and women.[33]

There is a dialectical problematic here. The right balance between our duty and obligation to respect our fellow humans and our freedom to take exception to their views and behavior cannot be determined by any fixed formula. Gregory Vlastos proposes that all persons have an equal right to well-being and freedom, because we all are of equal worth as human beings; and yet he sees a role for unequal "merit-praise" in order to provide incentives for creative and productive efforts.[34] Others, including Rawls, and possibly Dworkin, believe that economic rewards may justly be allocated disproportionately (within the limits of "fairness") to those who are energetic and productive.

The general issue of equality of incomes is not as important as it has been supposed to be in the massive literatures that have defended or attacked "socialism" on the ground that this philosophy should aim at a society in which all have the same standard of living: a noble principle to some, and anathema to others.[35] Two aspects of this issue are in my view important. First, there must be a right to a minimum income, regardless of employment or unemployment: enough to achieve security for everyone, so that each person is guaranteed adequate nutrition, shelter, and other necessities of life, requirements not only for survival and good health, but for individual dignity and self-respect. Second, there must be a right to equal pay for equal work, as a principle of fairness; for to be treated fairly, to the extent that people are still paid according to their work, not according to their need, is necessary (but by no means sufficient) to provide institutional support for self-respect.[36]

What matters concerning equality is equal respect and equal dignity, not the dollars and cents value of equal pay. To use Dworkin's felicitous phrase once more: what matters is not equal treatment, for human beings are individually different with respect to personal tastes and objectives; what matters is treatment as equals.

What matters, then, is political equality. This is necessary, but not sufficient, as an institutional support for self-respect. There can be political equality among slaves; and among citizens of so-called democratic political systems who are told that, collectively, they are the boss, but who know very well that they have virtually no say on the major matters that affect their own lives (peace or war, for example; or ownership of wealth). Many citizens, consequently, are neither active nor knowledgeable about the relatively minor issues that may be influenced significantly in an average election contest.

The conventional citizenship virtues—the product of political socialization in North America, including high school civics courses—are essentially passive: what mainly matters is loyalty, obeying the law, and voting.[37] Influential political scientists of recent years, all liberals and political behavioralists, have concluded that modern politics requires, to ensure stability, a fair amount of political apathy; and yet they have been writing as if it is democracy that requires low or moderate amounts of participation.[38]

With this stance these writers have ignored Marx's challenge, made more than a century ago, to the liberal Enlightenment's idea of individual rights: while man's species-nature, social man, was being alienated or even destroyed under the capitalist economic system, Marx wrote, all the alleged rights that the Enlightenment ideologists cared about were the individualist liberties of the private person, of the bourgeois, whose way of life and political concerns were entirely lacking in solidarity with the large community and society: " . . . the citizen is declared to be the servant of egoistic 'man', . . . it is man as a bourgeois and not as a citizen who is considered the *true* and *authentic* man."[39]

The American Bill of Rights stresses, of course, civil and political rights, and initially these were the rights stressed by the American side in the arguments within the United Nations, which led to the Universal Declaration of Human Rights. It has taken some time and some prodding from other regimes, but there was in recent years an increasing emphasis on social and economic rights in American foreign policy and it remains important in the general international debate on human rights. Yet, in our textbook discussions of liberal political institutions there is even today scant analysis of socioeconomic and sociopsychological prerequisites for intelligent political participation.

One such prerequisite is self-respect. That means, for every human being, a sense of being treated as an equal by right. It means, moreover, not only having equal legal rights, but having equal opportunity to participate in the political processes, in the broadest sense: in all decision processes affecting oneself and one's community.

Psychological Prerequisites of Asserting Right-Claims

It is important to acknowledge and stress a philosophical assumption here: a human right is not to be defended on the ground that it serves the public good; for example, the cause of democracy, or of community building. Human rights are universal and paramount entitlements that should be made enforceable by law, because they serve fundamental human needs: survival, health protection, belongingness, and basic liberties. Self-respect is a human right because human beings cannot live well without community solidarity; self-respect requires the symbols of political equality and the practice of community participation. In turn when these conditions prevail, self-respect facilitates a sense of personal power and the motivation to participate in one's community.

Carol Pateman and some of the democratic writers she cites have made a persuasive argument for the merit of participatory democracy, as distinct from ordinary constitutional liberal democracy. Moreover, she shows that participatory democracy is practicable in industrial as well as political settings, and that so-called political democracy within the state is likely to remain a matter of form rather than substance until most people gain experience in taking part in governing their own working lives. She quotes G.D.H. Cole on the important point that "the industrial system . . . is in great measure the key to the paradox of political democracy. Why are the many nominally supreme but actually powerless? Largely because the circumstances of their lives do not accustom or fit them for power or responsibility. A servile system in industry inevitably reflects itself in political servility."[40]

Prior to our working lives, we live in families, as children and young people. Before the era of feminist self-assertion, in some classes at least, the father was as a rule (or occasionally the mother) the sole order-giver, judge, and jury within the family. This, too, provided training in servility, instead of preparation for a sense of personal power and self-respecting political participation. The advent of feminist self-assertion has in many families considerably improved, I believe, prospects for dialectically achieved rather than dictatorially laid down family decisions; this offers some hope for improved development of self-respect, along with a sense of personal power over one's own life, within the next generation, in many families.[41]

Schools and universities during the 1960s often provided new arenas for the experimental exercise of personal political power, when students clamored for treatment as political equals, and sometimes gained concessions of rights to take part in governing their own lives, or even their institutions. Few of the more radical reforms survived, and yet I suspect that today's students are not quite as powerless or as defenseless against arbitrariness in high places as they were before the 1960s.[42] It remains to be seen whether the next big campus issue will bring larger, or sturdier, gains for political equality and for adult self-respect among students.

Attribution research in modern psychology powerfully supports the view that self-respect requires experience in making decisions affecting our own lives. Our self-concepts are based on the inferences we draw from our own acts and behavior, as a growing empirical and largely experimental literature amply confirms.[43] While it is true that self-respecting persons are more likely than others to act politically (rather than merely react, or be passive), the point to stress is that the practice of acting politically is necessary to build self-concepts that not only demand respect as equals from other people, including those who claim authority, but that also develop a sense of personal power and resourcefulness with which to back up such demands. This process proceeds in a self-reinforcing cycle.

The practices of nonparticipatory liberal democracy are antithetical to the building of self-respect: we keep hearing that we as citizens "have the power," and that we are the real and responsible originators of our governments and our laws, so that it is our fault when the laws and policies are monstrously unjust; and our actual powerlessness, which we sense, most of us, then becomes evidence of our weak and worthless selves.

The Struggle for Human Community

To develop the structural requirements for self-respect as a human right we must struggle to develop authentic human communities, and thus to free ourselves from the crushing weight of alienating hierarchies and pseudo-communities. Paraphrasing a familiar item of rhetoric, I would say that "eternal vigilance is the price of community"; as well as of liberty.

There is an important sense in which hierarchies are natural. The jungle is natural, in the same sense. Yet I shall argue that there is another important sense in which authentic communities are natural. I employ the following exacting definition of "authentic community": any group or aggregation of persons who share a sense of solidarity and who practice political equality, that is, equal rights, including an equal right to express views and to influence community decisions.

Pseudo-communities, on the other hand, are not natural, for they require manipulative deception. I use this term to refer to groups or aggregates that are hierarchically governed or dominated, and yet claim to be and perhaps in a formal sense are organized according to democratic principles; the claim is to serve legitimacy purposes and promote loyalty and obedience. All nation states, and especially those that claim to practice democracy or socialism, are pseudo-communities in this sense. Unlike authentic communities, in which the solidarity of their self-respecting members comes naturally, every pseudo-community requires never-ending campaigns of ideology and indoctrination; every state requires continuing heavy doses of patriotic symbolism and rhetoric to preserve and enhance loyalty.

The pseudo-community can be seen as a stage between outright (natural) hierarchy and authentic (natural) community. In what sense is the authentic community natural? In the sense that this is how human beings, to the extent that they are sufficiently secure and free, actually want to live together; for this is indeed the only way to live together which ensures that the most basic human needs will be met, to the fullest possible extent. In so far as the fears of jungle-like conditions and the anxieties of liberal individualist exploitation and competitive struggles can be left behind, most people will naturally prefer conditions under which self-respect becomes available to everyone, sustained by affectionate bonds with some and by a sense of solidarity with all community members. Surely people would make this choice in a Rawlsian original position.

It is natural to want authentic communities, and yet they cannot be achieved or preserved without continuing struggle, for hierarchies, and therefore hierarchical tendencies, are also natural, as we have seen. This is another dialectical process. As Robert Michels was the first empirical social scientist to document in some detail, organizations tend to become more hierarchical, the larger and more powerful they are.[44] States are large and powerful organizations, and so, above all, are the "superpowers." They invest vast economic and other resources to strengthen the symbols and rituals of obedient patriotism and to polish the democratic, or socialist, veneer that covers over the oligarchical realities; this veneer has to be thick enough for the ideologies of loyalty to take firm root.

The states show no signs of withering away. They are today the prime obstacle to the achievement of authentic human communities. With their fixation on military preparedness and on accumulating the most effective modern means of inflicting mass destruction, national governments have become the gravest threat to the survival of mankind.

Yet, states are necessary today, and not only in the sense of being inevitable. It is to the state that we must look, for now, for support in the vindication and enforcement of human rights. We must look to the state, for now, for crucial assistance in the struggle to tame the private economic superpowers, the multinational corporations. At the same time we must struggle to build authentic human communities, in spite of and against the state. In fact, I think this struggle represents our best hope for eventually taming and democratizing, and ultimately doing away with, our inherited Leviathan, in democratic garb.

Through practicing vigilance for human rights as self-respecting, self-governing, community-rooted individuals, we can gradually develop the fine art of defying and resisting, piecemeal, the designs of the state, or initially the most lethal of them. We will then be ready to discover, I think, that our only loyalty to very large human aggregates, those that are too large to constitute authentic communities, must go to the human race itself. At last we will be ready to build toward a peaceful world of human communities, which must gradually come to replace our familiar world of oppressive, incendiary nation states.[45]

NOTES

1. Morris Rosenberg, *Conceiving the Self* (New York: Basic Books, 1979), pp. 6–7 [Italics deleted]. I discuss the human self as the locus of freedom in *Strategies of*

Political Emancipation (Notre Dame, Indiana: University of Notre Dame Press, 1981), chap. 2.

2. "The Judging Self Observes the Identity Self and the Behavioral Self and says, 'Well Done!'" W. Fitts et al., *The Self Concept and Self-Actualization.* (Nashville, Tennessee: Counselor Recordings and Tests, 1971), p. 17. Quoted in L. Edward Wells and Gerald Marwell, *Self-Esteem: Its Conceptualization and Measurement* (Beverly Hills, California: Sage, 1976), p. 42.

3. See also my "What It Means to be Human," in Ross Fitzgerald, ed., *What It Means to be Human* (Rushcutters Bay, New South Wales: Pergamon, 1978), essay 7.

4. Milton Rokeach, *The Nature of Human Values* (New York: Free Press, 1973), pp. 14, 15.

5. See especially ibid., chap. 11.

6. Ibid., p. 229.

7. Rosenberg, *Conceiving the Self,* pp. 53–62.

8. Rokeach, *The Nature of Human Values,* p. 20.

9. John Rawls, *A Theory of Justice* (Cambridge, Massachusetts: Harvard University Press, 1971), p. 440.

10. Ibid.

11. Ibid.

12. Ibid., p. 302.

13. C.B. Macpherson. *Democratic Theory: Essay in Retrieval* (Oxford: Clarendon, 1973), p. 94.

14. Donald J.C. Carmichael, "Agent-Individualism: A Critique of the Logic of Liberal Political Understanding," Ph.D. dissertation (University of Toronto, 1978), p. 310. See also Bay, *Strategies of Political Emancipation,* pp. 16–23.

15. Carmichael, "Agent-Individualism," p. 43.

16. William James, *The Principles of Psychology* (New York: Dover, 1950), pp. 291–92; quoted in Rosenberg, *Conceiving the Self,* p. 34 [James's italics].

17. "Types of Identification and the Role of Self-esteem" in Christian Bay, *Structure of Freedom* (Stanford: Stanford University Press, 1970), pp. 172–79. On the logic of self-sacrificing identification, see Eric Hoffer, *The True Believer* (New York: Harper and Row, 1951).

18. Karl Marx, "On the Jewish Question" and "Economic and Philosophical Manuscripts of 1844," in Robert C. Tucker, ed., *The Marx-Engels Reader* (New York: Norton, 1978), pp. 26–52 and 66–125.

19. Abraham H. Maslow, *Motivation and Personality* (New York: Harper, 1954), chap. 5.

20. Herbert Marcuse, *An Essay on Liberation* (Boston: Beacon Press, 1969), pp. 10 and 11; and also see his *One-Dimensional Man* (Boston: Beacon Press, 1964).

21. William Leiss, *The Limits to Satisfaction: An Essay on the Problem of Needs and Commodities* (Toronto: University of Toronto Press, 1976). Also see his *The Domination of Nature* (New York: Braziller, 1972).

22. William Leiss comes close to adopting this position, in his otherwise cogent and important analysis of needs in relation to commodities. Leiss, *Limits to Satisfaction,* pp. 49–71.

23. See especially Marx, "Critique of the Gotha Program" in Tucker, *The Marx-Engels Reader,* pp. 525–41.

24. Maurice Cranston, *What Are Human Rights?* (London: Bodley Head, 1973), pp. 407 and 21–24.

25. Ronald Dworkin, *Taking Rights Seriously* (Cambridge, Massachusetts: Harvard University Press, 1978), p. 149.

26. Ibid., pp. 192 and 205. For a collection of critical essays on Dworkin, see "Taking Dworkin Seriously," a special issue of *Social Theory and Practice* 5 (1980) 3–4.

27. See Burton Zwiebach, *Civility and Disobedience* (Cambridge: Cambridge University Press, 1975), pp. 145–68, quoted at p. 160.

28. Richard E. Flathman asserts that, in so arguing, I proclaim a new dogmatism; my own construction is that I contribute rational input toward a dialectical clarification of issues that are of crucial importance to political theory as well as practice, issues that have for too long been left unattended by "dogmatically undogmatic" liberal theorists. See my paper, "Peace and Critical Political Knowledge as Human Rights" and the ensuing discussion between Professor Flathman and myself in *Political Theory* 8 (August 1980): 293–334.

29. Cf. Herbert Marcuse, *An Essay on Liberation,* p. 11; and also William Leiss, *The Limits to Satisfaction.*

30. Marcuse, *One-Dimensional Man,* pp. 4-9, and my "Human Needs and Political Education" in Ross Fitzgerald, ed., *Human Needs and Politics* (Rushcutters Bay, New South Wales: Pergamon, 1977), pp. 1–25, at pp. 2–7.

31. Paulo Freire, *Pedagogy of the Oppressed* (New York: Seabury, 1970).

32. See my "Foundations of the Liberal Make-believe," *Inquiry* 14 (1971): 213–37; and my "Acquisitive Liberties for Some: Toward a Constructive Critique of the Pluralist Persuasion," in *Social Alternatives* 1 (1977) 6–7: 22–34.

33. Harold D. Lasswell, *The Analysis of Political Behaviour: An Empirical Approach* (New York: Oxford University Press, 1948), p. 2.

34. Gregory Vlastos, "Justice and Equality" in Richard B. Brandt, ed., *Social Justice* (Englewood Cliffs, New Jersey: Prentice-Hall, 1962), pp. 31–72; especially pp. 52–53.

35. Richard H. Tawney has written the classic defense of socialist equality in basic rights, on the ground that it will make individualities flourish, in all social classes. See his *Equality* (London: Putnam, 1961).

36. One aspect of modern feminism is focussed on this issue of equal pay for equal work; but it is no recent discovery that women in the workforce are exploited even more severely than men. See Charlotte Perkins Gilman, *Women and Economics* (Boston: Small, Maynard, 1898); and Nona Glazer and Helen Youngelson Waehrer, eds., *Women in a Man-Made World: A Socioeconomic Handbook* (Chicago: Rand McNally, 1977).

37. See Stanley A. Renshon, *Psychological Needs and Political Behavior: A Theory of Personality and Political Efficacy* (New York: Free Press, 1974), especially chapter 1.

38. See Joseph A. Schumpeter, *Capitalism, Socialism, and Democracy* (New York: Harper and Row, 1952), part 4; Bernard R. Berelson, et al., *Voting* (Chicago: University of Chicago Press, 1954), chap. 14; Gabriel A. Almond and Sidney Verba, *The Civic Culture* (Princeton, Princeton University Press, 1963), chap. 15. Even Lester W. Milbrath and M. L. Goel, whose survey of many studies well documents

the wide extent of political apathy, conclude on the theme that "democracy seems to function more or less adequately with moderate to low levels of political participation . . ."; see their *Political Participation: How and Why do People Get Involved in Politics?* (Chicago: Rand McNally, 1977), chap. 6, p. 147. Papers representing various perspectives on the same theme are found in Henry S. Kariel, ed., *Frontiers of Democratic Theory* (New York: Random House, 1970).

39. Karl Marx, "On the Jewish Question" in Tucker, *The Marx-Engel Reader*, at p. 43. Marx's italics.

40. C.D.H. Cole, *Labour in the Commonwealth* (London: Headley Bros., 1918), p. 35. Quoted in Carole Pateman, *Participation and Democratic Theory* (Cambridge: Cambridge University Press, 1970), p. 38.

41. See Christian Bay's "Gentleness and Politics: The Case for Motherhood Reconsidered" in *Politics* 10 (1975), pp. 125–38.

42. One book with an apt title that bears on some of these issues is Edgar Z. Friedenberg, *The Dignity of Youth and Other Atavisms* (Boston: Beacon Press, 1965).

43. Three of the many relevant works are Daryl J. Berm, "Self-Perception: An Alternative Interpretation of Cognitive Dissonance Phenomena," *Psychological Review* 54 (1967), pp. 183–200; Edward E. Jones, et al., *Attribution: Perceiving the Causes of Behavior* (Morristown, New Jersey: General Learning Press, 1972); and Bernard Weiner, *Theories of Motivation: From Mechanism to Cognition* (Chicago: Markham, 1972).

44. See Robert Michels, *Political Parties: A Sociological Study of Oligarchical Tendencies of Modern Democracy* (Glencoe, Illinois: Free Press, 1949).

45. These last paragraphs draw on the more extensive discussion in Bay, *Strategies of Political Emancipation*, chap. 5.

PART TWO

APPLICATION OF NEEDS THEORY IN A GLOBAL SETTING

Part 2 of the book is composed of chapters that discuss the relevance of human needs for contributing to our understanding of global affairs. This is done by examining the role of human needs in a number of different areas: local individual and community involvement in world affairs, international development, the evolution of foreign policy, conflict resolution, the behavior of international governmental organizations, and international regimes. The concept of human needs has rarely been applied to global affairs. Therefore, these are formative efforts at linking needs theory to the study of world society.

CHAPTER SIX

Local Individual and Community Participation in World Society

CHADWICK F. ALGER

Chadwick Alger discusses the micro-macro problem and links individual action in pursuit of needs to global behavior. He is Professor of Political Science at the Ohio State University. He has a wide range of interests, including international relations theory, international organization, and the role of local publics in international relations. He is the author of many works, including You and Your Community in the World *(with David Hoovler; Columbus, Ohio: Consortium for International Studies Education, 1978).*

Alger demonstrates the presence and importance of individual and community action on world affairs. He begins by reviewing the basic assumptions of state system ideology and its tenacious hold on the minds of most people. He then discusses bold departures from the state system paradigm, emphasizing the importance of individuals and groups pursuing human needs in a local context. He goes on to illustrate the variety of local and community action that deeply affects world affairs as a function of individual action by reviewing interdisciplinary work on world history, culture and ethnicity, frontiers and border regions, Third World local contexts, the worldwide Green movement, peripheries in global cities, and voluntary community programs in industrialized countries. Alger clearly demonstrates not only that individuals and groups are important global actors, but also how people in local communities are integrally linked to the larger world systems (thus helping to bridge the theoretical gap between the individual and international systems).

Chapter 6 text reprinted in modified form by permission of the publisher from "Bridging the Micro and the Macro in International Relations Research," *Alternatives* 10 (1984-1985), pp. 319-344.

World order scholars are increasingly aware of the importance of individuals in local communities pursuing their human needs. Such scholars are calling increasingly for research and action that will empower people to participate in the transformation process in local places. Robert Johansen believes that "even small-scale efforts at local education and political organization for structural change [are] probably of greater usefulness than [the] more glamorous lobbying in Washington for incremental improvements in . . . legislation."[1] Local action, of course, need not and should not preclude action on a wider scope. Saul Mendlovitz, for example, has urged that "individuals and groups caught in 'local circumstances'. . . involve themselves in concrete political projects transcending state boundaries."[2] Indeed, there are already a host of localized popular movements agitating against deprivation, militarism, authoritarianism, and the like which have sprung up all over the world. And it is very important, Rajni Kothari stresses, to relate "to these grass-roots micro efforts [as well as] to macro movements around anti-nuclear, ecology, feminine liberation . . . to join in a common effort towards a global movement for peace and transformation."[3]

This growing tendency to make a place for local people in visions of global transformation is a paradigmatic breakthrough of overwhelming significance. Traditional visions of global futures have consisted primarily of innovative proposals for interstate relations and organizations. Even those schemes advocating simultaneous transformation within states have ignored local communities. But it has become increasingly apparent that local transformation and global transformation are but reverse sides of the same coin, as reflected in the now familiar phrase: "Think globally and act locally." Despite the growing response to this idea, as people increasingly experience "interdependence" in their daily lives, scholars espousing global transformation have yet to be very helpful. It is the purpose of this paper to contribute to the development of knowledge that will illuminate paths through which local action impacts on global change and transformation based on needs fulfillment.

One significant factor inhibiting more rapid progress is that world order studies are still limited by traditions in international relations research that place impermeable—although usually not perceived—barriers between the local and the global. Indeed, these traditions have made the perception of actual, as well as potential, links between the local and the global virtually "unthinkable." The first part of this paper will describe how state system ideology has isolated the local from the global and will briefly portray how a number of scholars have engaged in a painfully slow, and not altogether successful, effort to overcome the influence of this ideology. The second part of the paper will describe briefly the work of several scholars who have departed significantly from this mainstream tradition. The third and longest part of the paper will review some research from a micro perspective that we find useful in demonstrating the importance of the indivvdual pursuit of human needs in bridging the hiatus between the micro and the macro.

THE TENACIOUS HOLD OF STATE SYSTEM IDEOLOGY

We have seen vast changes in approaches to the study of international relations in this century as the emphasis evolved from diplomatic history, to international law, to international organizations, to politics and power, to decision-making, to quantitative studies, to regional integration, to linkage politics, to transnational relations, to bureaucratic politics, and to global issues. But despite these dramatic changes, the field has largely failed to address (actual) individual needs. Everywhere, people are involved in a variety of relationships—as consumers, workers, potential nuclear targets—and are therefore always affected by systemic events and problems over which they have little or no influence. This is largely because the field of international relations has not enabled people to perceive and understand their interactions with the world in the context of their daily lives though, of course, the responsibility for this inability, and perhaps even lack of interest, cannot be placed entirely on the discipline.

This failure has been largely based on the inability of international relations scholars to free themselves from the ideology of the state system. This is revealed in the painfully slow way in which the state system paradigm (often called a billiard ball model) evolved into a more complex paradigm that has become increasingly able to encompass the actual complexities of the world. We will briefly review some highlights in this process. An important landmark was the research on regional integration by two scholars (Deutsch[4] and Haas[5]): Deutsch offering a broad overview of the political, social and economic conditions necessary for a "no-war" community, and Haas focusing on the prerequisites for new political unions. Research on linkage politics (Rosenau[6]), and bureaucratic politics (Allison[7]) followed, challenging the assumption that states are unitary actors. Later, the shift of emphasis to transnational relations (Keohane and Nye[8]) undermined the assumption that states are the only actors worthy of attention, as it highlighted the activities of international governmental organizations (IGOs), international non-governmental organizations (INGOs), and transnational corporations (TNCs). The state paradigm has proved to be most tenacious in resisting territorial disaggregation, i.e., considering regions, provinces and localities (within countries) as viable actors. But this was achieved by Mansbach, Ferguson, and Lampert[9] who devised what they called a complex conglomerate paradigm. And yet, in all of these approaches, the state has tended to remain as the central focus, or the point of departure—sort of the North Star of international relations navigators. This is reflected in the widespread use of terms such as "non-state actors" for all actors but states, "high politics" for national security issues and "low politics" for all others, as well as in the fact that the main focus of regional integration studies was eventually the creation of regional states.

The ideology of the state system rests on two basic assumptions. First, states are assumed to be the inevitable constituent units of the world policy. A natural corollary then is that states are "the most important actors," a phrase often reiterated in scholarly texts. Second, international politics and domestic politics are assumed to be qualitatively different, to be analyzed with different concepts and guided by different norms. Accordingly, foreign policy has traditionally been subjected to far less popular control than domestic policy, even within democracies. It is widely assumed that only a small elite in the foreign policy establishment of the state is qualified to define and implement its foreign policy. Or, to use the terminology of the ideology, only they are able to "define the national interest." Both these assumptions are so deep-seated that they even permeate efforts to transform the state system: as when advocates of regional integration see the process as leading to a regional state, or when designers of world order schemes advocate a future world state. Obviously, not all international relations scholars fully accept the ideology. Indeed, I have just cited evidence of the struggle that is being waged to free research from the paradigm it dictates. But lack of forthright recognition of the ideology for what it is has delayed the development of an acute understanding of the more complicated realities of the world polity and alternatives for world futures that they imply.

The essential issue here is not whether some states have great military power, or whether some states have great economic power. A few obviously do, even on both counts. But many corporations have more economic power than most states, and some have tremendous influence over states, even over those with great military power. Indeed, in certain contexts, religious leaders, ethnic/national groups, liberation movements, INGOs, and so forth are also more powerful than many states. And yet, many who recognize the validity of these assertions nonetheless continue to employ research paradigms which give primacy to only one of the contending units, the state. This makes it difficult to assess realistically the actual capabilities and potentials of other actors, including those in local contexts. Fortunately, efforts less constrained by the state system ideology are beginning to appear.

BOLD DEPARTURES FROM THE STATE SYSTEM PARADIGM

Rare have been the efforts to escape the ideology of the state system altogether and create paradigms that transcend the fixation on the state as an origin point. But sharper breaks are beginning to appear. We will briefly describe the essential developments by using three examples.

One such effort is the issue paradigm of Mansbach and Vasquez,[10] which is heavily influenced by the work of David Easton. Easton, who is not an international relations scholar, had written in 1953 about the impact of state ideology on empirical investigations in political science:

> Bearing in mind the actual history of the political use of the concept [of state], it is difficult to understand how it could ever prove to be fruitful for empirical work; its importance lies largely in the field of practical politics as an instrument to achieve national cohesion rather than in the area of thoughtful analysis . . . . Basically the inadequacy of the state concept as a definition of subject matter stems from the fact that it implies that political science is interested in studying a particular kind of institution or organization of life, not a kind of activity that may express itself through a variety of institutions.[11]

Easton rejected power as an organizing concept for political inquiry because it "is only one of the significant variables," omitting "an equally vital aspect of political life, its goals other than power itself." Instead, Easton used as a starting point the "authoritative allocation of values." Building on Easton's work, Mansbach and Vasquez developed an approach stressing contention over issues. The assumptions of the Mansbach and Vasquez paradigm are:

1. Actors in global politics may include any individual or group that is able to contend for the disposition of a political stake.

2. The fundamental causal processes that govern political interaction are the same regardless of whether contention occurs between or within groups. A single theory of politics, domestic and global, is therefore possible.

3. Politics can be defined as the authoritative allocation of values through the resolution of issues: i.e., through the acceptance and implementation of a proposal(s) to dispose of the components at stake in the issue under contention. Substantive issues lie at the heart of politics, providing not only an overall purpose to contention, but having a major impact on the way in which contention is conducted. Politics, then, consists of the raising and resolving of public issues. To explain and regulate that process are the empirical and normative goals of political inquiry.

4. The shape of political contention is a function of three general factors—the characteristics of the issues on the agenda, the pattern of friendship or hostility among contending actors, and the nature of the institutional context in which allocation decisions must be made.[12]

Thus Mansbach and Vasquez assert their intent to break out of the predetermined framework of state units altogether and examine all "actors who have a measure of autonomy, unity, capability, and conjoint purpose." These actors "may range from individuals acting on their own behalf to large collectivities bound by common purposes and functioning in collaborative fashion."[13]   These would, of course, include local actors engaged in activities that transcend state borders.   They are not relegated a priori to a separate domain (domestic politics), to be studied there with different concepts and theories.   Instead, Mansbach and Vasquez reject the "alleged dichotomy between 'international' and 'domestic' politics."   After all, humanity has produced a vast array of territorial units (political, economic, ethnic and national), ranging from the very small to very large.   A diversity of organizations and activities transcend these territorial units, and all these border-crossing activities are subject to the same "causal process."   This is not to say, of course, that states are necessarily unimportant, nor that state borders may not have special significance.   But these are questions to be answered by empirical investigation, not a priori assumptions.

John Burton makes an even bolder break with tradition by adopting a problem-solving approach, given full scholarly treatment in *The Process of Solving Unsolved Social and Political Problems*,[14] and a more popular exposition in *Dear Survivors*.[15]   The focus of attention for Burton is not actors with specific kinds of qualities, as is the case with Mansbach and Vasquez.   Rather, he sees "human needs as the navigation or reference points, not only for psychologists, but no less for sociologists, and students of politics and international politics."[16]   Thus, Burton takes a significant step beyond Mansbach and Vasquez as their focus on actors who have a "measure of autonomy, unity, capability, and conjoint purpose" is still mildly reminiscent of the traditional international relations emphasis on powerful actors.   Burton's emphasis on needs extends his paradigm to include those presently powerless whose needs, he assumes, will eventually make an impact on "structures and institutions."   He succinctly summarizes the basic principles of his needs approach as follows:

1. There are certain human needs and desires that are specific and universal.

2. These will be satisfied, even at the cost of social disruption and personal disorientation.

3. Some structures and institutions that have evolved over time, as a result of differentiation of power and of socialization, do not necessarily, either in the short or the long term, reflect these needs and desires, and frequently frustrate them.

4. Disruptive behavior is the consequences of interaction between the pursuit of human needs and the institutional framework created by power differentiation.

For Burton, "the individual must be the unit of analysis, because it is individual human needs that ultimately have to be catered for in the interests of public policy at all levels."[17]   Appropriately enough, his book ends with this quotation from David Singer:

Finally, my conviction is that we must, in one fashion or another, break away from the normative assumptions which seem to be implicit in so many of the formulations found in contemporary social science. Whether the orientation is toward national interests, social order, political stability, economic growth or one or other of the many structural-functional paradigms, we seem to be in increasing danger of forgetting that the basic unit of any social system is the individual human being, and that any scientific formulation must take cognizance of that fact. In my judgement, no theory which ignores the single person is scientifically adequate or morally defensible. In sum, what is proposed is that we begin some systematic research which can simultaneously 'think big' and 'think small,' and which embraces in a rigorous synthesis both the lone individual and all of mankind.[18]

Burton suggests that, in actuality, individuals identify with each other in groups—ethnic, religious, economic, liberation movements, etc.—in order to pursue the fulfillment of their individual needs. Such identity groups serve for Burton as the building blocks for linking the individual to global processes and outcomes.

Johan Galtung also places the needs of the individual at the center of concern. In *The True Worlds,* he asserts: "The basic focus of this book is the *human individual,* in a social setting, domestically and globally."[19] Galtung's "theory of progressive action" designates self-reliance as "the overriding strategy"[20] and advocates "tasks for everybody."[21] But in contrast to Burton, Galtung strongly argues for empowering all people for participation in world affairs. According to him, citizens' initiatives can produce "a plurality of revolutions at the micro level,"[22] and intellectuals can contribute too by making the world "more transparent for citizens."[23] Clearly, in the context of the ideology of the state system, and most scholarly research on international/world affairs, these positions would be, literally, unthinkable.

I have argued extensively[24] that individual activation would require research that illuminates for people their specific encounter with the world. In a sense, I advocate that the needs approach encompass the need of all individuals for knowledge about their involvement in world systems, and about the impact of their lives on people linked to them through world systems. From this perspective, research would extend beyond studying the individual as object and instead contribute to activate the individual as subject, or as purposeful actor. This, of course, would require the creation of new local agendas, and organizations through which "ordinary people" could participate in world affairs decision-making. Such participation would include, but not be limited to, the foreign policy decisions of national governments. Indeed, the "foreign policy" decisions of a variety of voluntary associations—religious, labor, business, agricultural—and subnational governments would be considered as well.

These examples show that paradigms with the potential of offering local people enlightenment about their encounter with worldwide processes and to encourage them to become self-conscious and self-reliant participants are now being developed. This has been made possible by eliminating the preeminent position of the state in research paradigms, by focusing on needs, by entertaining the notion that it is feasible for individuals and groups in local situations to respond to (and possibly overcome) the encroachment of world systems on local space, and by urging scholars to provide opportunities for people to gain knowledge so that widespread intelligent responses are possible.

RESOURCES FROM A MICRO PERSPECTIVE

The intellectual developments we have been describing can be characterized as macro scholars at last discovering the micro. However, the reverse is also true—scholars whose work is primarily local are moving more frequently and further beyond their traditional concerns to inquire and examine how and what links local places and events have to the whole world. For the remainder of this paper, we will use a few examples to show how people working in a variety of disciplines and local milieus are enhancing our capacity for serving the knowledge needs of "ordinary people" in their efforts to cope with global systems and events. We will draw briefly on materials focusing on the following: world history; cultures, nations, peoples and ethnic groups; frontiers and border regions; local contexts in the Third World; the world-wide Green movement; peripheries in global cities; and voluntary community programs in industrialized countries. Examples will be chosen from scholars working in an array of disciplines: anthropology, economics, history, political science and sociology. It is important to stress that these scholars are not attempting to directly challenge traditional approaches to international relations through efforts to develop holistic paradigms. Rather, the examples reveal that researchers working in a variety of contexts are uncovering new information on human needs and micro-macro linkages, acquiring new perspectives on their significance and suggesting new possibilities for the future.

World History

Most of our examples here emphasize the ways in which the state paradigm has isolated people from world affairs by virtue of its spatial representation of the world. But local actors have also been deprived of knowledge about the intricate historical relationships between their local communities and the world. With the incorporation of transnational relations into the state paradigm, the impression has been created that so-called nonstate actors are entirely new, a product of modern transportation and communications.

Certainly, jet engines and satellite communications have greatly changed the nature of global interaction among peoples. But sustained contact between local peoples over long distances is not new. Widespread patterns of migration and commerce, the diffusion of religions, philosophies, science and technology, had all occurred before the Western state system was established, continued after its founding, and persist to the present. Yet, this more encompassing perspective has not been incorporated into mainstream international/global research, thus serving to wall off people from understanding the historical links of their local community in what William McNeill has called the "ecumene."

As McNeill puts it, "I deplore the effort to dissociate humanity's deeper past from the contemporary encounter with the world."[25] McNeill offers an interesting historical perspective on the links between the major civilizations of the world by employing the concept "ecumene." According to him, the first "closure of ecumene" occurred around 200 A.D.: which is to say, by that time, there was more or less continuous contact and exchange among civilizations that stretched from Spain and North Africa (in the Roman Empire) to the China Sea (the Han Empire). Contact was by sea over the Mediterranean and the Indian Ocean, by land routes passing through present-day Iran and Afghanistan, and by the movement of steppe nomads from the Han Empire to the Roman Empire. Diseases moved with ease across the ecumene; substantial migrations of useful plants and animals occurred. For example, "familiarity with cotton, sugarcane, and chickens, all first domesticated in India, spread to both China and western Eurasia during this period."[26] Significantly, however, technological secrets moved much more slowly. "Indian steel attained a peculiar quality that commanded a market in the Roman Empire, but could not be duplicated there; Chinese silk was exported to India, the Middle East, and Rome, but the secrets of its manufacture did not reach the outer world until the sixth century A.D."[27] In this provocative vein, McNeill leads up to the "global ecumene" created by European explorers in the fifteenth and sixteenth centuries and the eventual transformations in this ecumene brought on by air travel and satellite communications.

A western-centered world view had developed, in large part from the "discoveries" of the great European explorers in the fifteenth and sixteenth centuries. But recent developments in world history are placing these "discoveries" in a new light. Says the French historian Fernand Braudel, "Man had already explored and exploited the whole world for centuries or millennia before the triumph of Europe. . . . Even the inventory of vegetable wealth had been drawn up so precisely since the beginning of written history, that not one single nutritious plant of general usefulness has been added to the list of those previously known."[28] Another historian, Kenneth Neill Cameron, believes "there was certainly influence from Asia on developing civilized society in America," although "it is not easy to say when or how such influences came about." Cameron bases his judgment on concrete similarities between Asian and American cultures and argues that "if such direct contact seems hard to believe, we have to remember that a thousand years before Columbus, ships were crossing from Ceylon to Java with 200 passengers, that by the time of Augustus, ships of 75 tons (the Nina was 60 tons) were crossing the India Ocean, [and] that the Chinese had ships of 500 to 800 tons by 700 A.D."[29]

Diplomatic history has long been a key component in international education. This history has been significantly shaped by what Edwin Morse calls "The Heroic Framework." The origins of this framework, says Morse, are to be found in the emergence of the present state system,

> in a period of political heroism that idealized the capacities of 'master-builders' of the new political order. Even as the significance of political leadership diminished with the consolidation of nation-states, a heroic cast remained one of the characteristics of the ideal conduct of diplomacy. . . . The result was the personification of the nation-state that has confused more than it has informed diplomatic rhetoric.[30]

Indeed, because of the legacy of this heroic framework, it is difficult to convince people that their everyday life has a transnational dimension that affects their quality of life, and that of people in distant places.

This weakness of the heroic framework was severely criticized by the French Annales school of historians founded by Lucien Febvre and Max Bloch in the 1920s. Peter Burke, a scholar familiar with that tradition, has observed that "Febvre was always most severe on diplomatic historians who wrote about foreign policy without reference to the economic and social background . . . he opposed any history that was less than total."[31] And actually, the emphasis of the Annales school on the history of daily life offers a provocative context for rethinking the global significance of everyday, local relations. Fernand Braudel, one of the most prominent proponents of this school, offers the following remarks:

> I think mankind is more than waist deep in daily routine. Countless inherited acts, accumulated pell-mell and repeated time after time to this very day, become habits that help us live, imprison us, and make decisions for us throughout our lives. These acts . . . more frequently than we might suspect—go back to the beginnings of mankind's history. . . . This material life as I understand it is the life that man throughout his previous history has made a part of his very being, has in some way absorbed into his entrails, turning the experiments and exhilarating experiences of the past into everyday, banal experiences. So no one pays close attention to them any more.[32]

To Braudel the "banal" is exciting and profoundly important as when he discusses the influence on history of the choice of wheat, corn or rice as a staple crop by specific peoples:

> We might also discuss the number of calories that these plants represent and inadequacies and changes in diet across the ages. Aren't these questions just as exciting as the fate of Charles V's empire or the fleeting and debatable splendors of the so-called French primacy during the reign of Louis XIV? And they are surely questions with far-reaching implications: Can't the history of the old drugs, alcohol and tobacco, and the lightning swift manner in which tobacco in particular circled the globe and conquered the world, serve as a warning about today's drugs, different but equally dangerous?[33]

Cultures, Nations, Peoples and Ethnic Groups

The statist paradigm, with its view of a world of (only) some 160 states, inhibits perception of, or designates inferior status to, thousands of cultures, nations, and ethnic groups. In an assessment of the persistence of small cultural enclaves, "or persistent peoples," George Pierre Castile offers this challenging statement:

> The history of states is one of constant fluctuation; many if not most of the peoples have outpersisted two or more states. Perhaps it would be more appropriate to ask why states have been so ineffective at absorption of the peoples or even why states are so fragile compared to peoples.[34]

Subnational (and often transnational) cultures, nations, and ethnic groups have either no place in the statist paradigm or have tended to be seen as destabilizing, as inevitable "subnational units," or as elements in state-building. Yet they are vitally important actors on the present world stage themselves: to wit, the increasing prominence of fundamentalist religious movements and self-determination movements. Unfortunately most of these groups tend to be invisible to the outside world unless they respond to state policies with "terrorism." Increasingly, however, publications such as those of the Minority Rights Group and Human Rights Internet are making their existence more visible. Broad assessments by Crawford Young and Gunnar P. Nielsson have also been very useful in coming to grips with the significance of these groups as important global actors.

Young, especially, has decried the success of the state system in relegating "Third World" groups to relative oblivion. In the *Politics of Cultural Pluralism,* he argues eloquently for a reassessment of this oppression:

> We need, then, to examine more closely this cast-iron grid superimposed upon the culturally diverse populace of the third world. So much is the state system a part of our routinized perceptions of the world that its existence seems utterly banal and ordinary—yet we would suggest that it exercises a transcendent despotism over reality.[35]

Instead of the prevailing classification of Third World countries according to wealth or level of development, Young offers two revealing typologies: one is based on the modes of colonial intervention and their relationship with local groups, and the other on the number and distribution of cultural groups in specific countries.

Nielsson's work[36] came later, is global in scope, and makes a clearer break with the state as an exclusive unit of analysis. In addition to the state, he also employs two other units of analysis: ethnic groups with attributes such as common racial identity, language, religion, kinship, social customs, history, and stable geographic continuity; and nation groups which are ethnic groups that have become politically mobilized on the basis of ethnic group values. With these units of analysis, Nielsson is able to develop two views of the world. The state-centric view portrays the distribution of ethnic and nation groups within states while the ethnic-centric view portrays the distribution of ethnic and nation groups, whether they be within single states or several states. Based on this framework, Nielsson's world is one of 168 states and 589 ethnic groups. Significantly, were his analysis confined to the state-centric view, he would have had 1357 ethnic groups within the 168 states. But the ethnic group perspective reduces the number to 589 because many are spread across the boundaries of more than one state. Indeed, given the widespread use of the term nation-state, it is significant that only in 13 cases do all members of an ethnic group reside in one state and comprise a majority in that state. Rather, 56% of the ethnic groups (328) are minorities within a single state, and more than two-thirds of all ethnic groups are single or multi-state minorities.

At this point, Nielsson's largely classificatory analysis raises more questions than it answers. But his work is definitely a significant analytic break-through in portraying a world based on ethnic/nation groupings. And actually, self-determination movements based on ethnic/nation identity are now widespread, and the literature on specific groups is growing. Nielsson has enabled the international/global scholar to begin to conceptualize the place of these actors on the world scene as something other than irritants and disrupters of the state system. At the same time, he has also enabled members of these groups to see more clearly their place in the world.

Frontiers and Border Regions

Many ethnic/nation groups are bisected by state borders, much as modern urban highways divide neighborhoods. The special problems of state border areas are eloquently described by P. Orianne thus: "Time and mankind patiently strive to put together again what treaties and systems of laws once tore asunder to meet the requirements of a particular type of political organization."[37] In a report to the Council of Europe, he delineates three handicaps faced by people in frontier regions: they are usually far away from the capital or regional center; their most favorable trading area is often abroad; and some of the local authorities they have to deal with are in another country.[38] As a result, he says, they "have their backs to the wall," because "frontier municipalities and regions are themselves without the means of dealing with their counterparts abroad, to the extent that competence in the field of 'foreign policy' is the exclusive preserve of the supreme authority."[39]

Scholars at the Institute of International Sociology, Gorizia, have extensively probed the predicament of people living along border areas from their unusual vantage point on the Italian-Yugoslav border. R. Strassaldo and R. Gubert assert:

> The only difference between national frontiers and other kinds of boundaries is that the States have elaborated powerful armed organizations to defend them, a complex system of international law to prevent any undesirable 'input', and a religion of Nationalism to make them sacred and inviolable.[40]

Hence, they argue against the treatment of border regions as though they were "but an 'epiphenomenon' of something more basic" and urge that border regions be liberated to reestablish the functional linkages which competing national capitals have torn asunder. In this way they would see "the transformation of border regions from locus of division, hostility, disputes and wars to locus of cooperation and integration."[41]

The point here is that areas surrounding national borders can be usefully considered as units of analysis in their own right. Indeed, important perspectives are obscured when these border areas are perceived only as peripheries of states. When viewed as the center of concern, however, new possibilities are perceived for dealing with problems in border areas. People living in these areas thereby gain insights about their place in the world and new perspectives on the international problems of their daily lives. A good resource is the work edited by Strassaldo and Zotti, which contains case studies as well as more theoretical pieces.[42] Other examples are B. De Marchi and A. M. Boileau's *Boundaries and Minorities in Western Europe*[43] and Niles Hansen's *The Border Economy: Regional Development in the Southwest*, a study of the U.S.-Mexican border.[44]

Local Contexts in the Third World

As illustrations of work on local contexts offering resources for international/global studies, we find Richard N. Adams' volume on social structures in Guatemala from 1944 to 1966 and D. L. Sheth's article on grass-roots politics in contemporary India very useful. Writing in 1970, with no apparent knowledge of the emerging transnational relations literature, Adams offers a remarkable study of the place of the Guatemalan farm laborer and coffee farmer in world systems. This makes his comment on state power all the more interesting:

> In the case of Guatemala, it is evident that the power system, while defining the nation-state, is not in any sense restricted to that unit. Quite the contrary. The power relations indicate where the boundaries are, but, like kinship and economic systems, have ramifications and linkages around the world.[45]

And speaking of development, Adams observes:

> It is important in discussing development to make clear what unit is developing. In the contemporary world, the nation-state is often assumed to be the only appropriate one. If, instead of the nation, we say that development may be an issue of any organized set of human beings—a poor family, a local community, a clique, a business firm, a military junta—that any such unit is concerned with maintaining and assuring, if not improving, its adequate control over the environment, then quite obviously there will be conflict between one of these and another.[46]

Adams offers two striking diagrams, Figure 6.1 with the coffee farmer (finquero) in the center, and Figure 6.2 with the laborer (campesino) in the center. Using these diagrams, he discuss the ways in which each is affected by labor, commercial, political, religious, and military activities ranging from the very local to the global in scope. What is especially significant is the variation in the domains perceived and understood by different actors. Thus the campesino tends to operate in a very local framework, while the finquero operates within a somewhat broader framework that includes markets where he buys seeds, fertilizer and equipment, hires migrants, and interacts with the Guatemalan government and military. But other actors see the situation in a much broader light. The United States, for example, exercises considerable control through international coffee agreements and the U.S. market for coffee, as well as threats about armed intervention and the availability of loans.

Writing from his experiences with the Lokayan movement in India, Sheth observes a growing partnership between intellectuals and grass-roots activities in the Third World. He advances three principles on which this new politics will be based. First, there is rejection of "modern (Western) politics" and a search for a process consonant with the local social and cultural continuities. Second, there is an awareness that the local power structures against which (local) people are fighting derive power from macro structures of the prevalent national and international order. Third, the new perspective

> is based, to a large extent, on the day-to-day experience of ordinary people. . . . It is the experience of hunger, destitution and terror, on the one hand, and of the sheer inability of established institutional order to protect them from the rapacious exploitation and crushing domination of the local power structures, on the other.[47]

Figure 6.1 Idealized *Finquero*-Centered View of Relations Among Selected Domains

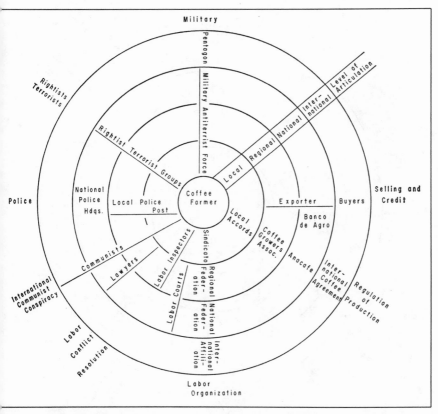

Source: Crucifixion By Power: Essays on Guatemalan National Social Structure, 1944-1966, by Richard Newbold Adams © 1970. Reprinted by permission of the University of Texas Press.

Figure 6.2 Idealized *Campesino*/**Laborer-Centered View of Relations of Selected Domains a**
Different Levels.

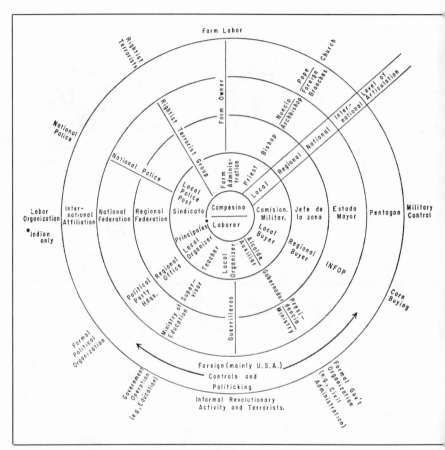

Source: Crucifixion By Power: Essays on Guatemalan National Social Structure, 1944-1966, by
Richard Newbold Adams © 1970. Reprinted by permission of the University of Texas Press.

Sheth places particular emphasis on the need for linking research with action. He describes how Lokayan operates as an example:

> Lokayan operates at the interface of social knowledge and social action, of academic institutions and activist groups. It aims at changing the existing paradigm of social knowledge in India, the generation of new social knowledge and its use with a view to making it more pertinent to the issues of social intervention and transformation. Rather than depend on the conventional methods of social research, Lokayan identifies action-groups and micro-movements and the key participants and then brings them together in dialogues among themselves as well as with intellectuals, journalists and, when possible, even concerned public officials.[48]

Sheth perceives a new mode of politics arising across regional, linguistic, cultural and national boundaries. It encompasses peace and anti-nuclear movements, environmental movements, women's movements, movements for self-determination of cultural groups, minorities and tribes, and a movement championing non-Western cultures, techno-sciences and languages. Importantly, this new politics is "not constricted by the narrow logic of capturing state power." Rather, Sheth discerns the need for new insights on micro-macro linkage. He concludes:

> It is the dialectic between micro-practice and macro-thinking that will actualize a new politics of the future. . . . In brief, a macro-vision is the prime need of these groups and movements, and this can be satisfied only by a growing partnership between activists and intellectuals in the process of social transformation.[49]

Worldwide Green Movement

Swedish economists Mats Friberg and Bjorn Hettne see a worldwide "Green" movement emerging that offers an alternative to the "Blue" (market, liberal, capitalist) and the "Red" (state socialism, planning).[50] They reject "mainstream development thinking" in which "the state is always seen as the social subject of the development process." Instead, from the Green perspective, they see that "the human being or small communities of human beings are the ultimate actors. The state can at most be an instrument for this ultimate actor."[51] In other words, Friberg and Hettne consider that "the tribes and nations of the world are much more basic units of development" than states.

Like Burton, in explicating the Green approach to development, they use human needs as a starting point from which the following are derived:

- *Cultural identity*: The social unit of development is a culturally defined community and the development of this community is rooted in the specific values and institutions of this culture.
- *Self-reliance*: Each community relies primarily on its own strength and resources.

- *Social justice*: Development programs should give priority to those most in need.

- *Ecological balance*: The resources of the biosphere are utilized in full awareness of the potential of local ecosystems as well as the global and local limits imposed on present and future generations.[52]

The Green approach sees the capitalist societies of the West and the state socialist societies of the East as "two variants of a common corporate industrial culture based on the values of competitive individualism, rationality, growth, efficiency, specialization, centralization and big scale." According to Friberg and Hettne, how these values came about can only be partly explained by economic factors. Rather, "their roots have to be sought, ultimately, in the cultural projects of Western civilization."[53] Thus, for the Greens, the "unbalance between the modern large-scale rationalized sector and the non-modern small-scale personalistic sector" would be an essential element of the predicament of Third World people in all regions of the world. More generally, their problems would not be simply those arising from capitalism or socialism, but have to do also with "the nation-state, bureaucratic forms of organization, positive science, the patriachate and the urban way of life."[54] Friberg and Hettne do not wish to eliminate states, only to make them serve the human needs of individuals in local communities better. Like other works we have discussed, they too are concerned with micro-macro linkages. They see the "Green project" requiring "stronger institutions on the global and local level," as well as the deemphasis of the state. But they do not present concrete ideas for global institutions which fit the Green approach nor do they indicate whether these institutions should be linked directly to local peoples.

Like Sheth's "new mode of politics," Friberg and Hettne's Green movement transcends single countries and regions. Their "main hypothesis is that the Green movement derives its strength from three rather different sources":

- *The traditionalists*, who resist modern penetration in the form of commercialization, industrialization, state-building and professionalization. They derive their strength from "non-Western civilizations and religions, old nations and tribes, local communities, kinship groups, peasants and self-employed people, informal economies, women, culture, etc."

- *Marginalized people*, who cannot find a place within the modern sector, "the unemployed, temporary workers, women, youth, the uneducated, workers with soulless jobs, etc."

- *Post-materialists*, who experience some sort of "self-emancipation," often through "opportunities provided by an affluent modern society. . . . They are young, well-educated and committed to non-material values. Their occupations are person-oriented rather than thing-oriented."[55]

Friberg and Hettne perceive these three groups to be at different places in the "center-periphery structure of the world." The traditionalists are to be found primarily in peripheries, the marginalized at the middle level and the post-materialists near the centers. They are now not part of a single Green movement. Rather, Friberg and Hettne see all three as potential elements of a worldwide movement.

Peripheries in Global Cities

Robert Ross and Kent Trachte[56] disagree with Immanuel Wallerstein's division of the world into core, semi-periphery and periphery.[57] In Wallerstein's view, the core concentrates on the production of goods requiring relatively more advanced skills and high wage labor, higher levels of capital intensity than the periphery, and hence receives higher profits. Within the core, certain cities are "global cities," the command and control centers for resource allocation throughout the world; these cities, presumably, have a comparatively privileged working class. However, using data on New York City, Ross and Trachte attempt to demonstrate that the internationalization of global production is actually producing a peripheralization of the labor force in global cities. Their mode of analysis offers additional insight on linkages between subnational units and world systems.

Ross and Trachte seek to respond, in particular, to Arghiri Emmanuel's characterization of cooperation between workers and capitalists in core areas.[58] Emmanuel has asserted that "the core working class not only enjoys a relatively privileged condition but has become a partner in the exploitation of the underdeveloped countries."[59] Furthermore, the world systems tradition accepts the notion that the core working class enjoys an improving standard of living. Ross and Trachte's challenge to these assumptions was stimulated by Chase-Dunn's testing,[60] over a 1200 year period, of the world systems assumption that global cities have a hierarchical relation to other cities. When Chase-Dunn found a flatter distribution than expected, interest grew in researching the political and economic demands of workers and other oppressed groups in global cities, and in the tendency of corporations to avoid these demands by leaving for more favorable locations.

Ross and Trachte would readily admit that the working class in the core is undoubtedly better off than the working class in the periphery. They have problems, however, with the "argument that core workers are the allies of core capitalists in the exploitation of the periphery [because it] neglects the ongoing class conflict and struggles for power within core regions."[61] Pointing to work on labor market segmentation by economists concerned with labor and race in the U.S. and Western Europe, they assert that "labor market segmentation is a phenomenon beyond the immediate conceptual reach of core/periphery imagery and reveals a serious limitation in its structural logic."[62] Indeed, they believe that the "very use of the term 'core labor' tends to conflate class with space."[63]

Ross and Trachte attempt to demonstrate that "there is a local reserve army of labor and that it is joined in a global reserve, any national or local fraction of which capital can choose to favor with investment"[64] by using New York City as an example. They use rising unemployment, declining wages, nonunion jobs, housing conditions, and households with incomes below the poverty line, as indicators of vulnerability to capital mobility. From their analysis of New York City data, Ross and Trachte conclude that "New York allows the proposition that the periphery is reproduced within the global city."[65]

In terms of international/global theory, the value of the work of Ross and Trachte lies in their challenge to the development of a world systems approach based on state units. To this extent, it is all the more surprising that Ross and Trachte, in their conclusions, stress the "obvious need . . . that *national* fractions of the global working class . . . develop the diplomatic infrastructure by which they may confront capital in a unitary fashion" (emphasis added).[66] While this could well be one way in which labor can respond to the mobility of capital, it is surprising that Ross and Trachte do not see other possibilities for transnational labor cooperation. Thus we have further evidence of the lingering impact of state ideology on analysis. This is in dramatic contrast with the perspective assumed by Sheth and Friberg and Hettne.

Voluntary Community Programs in Industrialized Countries

Also to be found in industrialized countries are the more traditional voluntary organizations devoted to a variety of international concerns. Despite widespread public ignorance about world affairs in the United States, and often considerable lack of interest as well, many people are making valiant efforts to relate to the larger world through local programs. Educational programs of World Affairs Councils, Great Decisions discussion groups, and UN associations are everywhere to be found. There are foreign aid programs such as CARE, CROP/Church World Service, and Project HOPE; extensive refugee programs often rooted also in religious denominations; and widespread exchange programs such as Youth for Understanding, AFS, local councils for international visitors, and People to People. Most of these programs, however, tend to involve only a small minority of people with relatively high economic and social status. Similarly, the activities of local "internationals" deal, to a considerable degree, with the consequences of the policies of other institutions, particularly states, rather than directly confronting the causes. For example, local "internationals" tend to administer to the local needs of refugees and the needs of the poor in other countries, rather than directly opposing the policies of transnational organizations and states that created these needs in the first place.

The state system paradigm has contributed to an effective division of labor between the role of the state and that of "ordinary people" in world affairs. Indeed, it is widely accepted that the really "big" issues relating to peace, security, and international economics are too difficult and complicated for most people to understand. Instead, an array of more limited tasks, in a sense "cleaning up the mess" made by the state system—such as poverty, hunger, malnutrition, homelessness—is relegated to voluntary organizations. National governments often encourage and even subsidize these organizations, so long as their activities do not challenge state policies. Significantly, this division of labor is generally accepted even by highly educated and well informed people who lack confidence in their own judgment on "big" foreign policy issues.

Nevertheless, challenges on these "big" foreign/global policy issues are emerging, as revealed in the municipal, county and state votes on disarmament and nuclear freeze in Canada, Japan and the United States.[67] Another example is the campaign in the United States for state and local authorities to pass legislation prohibiting public investments in corporations doing business in South Africa.[68] Still other examples are the successful INFACT campaign to require the Nestle corporation to adhere to standards for marketing infant formula in the Third World, and the Lucas Plan for converting Lucas Aerospace in the United Kingdom from production of arms to production of goods for human needs.[69] Many other examples could be given as more and more people proclaim: "Think globally and act locally."

There have also been efforts to develop community-wide approaches to local relations with the world, such as the establishment of sister cities and town-twinning. Sometimes these involve a very limited exchange of elites, but they can also reach out to link people in a great diversity of occupations, such as barbers and hairdressers, with their counterparts in other countries. Another approach, mundialization, often involves a sister/twinning relationship with other towns and cities, but includes also an affirmation of affinity with the world community, such as a declaration of adherence to the UN Charter, flying the UN flag, and so on.[70]

The movement toward the direct participation of local representatives in world affairs has led to two even more radical approaches. One is direct elections to an international assembly, such as the People's Congress organized from Paris.[71] Another is the effort within the Council of Europe to add a third main body, alongside ministers and legislators, through which local authorities would be directly represented.[72]

This very brief overview of local efforts at international/global participation in the industrialized world has revealed a great diversity of approaches, although the number of people involved is still relatively small. For the most part, these activities have not attracted the serious interest of international relations scholars. This neglect detracts from the visibility of these activities, undermines the belief of current and potential participants in the significance and potential of these activities, and deprives participants of knowledge that would enable them to strengthen their programs.

CONCLUSION

We have attempted to bring together examples of research that are generating new insights on how people pursuing their needs in local communities are linked to world systems. We have focused on several salient topics and have deliberately drawn on scholars from an array of disciplines: anthropology, economics, history, political science, and sociology. This kind of research is more attentive to local contexts, and is beginning to engender concepts and theories of international/global systems and issues that are more useful to "ordinary people" than the more traditional international relations literature. In addition, it can also suggest new possibilities for participation and problem solving. Such research is vitally necessary to complement approaches such as those of Burton and Mansbach/Vasquez that have successfully overcome the statist paradigm but still have not responded explicitly to the need to place "ordinary people" in paradigms that might serve their knowledge needs.

We have demonstrated how world history can help local people to understand their long-term encounter with humanity, as well as that of their parents and more distant antecedents. Some world history is particularly useful because it deals with the history of daily life, rather than the traditional "Heroic Framework."

We discerned a growing capacity to overcome the conceptual tyranny of the wall map, with its colored blotches (states) and stars (state capitals), thereby permitting the portrayal of a world of cultures, nations and ethnic groups. The growing literature concerned with these constituent units of humanity makes it no longer possible to use the ideologically laden term "nation-state" without more precise definition. Also, work on frontiers and border regions highlights peoples and problems that have so easily been placed in the periphery.

Throughout the literature reviewed, we have encountered strong objections both to the state as the dominant unit of analysis and the state as a dominant actor. This has come through most strongly in Orianne, Strassoldo/Gubert, Sheth, and Friberg/Hettne. Sheth and Friberg/Hettne discern new possibilities for global coalitions in the context of what Sheth would call a "new mode of politics," and Friberg and Hettne "a worldwide Green movement." Significantly, both conceive of widespread movements whose prime goal is not to control the old state apparatus but to create new possibilities for satisfying human needs. In the end, Ross and Trachte were not sufficiently able to free themselves from the constraint of the state paradigm to see that one possibility for peripheral labor in core cities might be transnational labor movements separate from national movements, and another might be to link up with "a new mode of politics" or Green movements. Nevertheless, their work raises these possibilities.

The research reviewed raises challenging questions about the kinds of relationships between local action and institutions, on the one hand, and global action and institutions, on the other hand, that might better serve human needs than those that now exist. In this brief literature survey, only Sheth and Friberg/Hettne are explicitly concerned about global futures. Friberg and Hettne assert that stronger local and global institutions are needed to achieve the "greening of the world." But they do not explicitly deal with how the local and the global might be linked. Sheth asserts that "the process of moving from micro-practices of transformative politics to a macro-conception of a new politics for the future has . . . just begun."[73] He claims that "it is the dialectic between micro-practice and macro-thinking that will actualize a new politics for the future."[74]

It is significant that while Sheth sees a "macro-vision" as the "prime need" of grass-roots groups and movements, he does not ask international/global scholars, or any intellectuals, to provide this vision. Rather, he believes this "can be satisfied by a growing partnership between activists and intellectuals in the process of social transformation." It is in this sense that Sheth extends the challenge to traditional international/global research beyond that of others researchers discussed in this paper. He believes that a "macro-conception of a new politics" will "depend on how sensitive and concerned intellectuals, particularly social scientists, are about the need to abandon their received theories and methods to meet the challenges thrown up by stirrings at the grass roots of their own society."[75] He calls for the "emergence of alternative macro-thinking, alternative institutions, and even large-scale movements joined by activists and intellectuals at the national, regional and international levels" that address "basic issues" and "can sustain, agglomerate and integrate what at present are localized and isolated efforts of the grass-roots organizations and movements. In effect, he is telling international/global scholars that problems with respect to micro-macro linkage can only be worked through practice and that scholars who would contribute to the enterprise must adopt new methods of partnership with activists.

To those who are concerned about international/global relations theory, these examples highlight the importance of research that begins with individuals in local communities pursuing their human needs. Such research endeavors to understand the local community's place in the world without the assumptions of traditional international/global scholarship. These scholars seriously challenge traditional temporal perspectives and units of analysis, and propose new and revolutionary research methods. At the same time, they perceive the potential for new kinds of local participation and global movements. We are certainly not suggesting that this literature offers easy guidelines for researchers who desire to cope more effectively with a rapidly changing world. But one thing is certain: the challenge of the literature emerging in a number of disciplines suggests that research and teaching about what we have at various times called international, transnational, world and global relations are in the process of a revolutionary change. What is particularly significant is the growing ties between research and action on global relations and research and action on human development in local contexts.

NOTES

1. Robert Johansen, *The National Interest and the Human Interest: An Analysis of United States Foreign Policy* (Princeton: Princeton University Press, 1980), p. 396.
2. Saul Mendlovitz, "On the Creation of a Just World Order: An Agenda for a Program of Inquiry and Praxis," *Alternatives VII*, 3, Winter 1981-1982, p. 362.
3. Rajni Kothari, "Peace in an Age of Transformation," *Alternatives IX*, 2, Fall 1983, p. 205.
4. Karl Deutsch, et al., *Political Community and the North Atlantic Area* (Princeton: Princeton University Press, 1957).
5. Ernst Haas, *Beyond the National State* (Stanford: Stanford University Press, 1964).
6. James Rosenau (ed.), *Linkage Politics* (New York: Free Press, 1969).
7. Graham Allison, *Essence of Decision: Explaining the Cuban Missile Crisis* (Boston: Little, Brown, 1971).
8. Robert Keohane and Joseph Nye, *Transnational Relations and World Politics* (Cambridge, Massachusetts: Harvard University Press, 1972).
9. Richard W. Mansbach, Yale H. Ferguson, and Donald E. Lampert, *The Web of World Politics: Nonstate Actors in the Global System* (Englewood Cliffs: Prentice Hall, 1976).
10. Richard W. Mansbach and John A. Vasquez, *In Search of Theory: A New Paradigm for Global Politics* (New York: Columbia University Press, 1981).
11. David Easton, *The Political System* (New York: Alfred A. Knopf, 1953), pp. 112–113.
12. See Mansbach and Vasquez (Note 10), pp. 68–69.
13. Ibid., p. 69.
14. John Burton, *Deviance, Terrorism and War: The Process of Solving Unsolved Social and Political Problems* (Oxford: Martin Robertson, 1979). We use

the subtitle here rather than the misleading main title invented by the publisher: *Deviance, Terrorism and War*, dramatized by a cover showing a globe spattered with red.

15. John Burton, *Dear Survivors* (Boulder, Colorado: Westview Press, 1982).

16. Burton, *Deviance, Terrorism and War*, pp. 64–65.

17. Ibid., p. 216.

18. J. David Singer, "Individual Values, National Interests and Political Development in the International System," *Studies in Comparative International Development* 6, 9, 1970, p. 230.

19. Johan Galtung, *The True Worlds* (New York: Free Press, 1980), p. 421.

20. Ibid., pp. 398–413.

21. Ibid., p. 396.

22. Ibid., p. 416.

23. Ibid., p. 419.

24. Chadwick F. Alger, "'Foreign' Policies of U.S. Publics," *International Studies Quarterly 21*, 2, June 1977; "Role of People in the Future Global Order," *Alternatives IV*, 2, October, 1978; "Reconstructing Human Policies: Collective Security in the Nuclear Age," in Burns H. Weston (ed.), *Toward Nuclear Disarmament and Global Security: A Search for Alternatives* (Boulder, Colorado: Westview Press, 1984).

25. William McNeill, *The Rise of the West: A History of the Human Community* (Chicago: University of Chicago Press, 1963), p. 5.

26. Ibid., p. 357.

27. Ibid., p. 358.

28. Fernand Braudel, *Capitalism and Material Life 1400-1800* (New York: Harper and Row, 1967), pp. 30–31.

29. Kenneth Neill Cameron. *Humanity and Society: A World History* (Bloomington: Indiana University Press, 1973), pp. 386–387.

30. Edwin L. Morse, *Modernization and the Transformation of International Relations* (New York: The Free Press, 1972), pp. 28, 45.

31. Peter Burke (ed.), *Economy and Society in Early Modern Europe: Essays from Annales* (New York: Harper and Row, 1972), p. 1.

32. Fernand Braudel, *Afterthoughts on Material Civilization and Capitalism* (Baltimore: Johns Hopkins University Press, 1977), pp. 7–8.

33. Ibid., p. 12.

34. George Pierre Castile (ed.), *Persistent Peoples* (Tucson: University of Arizona Press, 1981), p. xxi.

35. Crawford Young, *The Politics of Cultural Pluralism* (Madison: University of Wisconsin Press, 1976), p. 44.

36. Gunnar P. Nielsson, "The Role of 'Nation-Groups' in Political Integration and Disintegration: Toward Global Systematic Comparative Analysis," April 1982, to be published in E. Tiryakian and R. Rogowski (eds.), *New Nationalism of the Developed West: Toward Explanation* (Winchester, MA: Allen and Unwin, 1984).

37. P. Orianne, *Difficulties in Cooperation Between Local Authorities and Ways of Solving Them,* Study No. 6, Local and Regional Authorities in Europe (Strasbourg: Council of Europe, 1973), p. 1.

38. Ibid., p. 6.

39. Ibid., p. 1.

40. R. Strassaldo and R. Gubert, *Boundaries and Regions: Explorations in the Growth and Peace Potential of the Peripheries* (Trieste: Edizioni LINT, 1973), p. 46.

41. Ibid., pp. 31–32.

42. R. Strassaldo and G. Delli Zotti (eds.), *Cooperation and Conflict in Border Areas* (Milano, Italy: Franco Angeli Editore, 1982).

43. B. De Marchi and A. M. Boileau (eds.), *Boundaries and Minorities in Western Europe* (Milano, Italy: Franco Angeli Editore, 1982).

44. Niles Hansen, *The Border Economy: Regional Economy in the Southwest* (Austin: University of Texas Press, 1981).

45. Richard Newbold Adams, *Crucifixion by Power* (Austin: University of Texas Press, 1970), p. 8.

46. Ibid., p. 44.

47. D. L. Sheth, "Grass-roots Stirrings and the Future of Politics," *Alternatives IX*, 1, Summer 1983, p. 709.

48. Ibid., p. 11.

49. Ibid., p. 23.

50. Mats Friberg and Bjorn Hettne, "The Greening of the World: Towards a Non-Deterministic Model of Global Processes," University of Gottenburg, Sweden (Xerox), 1982.

51. Ibid., p. 23.

52. Ibid., p. 22.

53. Ibid., p. 36.

54. Ibid., p. 35.

55. Ibid., p. 42.

56. Robert Ross and Kent Trachte, "Global Cities and Global Closure: The Peripheralization of the Labor Force in Core Cities," *Review VI*, 3, Winter 1983, pp. 393–431.

57. Immanuel Wallerstein, "The Rise and Future Demise of the World Capitalist System: Concepts for Comparative Analysis," *Comparative Studies in Society and History* 4, 1974.

58. Arghiri Emmanuel, *Unequal Exchange: A Study of the Imperialism of Trade*, translated by Brian Pearce (New York: Monthly Review, 1972).

59. Quoted in Robert Ross and Kent Trachte, "Global Cities and Global Closure: The Peripheralization of the Labor Force in Core Cities," *Review, VI*, 3, Winter 1983, pp. 393–431.

60. Christopher K. Chase-Dunn, "The System of World Cities," in Michael Timberlake (ed.), *Urbanization in the World Economy* (Orlando: Academic Press, 1985).

61. Ross and Trachte., p. 9.

62. Ibid., p. 10.

63. Ibid., p. 10.

64. Ibid., p. 23.

65. Ibid., p. 31.

66. Ibid., p. 55.

67. Hanna Newcombe, "Peace Action at the Municipal Level" (Dundas, Canada: Peace Research Institute, 1983); also, Sakio Takayanagi, "Peace Policies of Local

Governments: Survey Report on 'Nuclear-Free Municipality Declarations' by Municipalities in San-Tama Area in Tokyo," International Peace Research Association Conference, Gyor, Hungary, 1983.

68. Janice Love, *People's Participation in Foreign Policy Making: Evaluating the U.S. Anti-Apartheid Movement*, Ph.D. Dissertation, The Ohio State University, 1983.

69. Hilary Wainwright and Dave Elliot, *The Lucas Plan: A New Trade Unionism in the Making?* (London: Allison and Busby Limited, 1982).

70. Newcombe (Note 67).

71. Ibid., p. 69.

72. Alois Lugger and Kjell T. Evers (General Rapporteurs), "The Role of the European Conference of Local Authorities in Present-day Europe" (Strasbourg: Council of Europe, ECLA, Tenth Session, CPL (10) 1, September 1974).

73. Sheth (Note 47), p. 23.

74. Ibid., p. 23.

75. Ibid., p. 23.

International Development
in Human Perspective

JOHAN GALTUNG

Johan Galtung demonstrates the relevance of a basic human needs approach to international development. In doing so, he emphasizes the importance of a general theory of human needs that would be flexible enough to respond to the diversity of the peoples of the world. Galtung is a professor of Peace Studies at the University of Hawaii, Honolulu. A distinguished scholar from Norway with a wide range of interests, he was the founder of the Journal of Peace Research *and is the author of numerous works, including* True Worlds: A Transnational Perspective *(New York: Free Press, 1980).*

Galtung makes a powerful argument for a basic human needs approach as an indispensable ingredient to the study and practice of international development. Other approaches fail to make development human—in fact, they often lead to antihuman practices; while a basic human needs approach focuses on the individual and human development. In the same vein as Part 1, Galtung provides a broad discussion of the concept of "basic human needs," describing four classes of material and non-material needs (security, welfare, freedom, identity) and the role of need-satisfiers. He is extremely critical of developmental approaches based on a "hierarchy of needs"—empirically and normatively, for they tend to emphasize the growth of a narrow set of policies oriented toward material needs determined by Westernized elites (whether capitalist or socialist), thus preserving the status quo and failing to promote full human development. Galtung argues for the growth of a general theory of basic human needs that is responsive

Chapter 7 text excerpted by permission of the publisher from "The Basic Needs Approach," in Katrin Lederer, ed., *Human Needs: A Contribution to the Current Debate* (Cambridge, Mass.: Oelgeschlager, Gunn & Hain, 1980), pp. 55-125, with some footnotes deleted.

to individual diversity around the globe. Although he recognizes that there are a number of difficulties with the basic human needs approach to development, it does serve to set priorities; it provides a rich image of the human being, and it indicates a very rich future agenda.

WHY A BASIC NEEDS APPROACH?

From the very beginning let it be stated unambiguously: a basic needs approach (BNA) is not *the* approach to social science in general or development studies in particular, but one approach. There are others. They may focus on structures (particularly of production-consumption patterns of any type of goods and services), on processes (e.g., of how the structures change over time), and on how structure and process are constrained and steered by culture and nature, just to mention some examples. In more classical approaches there is also heavy emphasis on actors, their strategic games in cooperation and conflict and their motivations and capabilities. Nor is it assumed that one can pick any one of these approaches at will; they are probably all (and more could be added) rather indispensable for a rich picture of the human condition. The only thing that is assumed in the following is that a BNA, although not sufficient, is at least necessary; that a basic needs approach—or its equivalent in other terminologies—is an indispensable ingredient of development studies.

To justify this position we shall make use of two arguments, one negative and one positive. The negative argument would be based on the futility of other approaches as the single or dominant approach, because they fail to make development human. . . . In the name of a human theory, considerable antihuman crime can be committed.

Pitted against this stands the single and clear idea that development is development of human beings, because "human beings are the measure of all things." This does not mean that one cannot talk about development of things other than human beings, but that changes in these "things" can only be shown in relation to the development of human beings. If this is not the case, reification will set in—that is, what should be seen as means after some time attain goal character. Instead of difficult, complex, ever-changing, very often dissatisfied, contradictory human beings, infinitely diverse, manifold, and volatile, "development" escapes into production and distribution patterns, institution building and structural transformation, cultural "aspects," and natural balances. . . .

Thus, the negative argument is based on the futility of other approaches, not because they are not feasible, but because they are not valid—either theoretically or practically. Indeed, pragmatically they often lead to antihuman practices because there is no built-in guarantee that such development really aims at improving the condition of human beings. We may be free to have the intuition that democracy is better than dictatorship, that socialism is better than capitalism, and that democratic socialism (not the same as social democracy) may be the best of them all, but how do we know? These terms all refer to social formation, not to human beings. To assume that human beings *develop* inside them is like assuming that inside a beautiful house there must by necessity be beautiful people. We know well enough today that a rich country may have many very poor people, that a democratic country may very often evidence authoritarian relationships, that a socialist country may have very capitalist ways of doing things, and so on. In short, these other approaches are futile not only because they make development studies too easy by dodging the real issues; they may also lead to most dangerous development practices that ultimately serve only the interest of those managing the "things" singled out as the objects undergoing development—the production managers, distribution bureaucrats, revolutionary leaders, institution builders, nature conservers, and culture preservers.

The basic needs approaches constitute one answer to this type of dilemma, and this is where the positive argument starts. The expression "a fully developed human being" may have no precise meaning; and that may be just as well, for if such a being existed, he or she would in all likelihood either be rather arrogant or be lifted by admirers onto a pedestal from which the arrogance of power, as well as the power of arrogance, might be exercised. . . . However, we may still know something about what it is to be underdeveloped as a human being, and one approach here would be to say, "when basic human needs are not satisfied."

Development, then, would be seen as a process progressively satisfying basic human needs, where the word "progressively" would stand for both "more and more need dimensions" and "at higher and higher levels. . . . "

In the pages to follow some of the perplexing and difficult, but also highly interesting and fruitful, problems connected with BNA will be discussed. At this point let it be said only that other approaches for conceiving of human development should be explored.[1] . . . What is needed are very rich, many dimensional and many-faceted, views of human beings, ranging from the most material to the most nonmaterial aspects. As far as we know, the basic needs approaches are the only ones that bring that entire range of aspects under the same conceptual umbrella.[2]

WHAT IS A BASIC HUMAN NEED?

A need should be distinguished from a want, a wish, a desire, a demand. The latter are subjectively felt and articulated: they may express needs, but they also may not; and there may be needs that are not thus expressed. Thus, there is no assumption that people are conscious of their needs. . . . Correspondingly, it is well known that we may want, wish, desire, or demand something that is not really needed in the sense of being necessary. Necessary for what? For the person to be a human person—and this is, of course, where the difficulties start.

Thus, one aspect of "need" is tied to the concept of necessity, which means that we have an image of what is necessary to be human, or at least of what it is to be nonhuman. Moreover, we shall claim that there is something universal to this image. This does not mean that a list of needs can be established, complete with minima and maxima, for everybody at all given social times and social spaces as *the* universal list of basic human needs. The claim is much more modest, namely, that it does make sense to talk about certain classes of needs, such as "security needs," "welfare needs," "identity needs," and "freedom needs," to take the classification that will be used here, and to postulate that in one way or the other human beings everywhere and at all times have tried and will try to come to grips with something of that kind, in very different ways. It may even be fruitful to look for needs in the least common denominator of what human beings are striving for: if one were capable of making lists of what everybody at any time had wanted, as inferred from words and deeds, from conscious and unconscious wishes—and they would be many lists indeed—then there would be a certain overlap. That overlap would be a guide to (basic) needs.

When we say "something universal," this applies to the needs, not to the satisfiers: they may vary even more than the needs. Moreover, there is no assumption that needs can universally be satisfied. There are, as is rather well known, needs that cannot be met because of some empirical scarcity—even needs held by the same person. And there are needs, like a possible "need to dominate," "need to be dominated," "need to be more educated and/or healthy than my neighbor," "positional needs," that cannot be met by everybody for logical reasons. . . .

Let us then proceed to the second term from the end in the expression "basic human needs"—human. Our concern is with human needs, and by that is meant needs that are located, if not necessarily perceived, in individual human beings. The need-subject is an individual, but that does not mean that the satisfier, the "things" necessary in order to meet or satisfy the needs, are in the individual or can be met by the individual alone, without a social context. The problem is that the term "need" is also used for nonsubjects; there is talk about "national needs" (for prestige of a country), "social needs" (e.g., for a good urban sewage disposal system), and "group needs" (e.g., for a place to meet, to be together). The argument here would certainly not be that there are no necessary conditions for these social entities or actors to function, but that the term "need" will   only be used with reference to need-subjects—and the only subjects we know of in human affairs are individual human beings. It is only in them that the "click of correspondence" between need and satisfier can be experienced. That these individual human beings develop their need consciousness in a social context and that most of them have most of their needs satisfied in a social context does not change the circumstance that groups, cities, and countries do not have minds in which needs can be reflected or even articulated. On the contrary, the usual experience is—and this brings in the negative argument from the preceding section—that such "collective needs" usually express wishes and wants, the desires and demands of the ruling elites in these collectivities, more or less poorly disguised.

Then, the term "basic," which serves to further qualify the notion of a need as a necessary condition, as something that has to be satisfied at least to some extent in order for the need-subject to function as a human being. . . . Consequently, when a basic human need is not satisfied, some kind of fundamental disintegration will take place.[3] This is not an *obscurium per obscurius* definition, for we know at least something about fundamental forms of disintegration. At the individual level they show up in the form of mortality and morbidity, the latter divided into the two interrelated categories of somatic and mental diseases. However, even if needs are seen as individual, the disintegration resulting from deficient need satisfaction may not necessarily show up in the individual or be classified as such. It may also show up elsewhere, for instance as *social disintegration.* . . .

Two relatively clear types of social disintegration can now be identified, using the metaphors of freezing and boiling: on the one hand, the society that suffers from lack of participation, from apathy, withdrawal; on the other hand, the society that suffers from overactivity, mutiny, revolt. . . . Just as with individual biological death, social disintegration may not necessarily be bad; it may put an end to something that no longer is viable. But both are signs of disintegration. Whether societies disintegrate because individual human needs are not sufficiently satisfied or the societies are incapable of satisfying them because they are disintegrating is less interesting. The two would probably be part of the same process, and from our point of view social disintegration is an indicator (as opposed to a cause or an effect) of insufficient satisfaction of basic human needs in concrete historical situations.

All that has been said in this section now amounts to one thing:

although we do not want to be rigid in the conception of needs, one should not be totally free in the use of this term either. . . . No doubt all of this raises the important problem of who are to judge what constitutes basic human needs if the person himself or herself is not considered sufficiently capable of judging—and we shall have something to say about that later. In conclusion, as we have defined it here, needs equal basic human needs, for "needs" are (1) "human" and (2) "basic." For other concepts, other terms should be used.

TOWARD A TYPOLOGY OF BASIC HUMAN NEEDS

So far we have touched upon a distinction between material and nonmaterial human needs, preferring "nonmaterial" to the term "immaterial" because of the connotation of "unimportant" also carried by the latter expression. There are at least two ways of trying to clarify this distinction, one relating to the need-subjects, one to the satisfiers.

Thus, there is a tradition, and it is not Western in general nor Cartesian in particular, to distinguish between the bodies and minds of persons and, correspondingly, between somatic and mental (spiritual) needs. One of the difficulties with this, of course, is that mind and body are related. Thus, is the satisfaction that derives from eating food, even unappetizing food and in an environment devoid of good company and esthetic pleasures, really merely somatic? Of course, there are digestive processes that perhaps may be referred to as merely somatic, but there is also a feeling of hunger abatement, of increasing satiation that, if not spiritual, at least is mental. . . . In short, it does not appear that the body-mind distinction serves as a good guide here.

A distinction based on satisfiers is not unproblematic either. It is relatively clear what is held to be material satisfiers: military or police hardware, food, clothes, shelter, medical hardware, schooling hardware, communication-transportation hardware. All these objects are scarce, ultimately due to the finiteness of nature, so that they obey the principle, "if you have more, I have less, and vice versa. . . ."

Then there are clearly nonmaterial satisfiers, and the major example would be social structures or arrangements. But it is not quite so simple as that. To enjoy togetherness, proximity is needed if one's needs are not met by telecommunication; to enjoy loneliness, geographical distance may not be absolutely necessary, but it is helpful, and certainly sufficient (provided one avoids telecommunication). Both can be referred to as "human settlement patterns" and put in the category of "structural arrangements." But whereas the former does not require much geographical territory, the latter does, and geographical territory is scarce, given the finiteness of our globe. . . . There seems always to be material constraints somewhere and hence some opportunity costs.

Then, how would one classify human beings? It may be argued that it is not my wife who is a "satisfier," but her love—both her capacity to love and to be loved—and that has to do with some expression in her eyes, the tone of her voice, the feeling when we look at a full Easter moon together. It is hard to refer to all of this as material, but it certainly does obey the principle that "if I have more of it, somebody else has less." It may be objected that if I have more capacity to love or to be loved, that does not mean that somebody else has to have less of either, and this may be very true and very important; yet I may be less interested in love in general than in love in particular. That there is a scarcity principle involved here, most human beings who live and have lived and much of human literature can testify to. In short, there is some scarcity in the non-material sphere, too. . . .

Like the needs, the satisfiers do not fall from heaven, and they do not exist from eternity to eternity; they are produced in and by a social context and are dependent on that context. Since any social context can be looked at in at least two ways—as a set of actors and as a structure—it may make sense to distinguish between actor-dependent and structure-dependent needs.[4] Thus, an actor-dependent need would be one where the satisfaction depends on the motivation and capacity of some actor to meet or impede the satisfaction; a structure-dependent need would have the level of satisfaction more built into the social structure itself, as an automatic consequence, not dependent on the motivations and capabilities of particular actors. To this could be added a third category—nature-dependent. For social analysis, however, we shall take that one for granted and be more interested in how actors and structures—in other words the social context—impede or meet needs over and above what nature yields. . . .

The following very tentative typology (Table 7.1), giving four classes of needs, is based on the two distinctions made above.[5] It is readily seen that the distinction actor-dependent versus structure-dependent is also highly problematic. Thus in the case of security, the fact that military and police hardware relate to security is one reason for classifying it as a material need.

Table 7.1   A Typology of Basic Human Needs

	Dependent on Actors	Dependent on Structures
Material	Security (violence)	Welfare (misery)
Nonmaterial	Freedom (repression)	Identity (alienation)

No doubt insecurity may also stem from the evil motivations of capable actors. But then security may also be highly structure-dependent, something provided for by a structure that makes the members more able to resist any attack, violently and nonviolently.[6] And insecurity may also stem from structure—for example, from exploitative relations between groups in general and societies in particular. And then both factors may be operating together, as they usually are: the structures produce the "evil" actors, and those actors make use of bad structures.

Nevertheless, the typology may serve as a rule of thumb, as some kind of guide, at least sensitizing us to some problems in connection with satisfiers and need satisfaction. When people starve, for instance, it is usually not traceable to strong actors with a motivation to kill through starvation (except during a siege), but to structures that are distributing the fruits of nature and human production unevenly. The same applies to alienation: it is generally a nonintended rather than an intended effect of the workings of the social context. But repression is different: at least the forms reflected in human rights are highly actor-dependent (although also structure conditioned). . . .

As mentioned, the four types in Table 7.1 stand for classes of needs. One effort to spell them out in a way that may be particularly relevant for rich, industrialized countries is given in Table 7.2. . . . The list (Table 7.2) no doubt has a Western bias—and may be of some use as a check list to discuss problems of Western societies. There is certainly no assumption that the satisfiers to the right really meet the needs—they may do so in a way, up to a certain point. The hypothesis is that they are held to meet the needs. It should also be pointed out that these needs are posited; there is no systematic empirical research behind them. They are included here as an example of a need set to facilitate discussions. . . .

IS THERE A HIERARCHY OF NEEDS?

In most literature about needs there is an explicit or implicit assumption of a general hierarchy of needs. Usually, there is a distinction, putting some of the "physiological" or "animal"—in general very somatic or material—needs at the bottom of the hierarchy and mental or spiritual needs—in our terms identity needs and freedom needs—higher.[7] The thesis may be seen as an axiological thesis (the higher needs are higher in the sense that they are less shared with animals, for instance), as an empirical thesis (the lower needs are pursued, in fact), or as a normative thesis (the lower needs should be satisfied first before attention is given to the higher needs).

Any such thesis is dangerous because it limits the range of possibilities that should be opened by any good theory of needs. As such these theses

Table 7.2   A List of Basic Human Needs as a Working Hypothesis

Needs	Satisfiers Held To Be Relevant in Some Societies
Security Needs (Survival Needs)—To avoid violence:	
• Against individual violence (assault, torture)	Police
• Against collective violence (wars, internal, external)	Military
Welfare Needs (Sufficiency Needs)—To avoid misery:	
• For nutrition, water, air, sleep	Food, water, air
• For movement, excretion	
• For protection against climate, environment	Clothes, shelter
• For protection against diseases	Medical treatment
• For protection against excessive strain	Labor-saving devices
• For self-expression, dialogue, education	Schooling
Identity Needs (Needs for Closeness)—To avoid alienation:	
• For self-expression, creativity, praxis, work	Jobs
• For self-actuation, for realizing potentials	Jobs and leisure
• For well-being, happiness, joy	Recreation, Family
• For being active and subject; not being passive, client, object	Recreation, Family
• For challenge and new experiences	Recreation
• For affection, love, sex; friends, spouse, offspring	Primary groups
• For roots, belongingness, support, esteem; association with similar humans	Secondary groups
• For understanding social forces; for social transparence	Political activity
• For partnership with nature	Natural parks
• For a sense of purpose, of meaning with life; closeness to the transcendental, transpersonal	Religion, ideology
Freedom Needs (Freedom of Choice)—To avoid repression:	
• Choice in receiving and expressing information and opinion	Communication
• Choice of people and places to visit and be visited	Transportation
• Choice in consciousness formation	Meetings, media
• Choice in mobilization	Organizations, parties
• Choice in confrontations	Elections
• Choice of occupation	Labor market
• Choice of place to live	
• Choice of spouse	Marriage market
• Choice of goods and services	(Super-) market
• Choice of way of life	?

constitute threats not only to cultural diversity but also to human diversity within cultures and throughout any individual human being's life cycle. Thus, the idea that nonmaterial needs are "higher" than material needs can be seen as a way of legitimizing the position given to intellectuals in many societies and to ascetics as sacred or holy in some societies, presumably specialists of specializing in nonmaterial. As their lives seem to be built around higher needs, should that not also give rise to a higher position? . . . As theories about needs are more likely to be formulated by intellectuals than by nonintellectuals, the point is worth considering—for example, as reflected in utopias.

This does not apply so much to the hierarchy thesis as an empirical thesis: if it can be ascertained empirically that people in fact do pursue material needs first and then nonmaterial ones, even under conditions where they cannot be said to be forced to do so, then this is an important consideration. However, the basic point would be that as an empirical thesis, this is certainly not a generally valid rule about human behavior. People are willing to suffer both violence and misery—including the sacrifice of their own lives—in struggling for identity and freedom. What is a general rule might be the possibility that the thesis is valid at an extremely low level of material satisfaction—that in utter deprivation (hunger to the point of starving, thirst, exposure to pain inflicted by nature or by human beings, not permitted excretion or basic sanitation, no possibility of moving, suffocation, "starving" for sex) priorities are clear. These are the cases where the ephithet "animal behavior" is often applied—and reference is made to extreme behavior under, for instance, concentration camp situations.

There is no denial that a rock bottom basic physiology of human beings exists that—under what we are used to seeing as extreme situations—would seem to completely control human behavior. But this is not the same as saying:

1. That all human beings first pursue the satisfaction of these needs to a maximum, or at least quite completely, before any attention is given to other needs, under all circumstances;
2. That other needs, "nonmaterial needs," cannot be given immediate attention at least after extreme material deprivation has been overcome or that they are not there all the time, merely overshadowed by the activity to overcome material deprivation; or
3. That all human beings have the same minimum borders, the same limits where deprivation is concerned. It is assumed that some cultures and some individuals can stand physiological deprivation much better than others—that some thresholds are much lower, in other words—whether this is the result of conscious training and practice or not.

It is the normative thesis that is the most dangerous one as seen from diversity. In this thesis a presumed empirical regularity is elevated to the status of a norm with considerable political implications. What it says is, in fact, that concrete policies and strategies, on both the individual and the collective levels, should be ordered in time sequentially so as to give first priority to the satisfaction of material needs, and then the time may come for nonmaterial needs. In other words, the normative thesis may serve as a pretext for deliberate inattention given to nonmaterial needs, claiming that the "time is not yet ripe." Both individually and collectively, this may serve as a basis for indefinite postponement. . . .

In practice this will serve as a carte blanche for the type of policies that might guarantee security and economic welfare, but at the expense of considerable amounts of alienation and repression. . . . And the problem here is not only that nonmaterial needs are put lower down on the priority list. It is also that the structures that have been used in order to satisfy only material needs may later stand in the way of satisfaction of nonmaterial needs. . . .

If need theory is to have any purpose or positive political function in contemporary society, it should be to serve as a basis for revealing such social malconstructions or cases of maldevelopment and to indicate other possibilities. A society that is incapable of giving attention to nonmaterial needs, or a society that is incapable of giving attention to material needs for the masses of the population, may be acceptable or compatible with theories of historical processes that define them as inescapable, necessary stages of development.[8]   In the name of such theories, any kind of crime can be defended, and any kind of alleged privilege can be legitimized as "historical necessity" or as "the only historical possibility at this stage of development."

A theory of needs should serve as a basis for a rich image of human beings and should demand of social constructions that they respect this richness. . . . Hence, the argument is not against having priorities in concrete situations—all of us have—but against any theory of needs that tries to universalize the priorities, freezing them into a general law, thereby decreasing the diversity. Moreover, the theory of needs should also serve as a checklist, as a warning of possible basic problems that may ensue if priorities are organized in such a way that important classes of basic needs are pushed into the background for large sections of the society and for considerable periods of time. . . . Thus, the hierarchy thesis may serve status quo purposes—particularly in a structural sense. On the other hand, it should not be denied that the hierarchy thesis may also serve to give much more attention to the material deprivation so prevalent in the world at large and that it has served to build a certain consensus among people and groups that otherwise might have remained inactive because of disagreement about nonmaterial needs and how to meet them.[9]

The position taken here would be one of avoiding any built-in hierarchization of needs. Individuals and groups will have their priorities and indeed their own conceptions of needs. The purpose of need theory would be to inspire them into awareness, not to steer and direct them into well-structured need sets. . . . A major purpose of development theory and practice would have to be to expand the range of the possible, and this is better served by nonhierarchical than by hierarchical need sets where the priorities are universally given in advance. People should work out their own priorities, and the self-reliant ones will always have the courage to do so in dialogue with others.

NEEDS AND WESTERNIZATION: TEN PROBLEM AREAS

After this preliminary exploration, an effort will now be made to go into more depth. The basic assumption will be that human beings do have needs, that there is such a thing as basic disintegration or pathology that shows up at individual-personal or societal levels, or both, if and when needs are not met. . . . The expression "human beings" is used; thus, the assumption is seen as universal. On the other hand it does not say very much: needs are not specified, nothing is said in precise terms about the breaking points where the pathologies will start developing. Nevertheless, there is a position taken: human beings are not infinitely malleable. We do have goals, some of which take the form of basic human needs of which the individual may be more or less aware. Those basic human needs differ between individuals and groups and vary over time; they are malleable (although not infinitely so), but once they are sufficiently internalized in a human being, that individual is no longer malleable without considerable risk. Inside him or her, more or less consciously, some sort of reckoning takes place; satisfaction-dissatisfaction is the term used for that. Thus the theory of socialization will have to play a fundamental role for any theory of needs unless that concept is reduced to a physiological level held to be socialization-independent (and hence culture-independent). And it raises the problem that people may be socialized into trying to satisfy some needs that will stand in the way of their own satisfaction of some other needs or in the way of others trying to satisfy theirs—these others being present or future generations. Consequently, the theory of conflict is also around the corner of any theory of needs, particularly if one is searching for those patterns of development (meaning meeting basic human needs) that are not at the expense of others.

What we shall now try is to develop some ideas about the relation between this very broad concept of needs on the one hand and something referred to as "Westernization" on the other. Westernization is seen as a process that shapes anything in a Western direction. It is seen as a social code that leaves its imprint on whatever comes its way, transforming it so that the result is compatible with the code. . . . The problem is what happens, or can be expected to happen, to the notion of needs when exposed to Westernization. It is assumed that the code is expressed partly as some general assumptions about how the world in general and human relations in particular are organized and how they evolve—referred to as the social cosmology—and some more specific ideas about social structure. To describe the code, two short lists with five points on each will be used:

The Western social cosmology is characterized by:
1. A Western-centered, universalist conception of space
2. A unilinear, present-centered conception of time
3. An analytic rather than holistic conception of epistemology
4. A man-over-man conception of human relations
5. A man-over-nature conception of relations to nature

The Western social structure is characterized by:
6. A vertical division of labor favoring the center
7. A conditioning of the periphery by the center
8. Marginalization, a division between a social inside and outside
9. Fragmentation, separation of individuals from each other
10. Segmentation, separation inside individuals

Let it only be stated again that this is an effort to separate a general theory of needs from Western "perversions" that tend to slant the concept, including the criticism of the concept, in specific directions that are compatible with the Western code.[10] Thus, the position taken is that much of what has been done, both in theory and in practice, in the field of needs so far bears an unmistakable Western imprint; the following is an effort to help identify that imprint. But the position is not that the concept of need itself is Western—as pointed out above. . . . We shall consider each item on the above list and try to draw some kind of demarcation line between the Western and the general. It is not important that the line is sharp nor that it is generally agreed upon; what matters is the effort and the consciousness of the problem.

A Western-Centered, Universalist Conception of Space

Given the tendency in the West to see itself as a universally valid model to be imitated and in addition to promote and institutionalize processes emanating from Western centers, penetrating all over the world (at least to the level of the elites) implanting the Western code, it is obvious how the West will make use of a basic human needs approach. The first step will be to establish a list of needs so that it can serve as a basis for a universal conception of man. Leaving aside whether such lists are meaningful at all, the lists emanating from the West will have a Western slant, meaning that if people attempt to meet these needs all over the world, fewer changes will be needed or expected in the West than elsewhere. Whether consciously or not, some or many of the needs will be Western needs with universal pretensions, the West thereby being built into other countries as a model. Given the power of the West to institutionalize and implement its conceptions, not the least through intergovernmental (and other international) organizations, this is not an abstract exercise; it becomes political reality. Thus, the West may make use of such lists, with universal pretensions legitimized through UN and UN-related resolutions, to exercise pressure on other countries to conform and become more compatible with models from the West.[11]

The first answer to this point is simple enough: instead of universal lists of needs, stimulate the search for particular lists. The ultimate in particularlity would be one individual, here and now. However, it is generally assumed that there is sufficient overlap between individuals over some intervals in time and some distance in space not to have to disaggregate to that extent. But what, then, is the unit of aggregation sufficiently homogeneous to posit its goals in the form of its list of what for it are basic human needs—or at least to posit some of its goals in such terms? The honest answer would probably have to be that we simply do not know; much empirical research would be needed. But if we assume that there are two roots of human needs, one physiological and one cultural, transmitted through the socialization process, no doubt in interaction with each other, then a fruitful point of departure might be to think in terms of groups that, *grosso modo,* are physiologically in the same situation (as to underconsumption, adequacy, or overconsumption) and groups that belong to the same culture. . . .

A Unilinear, Present-Centered Conception of Time

There are two problems here, and the first one is similar to the problem just treated—some kind of Western time imperialism in addition to the space imperialism discussed in the preceding section. The basic logic is the same: a need list reflecting Western society today is postulated as valid for all times —is seen as timeless, in other words. History is seen as the gradual realization of this list, which is then constructed in such a way that approximation toward the West can also be seen as progress, so that the West as model and the idea of progress are both reflected. . . .[12]

There is however, another problem here, hidden in the term "unilinear." More precisely, it is the non- or even antidialectic view of processes reflected in this term that has some important implications for how needs are conceived of. Thus, looking at the terms used in most lists of needs, one is struck by their onesidedness. One hears much about the need for security, very little about any need for insecurity. There is much about the need for food, but where is any need for hunger? If there is a need for togetherness, where is the need for separateness, even for isolation? Where is the need for hatred if there is a need for love—perhaps even a need to be hated or at least disliked if there is such a thing as a need to be loved or at least liked?

The answer to this should not be seen in terms of adding the opposites to the lists; that would also be too mechanical. Rather, what is missing is a more dialectical approach to needs and need satisfaction. For the hungry there is a need for food, but for the well sated, the satisfied, there may be a need to be hungry again so as to have the need for food and (if it is available) the satisfier of that need and with it the enjoyment of need satisfaction. . . .

Thus, the need for food is seen as a process, with no beginning and no end, of satisfaction and dissatisfaction, undulating through time with sometimes slow, sometimes quick rhythms, with no resting point, full of contradications at any point. The "need for food" should be seen as a shorthand expression for this more complex need. In all needs for something there is also an element of the need for its negation—that is the thesis.

An Analytic Rather Than Holistic Conception of Epistemology

Western epistemology, it is often said, is analytic, following the Cartesian dictum of subdividing a problem into components that can then be attacked one at a time, starting with the simplest. The problem is whether a problem can be subdivided or whether anything for that matter can be subdivided and still remain the same. Elephants cannot be subdivided and remain the same; there is something irreducible, the elephant as *holisis,* that is (considerably) more than the sum of the trunk, legs, tail, and so on. A list of needs looks like a list of components. The question is, What is the whole that has been subdivided to deliver that list, and what, if anything, has been lost in the process? . . .

In a sense it is the human person that has been subdivided into components. Hence, there is a double problem here—the wholeness of human beings and the wholeness of our images of human beings. Both problems are difficult; they can be approached but not solved in what follows, written by an admittedly analytically minded Western researcher, probably the worst possible point of departure for this type of exercise.[13]

First, it should be mentioned that people in general, unless they have been trained through need analysis, do not see their own situation in terms of need lists and need satisfiers. If a verbal expression is asked for, the expression "state of well-being," used in the WHO definition of health, is probably as good as any. . . . The problem is what happens when powerful analysts subdivide a holistic experience of well- and ill-being into components called need dimensions, use them to construct images of human beings as need sets, and then propagate these images to the people they are images of, asking, or even demanding, that they accept these images as their own.

Second, however, the analytic versus holistic image is not a dichotomy of alternatives; it is or can be seen as a both-and rather than an either-or (using both halves of the brain). The problem is not how to suppress analytical thinking in this field, but how to facilitate and promote holistic thinking. (Some of the dangers of analytical thinking will be pointed out under the heading of Segmentation, below).

Third, how is that done? How can the researcher develop images that are not one-sidedly analytical? Probably best by learning from the people, by understanding, through dialogues, how they understand their own situations. . . .

A Man-Over-Man Conception of Human Relations

One way of expressing this part of Western cosmology would be in terms of verticality and individualism. Society is seen as some kind of a jungle where conflicts are resolved through processes defining winners and losers rather than through consensus and solidarity-building processes. If such processes are enacted often enough, the net result is a society of vertically organized, mutually detached individuals; as the process is built into the social code, this type of structure will be not only produced but also reproduced. The problem of how a code of that type would affect the theory of needs may be answered, in general terms, by emphasizing those aspects of needs that would give prominence to the three themes just mentioned: conflict, verticality, and individualism.

Conflict. One would expect Western theories of needs to emphasize the need, or the theories of needs that, when translated into political practice, would generate conflict rather than cooperation. One way of doing this would be by giving priority to material needs, remembering that one perspective on such needs is that the satisfiers are high on material components, that such components by definition have some element of scarcity (at least when pursued ad lib, because of the finiteness of the world), and consequently, that if I have more, somebody else will have less. This may be one factor behind the Western tendency to give priority to material needs: by doing so conflict is guaranteed, conflict that can serve to arrange human beings vertically and individually.

More emphasis on nonmaterial needs would, in general, produce fewer zero-sum games in society. As will be seen immediately below, there are exceptions to this: there may also be nonmaterial scarcity. The important point, however, is not whether the fine line between competitive and noncompetitive needs passes exactly between material and nonmaterial (thus, there are also material needs—e.g., for air—that at least so far can be seen as largely noncompetitive—but decreasingly so with increasing pollution). The point is only that other codes might steer people and societies in less competitive directions by emphasizing other needs more and the competitive ones less—but not, of course, by pretending there are no such things as human needs.

Verticality. There is the point already referred to of promoting images of human beings and their needs so as to foster competition and conflict, ultimately leading to vertical ordering. However, it should be noted that this can also be obtained in other ways. Thus, need dimensions may be used for vertical ordering even when the satisfiers are not competitive. . . .

Behind this is not only the possibility of ranking people, but a cultural norm pressing people to do so. Earlier generations might have talked about competitive instincts.[14] Does this mean that we should talk about a basic human need, at least in the Western context, not only to have and to be, but to have more and to be more? . . .

One possible approach would be to stipulate that what cannot even for logical reasons be met for everybody should not be referred to as a "need"— or at most as a "false" need—for if I shall have or be more than anybody else, others cannot be in the same position; that would constitute a logical contradiction. To rule it out, by definition, however, sounds a little bit like removing sin by outlawing it. The problem still remains that this value persists and certainly not only in the Western code. . . .

However we choose to look at this, neither conflict nor verticality can be said to be built into the need concept as such. But what about individualism?

Individualism. No doubt there is something individualistic in a need concept stipulating that the only need subjects are individual beings. Thus, the position taken is that the need for togetherness is felt inside human beings, nowhere else, and that it is inside human beings that a feeling of well-being—because that need is met—is generated, nowhere else—other positions being seen as obscurantist and lacking empirical referents and as politically very dangerous. The need to belong to a society of which one can be proud is also located in members of that society; a country outdoing others in wars or economic competition is a satisfier of such needs, but both the need and the need satisfaction (into the satisfier!) are individual. This trivial point, however, is not enough to label need theory in general as individualist.

A clearly individualist need theory would go further and demand that the satisfaction not only take place inside the individual, but inside the individual in isolation—in other words, that a social context is not needed. No doubt need theory can be slanted in that direction, and this will be discussed in some detail below (under Fragmentation). But nothing in that direction is built into the concept as such. What is built into it as here presented is an effort to rule out concepts of "social needs" because they seem so often to be felt only by ruling elites and to confuse satisfiers with needs. . . .

A Man-Over-Nature Conception of Relations to Nature

The assumption that only individual human beings are need-subjects draws a line not only against human collectivities of various kinds as legitimate need-subjects; there is another borderline with nature on the other side. Nature—animals, plants, and other forms of nature—is not seen as being a subject possessing needs. No doubt this is in line with the Western tradition of de-souling nature and be-souling man and only man and, as such, an item of Westernness built into the theory, subject to challenge and possible modification.[15]

In the meantime let it be noted that to deprive nature of the status as need-subject does not mean that there is no recognition of necessary conditions for the survival of, say, an eco-system—just as there are necessary conditions for the survival of, say, the capitalist system (only that we would not identify these conditions with satisfiers of human needs, at least not without having more evidence). . . .

A Vertical Division of Labor Favoring the Center

How this vertical division of labor works is obvious: by a group in the center telling the rest of the population what their needs are. Under point 1, the tendency toward a Western view is discussed in geopolitical terms. The point here is how the same structure is also found inside societies. There are those who work out lists of needs and satisfiers, thereby contributing to the programming of others, and there are those who have their needs defined for them. The system is found in capitalist and socialist countries alike: in the former the corporations play more of a role; in the latter, the state bureaucracies (and the party). . . .

As pointed out above, there will for several reasons be a tendency to focus on material needs; in the capitalist countries denying the reality of some of the identity needs, in the socialist countries adding to the denial list many of the freedom needs (they are all for "later").[16] The examples are chosen so as to make very clear how profoundly political the problem of needs and their satisfaction is, which means that the struggle for the right to define one's own needs is a highly political struggle. In a sense the situation is very similar to the situation that has reigned in the field of "development": the idea has been coopted by powerful elites, a combination of bureaucrats, capitalists, and intellectuals at national and international levels. That the idea can be abused by those in power is, of course, what power is about. The needs of human beings do not disappear because the idea of needs can be abused, nor does reality change if one should decide to use some other term. The same applies to "development": it can be used for political, even military, manipulation and for economic exploitation; the problems are still there, particularly if development is seen as a process aiming at meeting human needs.[17]

Consequently, the problem relates not to the concept of needs, however it is defined, but to the power of defining needs, particularly for others. If anything should relate to a need for identity then it must be the need to define one's own situation—including in this, indeed, the definition of one's own needs. Again, which is the unit defining needs—the individual, the group, the country, the region can be discussed, but regardless of what level is chosen, participation in the need definition would have to be the general norm. . . . In such dialogues, bureaucrats, capitalists, and intellectuals, national as well as international, should also participate; they are also people. But in the present structure they count too much. . . .

A Conditioning of the Periphery by the Center

This conditioning is not merely a question of potential and actual culturocide and depersonficiation to be expected when Western need structures (point 1) elaborated by elites (point 6) are beamed in all directions as universal norms to be pursued, but also a question of making people dependent on the satisfiers that will follow in the wake of the propagation of need structures. It is difficult at present to see fully the possibilities of conditioning the periphery by means of basic needs strategies—on another occasion[18] we have listed six:

1. The BN approaches as an effort to sidetrack the new international economic order (NIEO) issue
2. The BN approaches as a new way of legitimizing intervention
3. The BN approaches as an instrument to increase the market
4. The BN approaches as a way of slowing down Third World growth
5. The BN approaches as an effort to decrease technical assistance
6. The BN approaches as a weapon of defense against the poor

Whether such consequences are intended is of less significance; the problem is that a basic-needs-oriented strategy may work this way when operated from the center, including Third World centers.[19]

In a sense this is to be expected. When fed into a certain structure, steered by a certain code, needs will be structured so as to be compatible. It is only possible to do this, however, with a very truncated need set, singling out from more complete sets the needs that fit, including others (such as the need for self-actuation, for self-expression, for being active and a subject, for challenge, for creativity, etc.). . . . As it is now, satisfiers tend to define the needs rather than vice versa. Needless to say, this leads to an overemphasis on material needs.[20]

Marginalization, a Division Between a Social Inside and Outside

What could be better for reproduction of the marginalization of the masses of our societies than a hierarchy of needs, having at the bottom people whose major concern it should be to have material needs (physiological and safety needs in Maslow's parlance) well taken care of before they can or ought to (the ease with which one slides from descriptive to normative statements here is part of the mechanism) proceed to nonmaterial needs? The isomorphism between needs hierarchies and social hierarchies will reinforce either of them, giving a sense of confirmation to either. Elites will be the first in propagating the idea of "material needs first" under the guise of humanitariansim, thereby preserving the marginalization for generations still to come, giving the magnitude of the job of "meeting the basic needs of those most in need" when it shall be done the way these elites suggest—managerially. To meet those needs may even be a low price to pay to retain a monopoly on social management—as is done in the social democratic welfare state.

This becomes even more significant given what is probably a reasonable map of the real situation where need satisfaction is concerned (see Table 7.3). The elites in countries, poor and rich, in the world today certainly have basic material needs satisfied and in addition a lot of material satisfiers (often called "gadgets") beyond that. The masses have less of the latter; this is, in fact, how some of the borderlines between elites and masses are drawn. As to nonmaterial needs the conjecture is simply that in a modern, corporate society based on the typical bureaucrat-capitalist-intellectual top management (with somewhat more power to bureaucrats in the state capitalist and to the capitalist in the private capitalist countries), satisfaction of a broad range of nonmaterial needs is impossible and the consequence of this is probably found, among other places in the rates of mental disorder. For the masses in the poor countries, this is all different: the material

Table 7.3 The Level of Need Satisfaction: A Conjecture

		Material Needs		Nonmaterial Needs
		Basic	Nonbasic	Basic and Nonbasic
Elites		Yes	Yes	No
Masses	Rich countries	Yes	Yes/No	No
	Poor countries	No	No	No/Yes

situation is deplorable in most regards; the nonmaterial not necessarily so. If one of the keys to identity is closeness, this is where it may still be found; as many authors, often naively startled by this obvious circumstance, report: "in the slums I found the solidarity, the generosity, the warmth so often missing where I come from. . . ."

No doubt a theory of needs draws a line between those whose basic human needs are not satisfied and those whose are, given the specificities of the society. So does, incidentally, the whole tradition of caring for the ill: there is marginalization involved with the institutionalization of the ill, (temporary) nonmembership in society, separation from healthy people in family and work, and so on. A good theory of needs, however, should serve as a corrective by constantly reminding us that even if a person is deficient relative to one need dimension, need satisfaction cannot possibly consist in a trade-off that sacrifices other need dimensions in order to make up for the deficit. . . . If a theory of needs is to be of any value at all it would be to serve as a reminder of the needs of the total human being in such a situation. . . .

Our present society makes deficits in material needs visible: poverty can be seen; so can illness. Deficits in nonmaterial needs are less visible: alienation, lack of ability to love and be loved, are more easily tolerated than is poverty, both in the need-subjects and in others. Why? Because of the material bias of our societies, implying that material problems are the problems held to be resolvable within these societies, other problems are either defined away or given up—and that consensus for action is built around material "facts," not nonmaterial "values." But in a different culture, with greater emphasis on non-material dimensions, this may all turn out very differently. . . .

Thus, the Maslow hierarchy can be seen as a very precise sophisticated translation of Western culture into a theory of needs. But did we not argue against that? Yes, and on two levels: First, it is often offered with the pretension of being a universal hierarchy, of being something beyond merely a reflection of Western cultural biases. Second, it reinforces Western type social stratification, even class formation, further. Thus, the critique of that kind of hierarchy is found partly in the contradiction between the West and important parts of the non-West, partly in contradictions inside the West. Our personal bias would be that a society is best served with a theory and politics of needs satisfaction that place the material and the non-material on a more equal footing, as argued several times above. In that case a hierarchy drawing lines between the material and the non-material would be impossible; no marginalization could be built on that basis. But this is the type of struggle that has to be fought inside each culture and society.

Fragmentation, Separation of Individuals from Each Other

If the only need-subjects there are are the individuals, why should not this individualization be carried further? The problem has been mentioned above (point 4): "that the satisfaction not only takes place inside the individual, but inside the individual in isolation; in other words that a social context is not needed. No doubt need theory can be slanted in that direction. . . ." Actually, "that direction" splits into two, both of them meaningful within a Western tradition of individualism and fragmentation, but very different in their consequences: that the need-subject alone provides for the need-objects, the satisfiers; and that need satisfaction takes place in social isolation. The hypothesis would be that the Western tradition would pick up both possibilities and slant a theory of needs in these directions. . . .

The basic point is that there is and should be nothing in needs theory as such that would make this type of social formation a logical consequence of needs theory. On the contrary, under the need class of "identity" it would be strange if most need lists would not one way or the other include some reference to "togetherness." A society that systematically counteracts this need will be punished sooner or later, regardless of efforts that it might make to make a virtue of its vices by proclaiming that this is a "natural" tendency.

Segmentation, Separation Inside Individuals

We have discussed above—under marginalization—how hierarchies of needs may serve to reinforce social hierarchies, and—under fragmentation—how the individualization of the need-subject may spread to the production of need-objects or at least to their consumption. Here an effort will be made to discuss how lists of needs may serve to reinforce tendencies toward segmentation, or rather, toward a segmented mode of need satisfaction, as opposed to an integrated mode of need satisfaction. One way of exploring this may be as follows.

So far we have looked at why need-objects/satisfiers are consumed/ enjoyed (to meet needs), but not at how. . . . As time progresses—for example, from morning to afternoon to evening to night—a person's action line passes through new points in space and social space—perhaps with family in the morning, workmates in that afternoon, friends in the evening, and back to the family at night. This is the segmented mode; in the integrated mode time also progresses, but all these activities are carried out with the same people, more or less at the same place. . . . The continuity in space and people provides for a carryover, a social continuity from one activity to the next. The segmented mode is often referred to as "compartmentalized" because transition from one activity to the next implies a change of place and social partners—a new "compartment" in space. . . .

One may now be for and against either pattern. The segmented mode is disruptive, but it also provides for new experience; the integrated mode provides stability, but there may be too much of that. This is not the point, however. The point is that needs theory may be used to reinforce the segmented mode, by assigning to each point in the space . . . one type of need satisfaction, one need dimension, or at least one need class. . . . Without that separation, the place and the people, all the things around that do not change, will provide continuity from one satisfier to the other and from one need to the other. Thus, the integration on the satisfier and the social context side may constitute one approach to the problem of lack of holism in the basic needs approaches.

Concluding this survey of possible perversion of a general theory of needs, presenting what in reality is adaptation to Western social cosmology and social structure as if it were universal theory, let us now summarize: "Westernization" is like a machinery; something emerges that is recognizable, but twisted in particular directions. Thus, our assumption is that Western theories of needs will tend to claim universal validity; that the approach to time will be noncontradictory and mechanistic; that the epistemology of needs will be analytical, nonholistic, that needs whose satisfaction generates conflicts of scarcity will be overemphasized; that nature will be seen as without needs; that there will be a strong division of labor between those who define the needs and those for whom needs are defined and that the former will plan the lives of the latter; that the center will propagate not only need images but also satisfiers and thereby create or awaken needs; that needs will be ordered into hierarchies, thereby reinforcing current stratification into higher and lower classes, engaging in satisfaction of higher and lower needs; that need satisfaction will be individualized; and that need satisfaction will be increasingly segmented, one need at a time and context. If this were needs theory, the present author would be against it; a theoretical tree should be known by its theoretical and empirical fruits.[21]

But it is not. It is not even Western needs theory, although there are strong inclinations in these directions. . . . In this case the distinction made is between a general needs theory and a specification adapted to Western conditions along the ten lines indicated above. From this one should not draw the conclusion that the general theory is good and the Western specification bad. What is wanted are many more specifications, none of them pretending to be the universal truth. What is needed is a general theory broad enough to help us generate such specifications—in short, let one hundred specifications of need theory grow.

BASIC NEEDS APPROACHES: SOME STRENGTHS AND WEAKNESSES

Basic needs approaches are certainly not new. Just to mention two traditions, the Western-Christian and Indian-Hindu. "Give us today our daily bread" is an invocation for minimum satisfaction of basic material needs (it certainly does not stand for bread alone); John Ruskin's *Unto This Last* is filled with this idea (but the source of satisfaction is now more secularized); Marx' entire theory is actually based on thinking about needs; and in the history of the United Nations, Lord Boyd Orr's famous Quebec speech when FAO was founded in 1954 is certainly along the same line.[22] Gandhi, deeply inspired by Christianity and John Ruskin on top of his Hindu roots always had those most in need as top priority, in theory and in practice. . . .[23] The twin ideas, which focus on what is fundamental and on those who lack precisely this, run through history, but not as a mainstream: had it been a mainstream, then there might still have been inequality, even exploitation, but not so much abject misery. And that leads us straight to the major strength of and the major weakness of BNA.

The major strength is that BNA serve to set priorities. It is an effort to cut through rhetoric, focusing on what is essential and basic, and to provide individuals and societies with a measuring rod that lowers the focus of social attention downwards, "unto this last," saying this: "tell me how much material and spiritual misery there is at the bottom of society and I will tell you what kind of society you have." . . . Human suffering, deprivation shall count more and serve to set our priorities straight.[24]

The major weakness is that BNA say nothing about how misery is produced; they do not comprise a social theory. Thus they say nothing about inequity, for these are relations, even abstract ones, and it would be hard to assume that there is a need not to be exploited or not to live in a society with too much inequality. Equity and equality are social values, and so is social justice. As such they may be so deeply internalized that they attain need character, but one would assume such cases to be exceptional. What is felt inside a person would be concrete deprivation, leading to concrete tension, even suffering; and that is what needs theory is about, not about social analysis. Thus, by raising the floor above a certain minimum agreed to by people themselves so that misery is abolished, basic needs will be satisfied,[25] even when inequity and inequality are constant or even increasing. Thus, there is no automatic extension of BNA to cover all good social values; that would be to stretch the needs concept too far. And in this a major danger exists: it is quite possible, even when material and nonmaterial needs are put on a more equal footing, to combine BNA with many kinds of exploitative processes, channeling most resources toward the rich as long as the poor are above the minimum. One may impose a social maximum, a ceiling, but between ceiling and floor there may still be inequality and inequity; there may be need satisfaction at the expense of somebody else's need satisfaction. Needs theory does not automatically guard against that, except in the (postulated) need to be a subject.

The answer to this should not be to pretend that BNA can offer what is not within their paradigm, but to call for additional perspectives, theories, paradigms, approaches. Most important would be theories about how misery is produced and reproduced, and such theories exist—they are indispensable to get at the roots of the phenomena. . . . Further, a theory of conflict is an indispensable additional perspective: satisfiers are often scarce; there may be trade-offs and choices to be made.

A second strong point in BNA is the rich image they can give of the human being when they are not too narrowly interpreted. A list of needs like the one given in Table 7.2 can so easily be subdivided among the social sciences; and it is rather obvious what the psychologist, the social psychologist, the sociologist, politologist, and economist would focus on, deriving their *homo psychologicus* and so on till we reach *homo economicus*. BNA transcend such efforts at compartmentalization, aiming at rich biosocial, physiological-cultural images.

But another major weakness is that the empirical procedures for developing these rich images are far from clear. Survey research may get at values, depth interviews may probe more deeply into motivations. But for needs it is more complicated: what the subject says, in spite of being a subject, is not necessarily to be taken at its face value. To use the two distinctions made use of in this chapter, conscious versus unconscious (also called manifest versus latent) and true versus false needs: the subject is not necessarily conscious of her or his needs, and what is held to be needs may turn out to be false needs—they may not be that important.

The answer to this would be that empirical methods do exist, but they certainly have to go beyond simply asking the person what her or his needs are. The dialogue should be a much more promising approach, around the theme, What is so important that we cannot do without it. . . . A process of mutual probing into depth may reveal to what extent nonsatisfaction of the

Table 7.4 Empirical Approaches to Explore Needs

	Is it Possible to Do Without?	How Much Sacrifice to Have it Satisfied?
Verbal Approaches (through dialogue)	(A)	(B)
Nonverbal Approaches (observation of behavior)	(C)	(D)

need can really be held to be that crucial, and how much effort or sacrifice one would be willing to make for that need. This would still be verbal, only intense, so that it may explore the deeper recesses of the mind.

The second major approach would be through practice, again with the same subdivision. Empirical situations of deprivation might occur where satisfiers usually present disappear wholly or partly: does disintegration take place or not? And in the concrete situation, what do people in fact sacrifice in order to meet a certain need? More particularly, are they willing to sacrifice along other need dimensions, for if they do, that serves as an indication of relative priority. Thus, people are known to be willing to give up their lives for freedom and/or identity, so physical survival is not unconditionally the most basic need. But they are also willing to give up freedom and/or identity in order to obtain security and/or welfare— indicating the futility in trying to establish any universal linear hierarchy. From considerations such as these one arrives at a flatter need landscape in general. For particular situations and groups clear peaks may be visible; we do not deny hierarchies in concrete situations.

Thus we have essentially four empirical approaches, as shown in Table 7.4. This table can now be seen as an exercise in methodology, and one may discuss which method is more valid and which method is more reliable. The conclusion is probably that the nonverbal methods are more valid but less reliable, among other reasons because replication is less feasible; and the verbal method is more reliable, but also less valid. The verbal approach is certainly the easier to use.[26]

But the four approaches can also be seen as a form of social practice. Through dialogue people help each other, raising the general awareness and consciousness of their own true needs—manifest-conscious or latent-unconscious—meaning by that what they really cannot do without. . . .

A third point in BNA is that they indicate a future agenda for development and a very rich and open one. BNA do more than set a list of priorities, of things that must be done. Correctly understood they go beyond discussion of minimum level of satisfaction in at least three ways. First, they open for the whole exploration of true versus false needs, thereby potentially being a tool for enriching human existence. A condition for this, however, is not only to strip one's need set of false needs, but also to enrich it with latent, but true needs. This is where there is so much to learn from others—a reason why the union approach to universalism in the field of needs is so important. Second, they open for the whole exploration of true versus false satisfiers, questioning all the relationship in Table 7.2 with pretend satisfiers, precisely by being a theoretical construct, something nonobservable that can serve to define a class of satisfiers from which the best—the most adequate in terms of a range of needs and resources available—may be picked. Third, they open for the whole exploration of richer relations between needs and satisfiers, particularly how new satisfier contexts can be imagined relating to whole need complexes. . . . The point is to reason from the needs, combining them mentally, asking for rich satisfier contexts that may speak to new, more integrated combinations and not to be steered by existing satisfiers simply because they are there.

The major weakness corresponding to this strength remains: there is a difference between tension relief and human development; and the image is not holistic enough. The preliminary answer would be that needs theory never assumes that needs remain at the same level, a sort of basement level in a building where values constitute the upper floors. Needs can be developed precisely because they are biosocial in character. We have tried to point to the process: through internalization of values, to want so much to do what is good and right that it becomes a need to do so. But this will never exhaust any image of human beings because of our capacity of transcending whatever image somebody has constructed, in good directions, in bad, in both.

In conclusion, basic needs approaches are indispensable in any theory of development that sees development as development of human beings—in other theories BNA become unnecessary, even disturbing.[27] In one way or the other, BNA will be present, even under other names. Thus, instead of letting the needs creep up that building from the basement, one may let the values creep down, into the basement, insisting that it is all culturally conditioned. But one does not escape from the idea of a *conditio sine qua non*. No development theory worth its name can do without an anthropology of human heings, and however vast the variations, the concept of necessary conditions remains. That the approaches are beset with problems is obvious—and constitutes important challenges for future research. But the major problems are those people, adherents or critics, who see them as the only approaches and either pretend that BNA have answers when not even the question can be formulated within a BNA paradigm or attack it for the answers that BNA cannot and should not give.

So what we need are a rich range of perspectives, among which BNA are one, and a rich theory of basic needs, all of which will be very complex. And yet it will never be as complex as human life and social reality themselves, in their infinite variety. And that may turn into a virtue what to many seems like a vice built into basic needs approaches: they are not only complex, but also chaotic. But why not? Maybe they should be chaotic, to guard against the type of clarity that will only too easily serve as a basis for bureaucratic/corporate/intellectual manipulation! There is much wisdom in the tale related by Mushakoji[28] in defense of the alternative of chaos: King Chaos died when the Kings of the Northern and of the Southern Seas "structured" him by giving him eyes and ears, a mouth. For that reason we referred to the subject of this paper as "approach," not as "model" and not as "strategy"—knowing well that there are strong forces trying to pull basic needs in that direction. Some clarification is needed, but not too much; whether the present effort is adequate is for others to decide.

NOTES

1. Thus, there is something negative about the needs approach, very well expressed by Dorothy Lee, "Are Basic Needs Ultimate?" in *Freedom and Culture*, D. Lee, ed. (Englewood Cliffs, N.J.: Spectrum, 1959):

> The premise that man acts so as to satisfy needs presupposes a negative conception of the good as amelioration or correction of an undesirable state. According to this view, man acts to relieve tension; good is the removal of evil and welfare and the correction of ills; satisfaction is the meeting of a need; good functioning comes from adjustment; survival from adaptation; peace is the resolution of conflict; fear, of the supernatural or of adverse public opinion, is the incentive to good conduct; the happy individual is the well-adjusted individual. (p. 72).

No doubt, there is in the need concept the idea of tension relief. But these tensions are real, whatever the mix of the physiological-cultural basis. When Lee argues that "it is value, not a series of needs, which is at the basis of human behavior" (ibid.), she is obliterating the important distinction between values in general and values so basic that the tension resulting from nonfulfillment becomes destructive. Needs are in this latter category, and it is not a fixed category. We can turn values into needs; the question is, Which values should become needs?

2. Thus, world philosophies tend to be relatively silent on material needs, with the important exception of some of the basic Western philosophies in antiquity, important for the general materialistic bias of Western thought (but they may also have been misinterpreted, and at any rate, the Middle Ages were less materially bent). What is generally associated with Oriental thought (for a good survey see J. K. Fiebleman, *Understanding Oriental Philosophy* [New York: Horizon Press, 1976]) has a very nonmaterial bias.

3. Andrzej Sicinski "The Concepts of 'Need' and 'Value' in the Light of the Systems Approach," *Social Sciences Information* (1978): pp. 73f. speaks of a logical hierarchy of needs, namely:

(1) Needs whose non-satisfaction results in the annihilation system (these could be termed as in traditional terminology *fundamental needs*)

(2) Needs whose non-satisfaction results in the system's *inability* to perform *some of its functions*

(3) Needs whose non-satisfaction results in disturbances in the system's performance of *some of its functions*

(4) Needs resulting in disturbances in the *development* of the system (this applies to self-organizing systems in particular) [Emphasis in original]

4. For more on this distinction, see Johan Galtung, *The True Worlds: A Transnational Perspective* (New York: The Free Press, 1979), ch.2.

5. I am indebted to my colleagues in the World Order Models Project for stimulating discussions on this subject, especially during the meeting in New Brunswick, August 1976.

6. Thus, both Gandhi and guerilla type resistance are based on very decentralized, numerous, and autonomous units—so that the society cannot be hit at any central point and dominated from that point.

7. The best known author, most worthy of being discussed, is, of course, Abraham H. Maslow. His famous hierarchy was put forward in "A Theory of Human Motivation," *Psychological Review* L (1943):370–96; also see his books, *New Knowledge in Human Values* (New York: Harper and Row, 1959); *Toward a Psychology of Being* (Princeton: Van Nostrand, Reinhold, 1962); *Motivation and Personality*, rev. ed. (New York: Harper and Row, 1970); *The Farther Reaches of Human Nature* (New York: Viking Press, 1979). His hierarchy (from 1943) has five levels: at the bottom are physiological needs (hunger, thirst, oxygen, recovery from fatigue) and safety needs (freedom from pain, protection of physiological goals); in the middle, belongingness and love needs (friendship, love, and tender affection); at the top are esteem needs (prestige, achievement, status, and dominance) and need for self-actualization (expression of capacities and talents). We have grouped them in these three levels because that seems to correspond not too badly with what one may associate with lower, middle, and upper classes in our vertical societies, with the middle classes taking physiological and safety needs for granted but not able to actuate the highest group of needs; and with the upper classes deeply engaged in exactly that, while taking the others for granted—and maybe discovering that in the struggle for esteem and self-actualization, belongingess and love needs somehow get neglected. Any vertical ordering of needs is likely to be reflected in social stratification one way or the other, and a theory of needs hierarchy may therefore easily become a justification of social hierarchy.

8. Neither liberalism nor Marxism can be said to be strong on emphasizing the possibility of nonmaterial growth before or together with material growth.

9. Thus, a consensus in the UN around material needs would probably break down very quickly if the intricate "philosophical" problems pertaining to identity and freedom should be entered into, with the First World accusing the Second World of repression and the Second World accusing the First World of alienation (and the First World retorting with a *tu quoque*)—with the Third World obtaining nothing for lack of consensus. The spiritual poverty of liberalism and Marxism (compared, for instance to Oriental thought) may have been necessary for this consensus to be worked out—for good or for bad.

10. In so doing it is also a response to the critique of the needs concept by my colleague Gilbert Rist. . . . At least in earlier versions I perceived his critique as being directed not against needs theory but against the Western perversions of needs theory—or against some of them. For a more effective critique of that kind of needs theory, a map of Western social cosmology and social structure is needed to generate hypotheses about what kind of biases would be likely.

11. One might even say that this is the function of the UN system from a Western angle: what is profoundly Western may look more universal clothed in a UN resolution, at least until one starts asking questions about the degree of Westernization in the UN.

12. World history is seen then as some kind of rolling agenda, first welfare, then . . . , and so on—always assuming that the West is tackling the more advanced points on the agenda.

13. Hence, a major topic of research in this field is precisely how to develop more holistic images. In what language can it be expressed without becoming some type of bla-bla?

14. A difference between instinct theory and needs theory, and an important one at that, would be that whereas needs vary greatly and are not only biophysiologically, but also socioculturally determined, instincts would be seen as biophysiological, species-typical, and hence, universal. Thus, the transition from one theory to the other also permits much more flexibility and variation in general.

15. The efforts to try to draw a line between humans and animals are countless. My own favorite formula is something like this: "Both animals and humans are programmed, but it is given to humans to some extent to reflect on this program and to change it, again to some extent. It is this self-transcending character that renders distinctness to man." According to a view of this kind, animals do not have needs; they have instincts, because needs can be the objects of reflection. This certainly does not mean that there are not necessary conditions that have to be fulfilled for any form of life to continue and unfold.

16. "When time is ripe"—the "principle of unripe time" that may serve to legitimize almost any repression.

17. But not at meeting in any way possible; in a human way (as emphasized by Anders Wirak, "Human Needs as a Basis for Indicator Formation," *Papers*, CCPR [Oslo: University of Oslo]). One way of formulating this might be as follows: development is not only to satisfy the needs of the need-subjects, but to do so in such a way that the need-subjects can control the need-objects, decide over them. This is also one way of defining self-reliance, like the Chinese *tzu li keng sheng* (regeneration through own efforts). For a very interesting example, see *The Basic Human Needs and Their Satisfaction,* Sarvodaya Development Education Institute, Moratuwa, Sri Lanka, with a preface by the president of the Sri Lanka Sarvodaya Shramadana Movement, A. T. Ariyaratne. The needs are classified in ten classes: environment, water, clothing, food, housing, health care, communication, fuel, education, and spiritual-cultural needs. Thus the focus is on material needs, and the 167 satisfiers listed—based on dialogues with Sarvodaya villagers—are mainly material (no. 33: to have a raised raft built to keep pots and pans). But they are all within the reach of the villagers themselves, with modest means, and hence a basis on which autonomous development can start. Surely it will not necessarily stop at that level, either materially or nonmaterially. Needs are dynamic!

18. See Johan Galtung, "The New International Economic Order and the Basic Need Approaches" (paper presented at the Society for International Development North-South Round Table, Rome, May 18-20, 1978).

19. For a good analysis from one Third World point of view, see Firouz Vakil, "Basic Human Needs and the Growth Process: The Dimension of Conflict" (paper prepared for Aspen-Gajareh Workshop, Iran, June, 1977).

20. This is where the obvious linkage with market and sales promotion under capitalist economic structures enters: satisfiers can be promoted (a whole structure exists for that purpose), but they can only be sold and consumed if some kind of need

is created for them. That need has to be implanted in people (see Goulet). In some cases this may bring to the surface latent but true needs; in other cases artificial, false needs are created. The experience of children with toys is interesting here. There is a need for something that toys can satisfy—but what kind of toys? Children are fascinated by glittering, expensive-looking toys, get them, and get tired of them after one day—because they are too well made, too programmed, not sufficiently full of unexplored possibilities. The moment they are discarded, the child may turn to a heap of pebbles, some old brick, or the like. But the market does not press these upon her or him, which may mean that the child still has the capacity to be honest, to be faithful to true needs, rather than to give in to the forces of the market. Socialization into adult consumer behavior, then, is socialization into dishonesty toward oneself—in part.

21. Thus, there is agreement, by and large, with the points made by Gilbert Rist . . . , if they are seen as directed against a special interpretation of BNA, not BNA in general.

22. "The hungry people of the world wanted bread and they were given statistics—No research was needed to find out that half the people in the world lacked sufficient food for health." The words of Article 25 (1) of the Universal Declaration of Human Rights, of December 10, 1948, are very clearly basic needs oriented:

Everyone has the right to a standard of living adequate for the health and well-being of himself and of his family, including food, clothing, housing and medical care and necessary social services, and the right to security in the event of unemployment, sickness, disability, widowhood, old age or other lacks of livelihood in circumstance beyond his control.

And then there is the important report on "International Definition and Measurement of Standards and Levels of Living" (United Nations, 1954), listing categories of material needs and adding at the end "human freedoms." Thus, the idea has been with the UN from the very beginning, but in different terminology. The debate within the UN about the proper position of basic needs in development strategy, not to mention the selection of development strategies to meet basic needs, is terribly important and the steps forward should be appreciated, not belittled. At the same time, many watchful eyes are needed—there are strong forces at work.

23. The whole idea of "constructive work" and "positive action," so essential as part of a dialectic where "noncooperation" and "civil disobedience" constituted the other part, was aiming exactly at basic needs for the most needy.

24. That means lower priorities to elite nonbasic needs—hence not so strange if they are skeptical or outright against BNA. But a view of basic needs as leading to a zero-sum game between elites and masses overlooks the possibility of generating new satisfiers through self-reliance. Thus, it is hard to believe that the sarvodaya villages in Sri Lanka, based on much volunteerism and hard work, are competitive with elite interests. To many this would be an argument against them.

25. The history of the last generation or two of the rich developed countries under controlled, welfare state capitalism is about this. Is it possible for the whole world? My own view is yes. What capitalism presupposes is not misery or poverty at the bottom, but inequality, internationally, intranationally, to reward the entrepreneurs, to have vast differentials to play upon for motivation, and above all to be able to find new markets for old products when they have to cater to old markets

with new products

26. Thus, there is the usual trade-off known from the general methodology of data collection in the social sciences: what one gains in validity one usually loses in reliability and vice versa

27. And that is, of course, a major reason why it is rejected by those who have a vested academic, intellectual, political interest in some other theory; it becomes disturbing when development as defined by these theories may turn out to be not only ahuman, but antihuman.

28. Kinhide Mushakoji, "Scientific Revolution and Inter-Paradigmatic Dialogues" (paper prepared for the GPID project meeting, Geneva, October 2–8, 1978).

CHAPTER EIGHT

Human Needs and the Evolution of U.S. Foreign Policy

JEREL A. ROSATI

In this chapter Jerel Rosati develops a theory of foreign policy based on assumptions of the individual pursuit of human needs, then applies it to explain continuity and change in U.S. foreign policy since World War II. Arguing for the necessity to go beyond the traditional focus by students of U.S. foreign policy on intra-governmental relations, he develops a theory of the state and foreign policy change. The theoretical model posits that governmental foreign policy evolves dialectically as a state goes through different phases or periods over time: from a period of stability in which continuity in foreign policy is the norm to a period of transition in which change in foreign policy is most probable. The key to understanding the dynamics of foreign policy over time is the interaction of the state, society and the environment as they impinge on the satisfaction of individual human needs. The model is used to explain the existence of both continuities and changes in U.S. foreign policy since World War II.

Students of foreign policy, and U.S. foreign policy in particular, tend to focus on the role of the government. In U.S. foreign policy, the tendency has been to concentrate on the executive branch as the primary source of foreign policy. Moreover, most studies and analyses have revolved around the president—his personality traits, beliefs about U.S. society and the world, management ability, and leadership skills. Since the president does not operate in isolation, but is part of a larger governmental environment, it has also been common to integrate the role of executive branch policymakers and bureaucracies. Bureaucratic players and organizations, such as the National Security Council, the Department of State, the Department of Defense, and the intelligence community, among others, typically receive extensive analysis. With the Vietnam War and the resurgence of Congress, the legislature has often been incorporated as part of the overall study of U.S. foreign policy. Sometimes, non-governmental societal factors, such as the public, interest groups, and the media, have received attention, but this has usually been of peripheral concern. In short, a study of governmental actors essentially comprises the study of U.S. foreign policy.

This orthodox or mainstream approach to the study of U.S. foreign policy is too narrow. It is founded on the unrealistic assumption that the government tends to operate in relative isolation from the society and the world. It assumes that governmental elites are always the key players in the making of U.S. foreign policy. As a result, this orthodoxy yields a static view of time, focusing on the immediate role of governmental leaders and organizations. Yet it is unable to explain how political leaders acquired, as well as lost, their policy positions over time, how their beliefs developed, and how governmental institutions have evolved.

This almost-exclusive concentration on the role of the government in the making of U.S. foreign policy acquired scholarly legitimacy during the height of the cold war—a time of perceived national emergency, when "high" national security policy was dominant, and there was a tremendous increase in presidential power. In a sense it was natural to focus on the president and the executive branch during the fifties and the sixties because it was a time of consensus within U.S. foreign policy and a time of great wealth in U.S. resources and power—a time, many argue, of U.S. hegemony within the global environment. Yet, one cannot really understand U.S. foreign policy during the cold war years unless one places the president and the bureaucracy in a societal and global context.

As a result of the debacle in Vietnam, foreign policy scholars and analysts have begun to realize that the government is not the only, and possibly not even the primary source of U.S. foreign policy. Although there has been greater recognition of non-governmental sources of foreign policy, the legacies of the cold war years continue to hold sway over the contemporary study of U.S. foreign policy. The orthodox approach has broadened in scope, allowing for more diversity of inquiry, but the prevalent orientation continues to be the role of governmental players and organizations as the immediate, direct sources of foreign policy. This chapter attempts to open up the study of U.S. foreign policy even further.

In order to understand the complexity and the dynamics of U.S. foreign policy, one needs to take a broad and comprehensive view of the workings of the U.S. state and society within the global arena based on assumptions of the individual pursuit of human needs. Studies limited to the study of the government are necessary, but insufficient, both during the cold war years and the subsequent post-Vietnam years. This chapter develops a broader, more holistic and dynamic explanation of U.S. foreign policy. This is done by describing a general model of how foreign policy evolves due to the interplay of the state, society, and the environment. The model is then applied to the United States in order to explain continuity and change in its foreign policy since World War II.

A THEORY OF FOREIGN POLICY

The theoretical model developed in this chapter attempts to explain the major trends in the policies emanating from the state over time. Specifically, I am interested in explaining the dominant patterns in the evolution of U.S. governmental foreign policy at the macro-level[1]. The model posits that governmental foreign policy evolves dialectically as a state goes through different phases or periods over time: from a period of stability in which continuity in policy is the norm to a period of transition in which change in foreign policy is most probable. The interaction of three forces—the state, society, and the environment—are critical for understanding the dynamics of the policies of states over time. A brief overview of the theory of the state and foreign policy change is provided.

The existence of the state, and of the broader society in which it is embedded, is rooted ultimately upon individuals pursuing their needs. Individuals join groups in an effort to fulfill their needs, which coalesce with other groups that share similar values and beliefs, thus forming *social networks*. These different networks, representing different interests and beliefs, compete for control of governmental and societal institutions and for the allegiance of the mass population. Some social networks are more successful than others in penetrating and dominating the institutions of the state and society; the less successful networks end up as the principal challengers or exist on the fringes of society. Governmental foreign policy tends to reflect the beliefs of policymakers who come from those networks which most successfully dominate state and societal institutions. Thus, the interaction between the state and society is symbiotic—the state is a part of and interacts with society.

The foreign policies that emanate from a state, once formed, are highly resistant to change. Foreign policy continuity is the norm because the beliefs of the members of dominant social networks become institutionalized and they oppose challenges to their positions within the government and society. Thus, continuity in foreign policy tends to prevail because of the patterns of stratification that exist in the structures and beliefs throughout society and the state. During such times human needs tend to be perceived by most individuals as being, for the most part, satisfied. Such a *period of stability* continues as long as changes in the state's environment do not impede successful policy outcomes.

Although stability and policy continuity are the norm, changes in the environment over time eventually force changes within society, the state, and a government's foreign policy. Since resistance to change and continuity is the norm, change within the society and state and in foreign policy tends to be not continuous or evolutionary, but abrupt and of short duration. Changes in foreign policy tend to occur when the state's capabilities have altered over time because of changes in the environment, which make it more difficult for the government to successfully pursue its policies. During such *periods of transition*, more and more individuals perceive their needs as not being fulfilled, activating them to join groups and become part of social networks that increasingly challenge the beliefs and elites that dominate society and the state.

Thus, states go through different phases—a period of stability is eventually superseded by a period of transition where change in foreign policy may occur. The changes in foreign policy, produced from changes in the structures and beliefs of society and the state, soon result in a new period of stability in which continuity in policy is again the norm. The movement from a period of stability to transition, and its implications for foreign policy change, is dialectical and continues in perpetuity—a constant pattern in itself—as long as the state and society continue to exist. Such a depiction of social change is consistent with the observation made by Robert Nisbet. In *Social Change and History,* Nisbet reviewed the major theories of development throughout western civilization based on the metaphor of "growth" and concluded that social change is rarely continuous and evolutionary, but abrupt and periodic:[2]

> Despite the testimony of conventional wisdom in social theory, despite the first and abiding premise of the theory of social development, it is not change but persistence that is the "natural" or "normal" condition of any given form of social behavior. . . . Change in any degree of notable significance is intermittent rather than continuous, mutational, even explosive, rather than the simple accumulation of internal variations.

The remainder of this section will describe the theory of the state and foreign policy change in somewhat greater depth and provide a better understanding of the continuity and change in foreign policy that seems to be such a permanent part of the global landscape.

State-Society Relations and Foreign Policy

The *state* is a legal concept which refers to the governmental institutions through which policymakers act in the name of the people of a given territory. *Foreign policy* refers to the composite of the goals and plans of action that are selected by governmental policymakers to respond to the present and estimates of the future. In the United States, the government is composed of three central branches, as well as the state and local governments. In the making of U.S. foreign policy, the key participants are usually the president, policymakers within certain executive branch organizations, and Congress. *Society* refers to the social collectivity, and to the specific institutions, beliefs, and relationships people develop. In the making of U.S. foreign policy, the main social institutions include the media, parties, and organized interests.

Students of U.S. foreign policy have tended to emphasize intra-governmental relations within the state and de-emphasize the role of society. Students of international relations, on the other hand, have tended to reify the state and emphasize environmental constraints (usually the international structure), either ignoring the importance of domestic politics or assuming the state is a unified, rational actor. Stephen Krasner, in *Defending the National Interest*, has attempted to fuse these two positions, treating the state as an autonomous actor constrained by its environment. However, he ends up demonstrating that in liberal societies the state tends to be rather weak and heavily constrained by society, especially in the United States.[3]

The state and society cannot be examined solely in isolation, for as discussed above, there is a symbiotic process between the two—the state and society are interactive and mutually dependent. Although this has not been the orthodox approach to the study of U.S. foreign policy, political scientists and sociologists have long been interested in state-societal relations within the United States. Pluralists have argued that the state tends to be responsive to the outcomes of competing societal elites, none of which dominate society and, when aggregated, are representative of the mass public. Marxists tend to see an authoritative system in which the state is an instrument of the capitalist class and/or constrained by the structures and demands of capitalist society. Elitists see democracy only for a few because of the interlocking relationships between different private and public institutional elites. Although each approach provides insights into certain facets of state-societal relations, each tends to simplify reality to the point where the richness of the policy process is not fully captured.[4]

In order to more adequately explain the government's foreign policy, it is necessary to examine the linkages between individuals from various private and public groups, and their relationships to the public at large. Furthermore, it is important to determine the distribution of beliefs that exist within governmental and societal elites, as well as among the mass public. The concept of social networks (and their interaction) allows us to analyze the structural and belief system patterns that exist in state-society relations, for these patterns are responsible for the overall trends in governmental foreign policy. The role of the environment on foreign policy change is momentarily deferred until we discuss the period of transition.

The Period of Stability

States and societies are composed of structures and beliefs that are very resistant to change. Governmental policy results from the dominant beliefs of the people who are linked throughout the established institutions of society and the state. The dominant values and beliefs that prevail result in a narrow range of policy alternatives for consideration. The net consequence of the established structures and beliefs of society and the state is overall continuity in governmental policy. This describes a period of stability, which is the typical state of affairs for most states most of the time.

In other words, when an established set of institutions and structural relationships exist within society and the state, governmental policy becomes difficult to change. This resistance to change is reinforced by the dominant set of beliefs that pervade society and the state. This is not to say that no change in governmental policy can or does occur. Certainly modest changes may occur for particular governmental policies. However, the basic patterns in policy usually stay the same in their essentials throughout the stable period.[5]

Once an established set of structures exists for the society and the state, structural change is very difficult to achieve. Regardless of the type of structure—pluralist, hyperpluralist, class elitist, or institutional elitist—that permeates a society and its impact on the state, all dominant relationships are status quo-oriented.[6] Contemporary literature on inter-organizational and organizational behavior reinforces the trend toward continuity in governmental policy.[7] In other words, state and societal elites, groups, and institutions are difficult to alter once they are established—if for no other reason than that they exist, and the members of society who comprise them usually have vested interests in resisting change.

When you take into consideration the beliefs held by members of society, in addition to the structures of the state and society, the probability of policy change is extremely unlikely during normal times. Although it is possible for members of a society and state to adhere to a multitude of values and beliefs, this is rarely the case. Typically, only a narrow range of beliefs or ideologies is prevalent among social elites and masses.[8] The beliefs of members of the state tend to reflect the range prevalent throughout society. Therefore, only policies which are consistent with those dominant beliefs within society and the state have the opportunity of being formulated; those policies that are inconsistent are perceived as being illegitimate and are therefore ignored or combated by individuals within the established societal and state institutions.

This is not to suggest that all members of society share the same values or that all are content with their position within society. There are always some members of society who hold different beliefs and may challenge or act to alter the dominant institutions and beliefs of society and the state.

These people are often labelled "deviants," a term used in psychology and sociology and applied by mainstream members of society, especially people in high structural positions. Such non-mainstream members of society usually remain on the fringes of the state and society during routine times of stability. However, during a time of transition it is often these elements that generate the ideas and activity that lay the basis for challenging the dominant institutions, beliefs, and policies of the system.[9]

The Period of Transition

As long as the policies of the state are perceived to be successful by members of the society (as well as the state), the established structures and beliefs of the state and society are reinforced and therefore continuity in policy is maintained over time. When policies are perceived as being unsuccessful throughout society, more and more participants within society become willing to challenge the established institutions and beliefs of the state and society that formed the basis of the policies, thus opening up the possibility for change. The key for determining the potential for successful policy outcomes is the relationship between the state, society, and the environment.

The *environment* refers to the resources of a state (e.g., level of population, technology), as well as to the opportunities and constraints it faces in a societal and global context. The environment of a state determines its capacity or potential for the successful pursuit of governmental policies. "Capability analysis," according to Harold and Margaret Sprout, "is directed to the calculation of the opportunities and limitations implicit in the milieu, which will affect the operational results of whatever is attempted, irrespective of whether such factors are known or heeded by the decision-makers in question."[10]   The Sprouts have consistently theorized that the relationship between the policymakers' *psychological milieu* and the *operational milieu* determines the level of what government can accomplish. In other words, the greater the gap between what is perceived by governmental and societal elites and what exists in the environment, the less likely the foreign policy outcomes will be successful.

A government is likely to maintain continuity in policy as long as its resources are consistent with the opportunities and constraints that exist in the environment. When the policies were formulated and implemented initially they may have been appropriate for promoting outcomes perceived as successful by most members of the state and society, elites as well as masses. The state's resources may have been sufficient for satisfactory outcomes, and the beliefs on which they were based may have reflected some of the major aspects of the global environment. Satisfactory outcomes in governmental policy help to promote and maintain the legitimacy of the entire state-societal system.

The elites of the state and society attempt to maximize the support of the populace by promoting the legitimacy of the established institutions and prevalent beliefs of the society and the state. Karl Deutsch clarifies the importance of policy outcomes to the legitimacy of any regime:

> Most governments are obeyed most of the time by their subjects, and a great deal has to happen before an established government will lose its legitimacy in the eyes of its people. What will count most heavily in the long run are results—what difference, if any, the actions or omissions of the government will seem to make in the lives of those who count in politics, and eventually in the lives of the mass of the population.[11]

People tend to support the existing structures and beliefs of the state and society as long as policy outcomes tend to be successful and not harm them. This explains the importance of successful or unsuccessful policy outcomes on the individual pursuit of human needs and its consequences for continuity and change in the society, the state, and public policy.

Over time, however, governmental policy eventually fails to reflect changes that occur in the environment, thus damaging the legitimacy of the dominant structures and beliefs in society and the state. Changes inevitably occur in the environment, which alter a state's capabilities. Yet governmental policies, based on the structures and beliefs of society and the state, are locked in, preventing major policy adjustments to occur. Therefore, it is inevitable for contradictions to develop between the state, society, and the environment.

As a result, governmental policy begins to inadequately reflect the dynamic nature of the environment, which increases the state's and society's level of sensitivity and vulnerability to its environment.[12] The more likely that a state's capacity is insufficient to implement policies when confronting external constraints and obstacles, the greater the likelihood that governmental policies will be unsuccessful over time. This results in a greater investment in time and effort by the government for its policies to succeed. However, as long as the policies do not change—they can't, given the established institutions and beliefs of the society and state—the gap or contradiction relative to changes in the environment continues to grow, resulting in less successful policy outcomes for the state and, thus, for the society.

The more the policies are unsuccessful the greater the possibility that individuals within society and the state will feel that their needs are being deprived, and the more likely pressures will intensify on the government to change its policies. Those issues unsuccessfully addressed by the government become increasingly politicized, resulting in dissatisfaction by various elites and masses within society. This promotes new, politically active segments of society, possibly resulting in the creation of new organized interests and social movements.[13] According to John Burton, "altered environmental conditions, changed political and social relationships and altered differentiation of power, give opportunities for the overt expression and pursuit of needs."[14] As this dialectical process continues, unsatisfactory policy outcomes continue into the future, the unresolved issues dominate the political agenda, dissatisfaction increases, challenges become manifest and grow to the point that the legitimacy of the system is now questioned. Hence, the period of continuity has now been transcended into a period of transition and potential policy change. This may result not only in policy changes, but may change the structures and beliefs of the society and the state on which they are are founded.

Events are the catalyst for producing instability leading to a period of transition for the state and society. Events act as the immediate cause of change, reflecting the underlying relationship and contradictions which exist between the state, society, and the environment. As described by Nisbet:

> The very tendency of social behavior to persist, to hold fast to values and convenience, makes a degree of crisis inevitable in all but the most minor of changes. A given way of behaving tends to persist as long as circumstances permit. Then . . . the way of behaving ceases to be possible, as the result of some intrusion, some difficulty which is the consequence of event or impact, and a period of crisis ensues.[15]

In other words, the government produces continuity in policies until critical negative events force the society and the state to adapt to changes in the environment.

To be more specific, two general types of events are particularly important in affecting individual beliefs and participation within a society: spectacular events and cumulative events.[16] Domestic and international crises, for example, have a major effect on the institutions and beliefs of the society and the state, and subsequent state policies.[17] In foreign policy, war is a major agent of change for it is a set of events which is both spectacular and cumulative for the members of the society involved.[18]

An individual's interpretation of events is the major means available for evaluating state policies—whether they are perceived as being successful or unsuccessful in fulfilling their human needs. As Jervis describes it, "since events with major consequences for a nation absorb so much of the citizen's time and attention, they both socialize the previously unconcerned and change the perceptual predispositions of many people with established views."[19] There is no guarantee that major events, such as crises, will necessarily alter individual beliefs and action. Change will result only if events are perceived as having a negative impact, frustrating and harming the positions and motivations of individuals.[20] Positive events, those which are perceived as supporting or promoting individual positions and motivations, tend to reinforce stability and continuity in state policy.

The satisfaction and deprivation of human needs and desires affects the perception and evaluation of political phenomena and influences the nature of political participation.[21] As suggested by James Rosenau:

> There is nothing in the state of nature which enables a system to serve well all the relevant needs and wants of people. Whole systems and subsystems alike are limited in what they can accomplish. The former do poorly at providing the psychological rewards derived from a shared identity and the latter are ill-equipped to solve the material problems associated with physical security and well being.[22]

As governmental policy, reflecting the dominant institutions and beliefs of society and the state, fails to adapt to changes in the environment, the individual pursuit of human needs and desires becomes increasingly frustrated.

The Transitional Outcome

Changes must occur in the structures and beliefs of a society and state in order for public policy change to result. A period of transition may result in changes in societal and state institutions and beliefs, consequently producing a change in governmental policy. However, the outcome of a period of transition cannot be foreordained: the level and direction of change cannot be clearly surmised.

The substantive nature of critical events and their level of intensity will determine the scope of issues that will be affected. Some critical events (e.g., World War II) may politicize issues across the board and, consequently, have an impact throughout the entire society and the state—on the institutions, beliefs, and public policy. Other events may only politicize a few general issues, leaving other issues untouched. The outcome will ultimately depend on the nature of the critical events and their impact on mainstream social networks within the state and society, and their principal challengers. During such times of instability, fortune is often an important variable in affecting the outcome.[23]

In examining the range of likely patterns, four outcomes are possible:

1. *Intensification*: The dominant structures and beliefs of society and the state are reinforced, resulting in an intensification of governmental policy.
2. *Refinement*: Minor changes in the state-societal system (and, thus, in governmental policy occur).
3. *Reform*: Moderate changes in the state-societal system occur.
4. *Transformation*: Major changes in the state-societal system take place.

Intensification and refinement result in no or little change, thus representing overall continuity in foreign policy. Reform and transformation result in moderate and major changes, thus representing overall discontinuity in foreign policy.

The likelihood of overall policy continuity or change in a period of transition is an open-ended question. To state the obvious, given the existence of continuity in policy over a prolonged period of time because of the established institutions and dominant beliefs of society and the state, the likelihood of intensification or refinement is relatively high. It is much more difficult for the system to be successfully challenged, which would result in societal and state reform, let alone transformation.[24] This explains the importance of catastrophic events as a catalyst of societal, state, and policy change.

To summarize, a model of social change has been presented in order to explain continuity and change in policy over time.[25] Societies and states are fundamentally resistant to changes in policy. This is due to the dominant beliefs that exist within society and the state, institutionalized by their established structures. The result is a prolonged period of public policy continuity over time. However, the capacity of the state constantly undergoes change reflecting changes in the environment, resulting in increasing contradictions between governmental policies and their possibility for success. Eventually, unsuccessful policies result in negative events that politicize members of society, whose needs fulfillment is increasingly frustrated, to challenge the dominant institutions, beliefs, and policies. During such a period of transition, societal and state intensification, refinement, reform, or transformation are all possible depending on the circumstances. The net result is a new period of continuity for the society, the state, and public policy. Overall, the general pattern of social evolution is a dialectical process of continuity and transition over time resulting in the ebb and flow of policy continuity and change.

U.S. FOREIGN POLICY SINCE WORLD WAR II

Most people who study U.S. foreign policy argue that since the end of the Second World War the dominant pattern has been one of continuity. There are different interpretations as to the nature of the continuity, but there appears to be consensus that U.S. foreign policy has remained the same over the past forty years. The major source of disagreement revolves around the goals and instruments of policy.

The orthodox interpretation has emphasized U.S. efforts to prevent the spread of communism throughout the world based on a policy of containment.[26] Therefore, the United States became internationally active emphasizing a political-military response to the expansion of the Soviet Union in order to promote global security. Containment and deterrence were pursued through military spending and the development of nuclear weapons, the creation of alliances, the placement of military troops and facilities around the world, the overt use of military troops in Korea and Vietnam, the use of covert activities, the provision of foreign military and economic assistance to allies, and efforts to isolate and weaken the Soviet Union and its allies with economic sanctions. Although many scholars believe that the particular use of instruments has fluctuated over time, they agree that the U.S. policy of anti-communism and containment has consistently been the foundation of its foreign policy since the end of World War II.

Although the orthodox interpretation has been the most popular interpretation—consistent with the initial governmental version and the common interpretation throughout U.S. society—a revisionist literature has developed. The revisionist literature associated with the political left emphasizes the flip side of the coin focused on by the orthodox interpretation: they ignore what the United States was trying to negate, emphasizing instead what it was attempting to promote—global capitalism. They cite similar instruments of policy, but for the purpose of promoting American private investment and trade abroad. The fundamental goal was not to contain the expansion of communism, but to maintain and promote U.S. capitalism throughout the world.[27]

A third school of thought which also argues continuity in contemporary U.S. foreign policy is provided by the revisionists of the political right.[28] They believe that U.S. society has failed to contain the growth of communism as a result of the inadequacy of containment or, as some argue, by conspiratorial design. The conspiratorial vision posits that U.S. foreign policy has consciously promoted global socialism. The major individuals of high finance, such as the Rockefellers, have consistently pursued policies to create a world of socialism under their control.[29]

Although the dominant interpretations discussed above have each argued that U.S. foreign policy has been one of continuity, a close look at the empirical literature suggests that each interpretation is simplistic, for U.S. foreign policy—that is, the foreign policy that emanates from the state—has experienced both continuities and discontinuities since World War II. The dominant structures and beliefs of U.S. society and the state resulted in a period of stability and policy continuity during the late forties, the fifties, and the early sixties. However, changes in the environment affected U.S. capabilities, which resulted in a period of transition during the late sixties triggered by the Vietnam War. The consequence has been a moderate level of change in society and the state producing both continuity and change in the policies of the seventies and eighties. The brief description and explanation of U.S. foreign policy that follows is based on this theory of foreign policy.

Cold War Continuity and the Quest for Global Security

Continuity in U.S. foreign policy did occur, and lasted for two decades following the Second World War. Two principal and complementary goals formed the basis of the U.S. quest for global security: anti-communism and pro-capitalism. U.S. foreign policy attempted to prevent communism from expanding, at the same time attempting to maintain and promote a liberal global political economy.[30] These goals were to be achieved through containment, emphasizing political-military instruments, and expansion, emphasizing private investment and trade. Thus, both the orthodox and the left revisionist positions tend to be correct about the cold war years, but each interpretation tends to provide only half the story about U.S. foreign policy.

A variety of specific instruments were used by the government to directly promote anti-communism, at the same time indirectly supporting the promotion of capitalism. After the initial demobilization following World War II, nuclear and conventional forces quickly expanded to the point where the United States acquired a large, permanent, professional military for the first time in its history. Alliances (e.g., NATO, Rio Pact, ANZUS, CENTO, SEATO) and U.S. military base facilities were created with allies throughout the world in an effort to prevent communism from expanding beyond Eurasia. Foreign assistance, both military and economic, was provided to support allies. Presidential proclamations, such as the Truman and Eisenhower Doctrines, were made to communicate to the world the U.S. policy of containment. The enemy was to be economically isolated through trade sanctions in an effort to weaken their society and promote internal collapse. Although overt military force was occasionally used (e.g., Korea, Lebanon, Vietnam, Dominican Republic), U.S. foreign policy was premised on the existence of a national emergency which directly threatened its national security—a time of "cold war." Therefore, covert activities were the major means used to prevent any change U.S. leaders perceived as counter to U.S. interests. As suggested by the orthodox school, the United States became very much a status quo actor as a result of its foreign policy of anti-communism and containment.

These policies, which emphasized a response to the threat of communist expansion, also supported U.S. efforts to maintain global capitalism and promote the role of the United States within the global economy. Multilateral efforts were designed to restore and manage the liberal global economy based on the Bretton Woods system of fixed exchange rates and free trade via the creation of the International Bank for Reconstruction and Development (IBRD), the International Monetary Fund (IMF), and the General Agreement on Tariffs and Trade (GATT). Such multilateral efforts, however, collapsed due to the inability of Western European economies to recover from the depression and the war. As a result, the United States unilaterally attempted to revive the European economies, which were seen as vital to enhancing global capitalism and world prosperity, by providing massive capital outlays in the form of assistance (the Marshall Plan), private investment and loans by U.S. multinational corporations, and trade based on opening the U.S. domestic market and allowing the Europeans to close theirs. Although primarily European-oriented, the United States was active in promoting global capitalism in the Third World through its support for private investment abroad as suggested by the left revisionist school.

Four important developments within the state and society of the United States provided the foundation for the policies of anti-communism and pro-capitialism. First, there was the rise of the national security state. Second, there was the rise of the foreign policy establishment—the social network responsible for linking societal and governmental elites and institutions. Third, there was the rise of an anti-communist consensus in beliefs throughout the state and much of society. Finally, there was the rise of a national security infrastructure throughout society. These four patterns became prominent at the same time and reinforced each other, producing continuity in foreign policy until the mid-sixties.

The key governmental institution responsible for directly formulating and implementing foreign policy was the executive branch. The key governmental agencies included the National Security Council, the State Department, the Department of Defense, and the intelligence communities. The executive branch was dominated by the president, his closest advisors, and other high-level officials. Due to World War II and the cold war, power in the area of foreign policy moved toward the president and away from Congress, to a point, in fact, where the presidency dominated decisions of war and peace.

The people who were appointed by the president to lead and staff the executive branch were recruited from major multinational corporations, law firms, universities, and think tanks—usually moving readily from public institutions to private institutions and back, although many individuals became permanent members of either private or public bureaucracy. Therefore, a network of a relatively small number of individuals from public and private institutions came to dominate the making of U.S. foreign policy.[31]

The existence of a foreign policy establishment or network directly linking the state and society resulted because of the development of a shared consensus. This was a time of bipartisanship in foreign policy. Most individuals within the society and the state, whether they identified with the Democratic or Republican Party, perceived a similar world, and they agreed as to the general goals of U.S. foreign policy. Differences may have existed over the particular importance of an issue and the specific use of instruments needed to respond, but the general foreign policy orientation was based on shared values of anti-communism and pro-capitalism.[32]

U.S. leaders, throughout the society and the state, perceived a world which was radically transformed following World War II. Where Europeans were the dominant global actors before the war, the United States and the Soviet Union were now the superpowers. They perceived a bipolar world where conflict was endemic due to the expansionism of the Soviet Union and its communist system—as demonstrated by its occupation of Eastern Europe, the "fall" of China, and the invasion by North Korea of the South. Given the perception of a monolithic communism dominated by the Soviet Union and its promotion of values antithetical to the American values of democracy, capitalism, and freedom, it was imperative for the United States to contain the enemy.

One of the lessons learned by post-war U.S. leaders was that one should not appease aggressors, for this led to more aggression and eventually war. The "Munich Syndrome" led U.S. leaders to perceive the Soviet Union under communism and Stalin as resembling Germany under fascism and Hitler. Therefore, unlike before World War II, the state was "forced" to become internationally active and to contain the threat of communism.[33] The world was a bipolar, zero-sum contest between the United States and the Soviet Union. Any losses by the United States, anywhere in the world, were considered gains for the Soviet Union. Hence, global containment through the militarization of U.S. foreign policy was necessary to prevent changes in the status quo in order to promote global security.

The collapse of the global economy and the economic depression were considered the major cause of the rise of Hitler and fascism. This is why it was so important for U.S. leaders to revive the global economy and regain prosperity. Europe initially was the key, for it was the center of global capitalism before the war and was still crucial. The recovery of the European economies would allow the U.S. economy to grow, and eventual European and U.S. prosperity would allow for global economic recovery, growth, and prosperity.

Once the cold war became reality, most members of U.S. society supported—or at least condoned—U.S. foreign policy.[34] Most people in the United States really feared the threat of communism during the fifties, especially because of the rise of McCarthyism. They identified their values of liberty and democracy with U.S. global responsibilities.

The development of a national security infrastructure throughout the economy and the society was the final element that contributed to policy continuity in the post-war years. Much of U.S. industry, for example, was directly involved in supporting the government's defense build-up. The overseas activities of private corporations also complemented the government's efforts to promote a liberal economic order. Furthermore, as the United States became the world's policeman and banker, most private companies were able to benefit economically from the country's favorable position. The U.S. economy never really suffered after the end of the war, and its continued growth resulted in more jobs and benefits for labor—most people benefited materialistically. Activity by business and labor was further reinforced by behavior in the scientific, research, educational, and even intellectual communities which supported the cold war effort.

Transition and The Vietnam War

The U.S. quest for global security based on anti-communism and pro-capitalism through containment and expansion was perceived as being relatively successful throughout the fifties and early sixties. Therefore, the dominant structures and beliefs of society and the state were reinforced, resulting in continuity in U.S. foreign policy for roughly twenty years following the Second World War. However, U.S. involvement in Vietnam began a series of events that resulted in a large segment of the society questioning and eventually challenging U.S. foreign policy, which in turn resulted in a period of transition.

By the middle and late sixties U.S. capabilities had altered because of changes in the environment. In actuality, following World War II there was only one superpower in the world: the United States, which had become the most powerful actor the world had ever seen—the hegemonic power of its time.[35] By the 1960s, although the United States continued to grow more powerful on an absolute scale, the changes that were occurring throughout the globe resulted in a relative decline in power. This was inevitable, for U.S. hegemony could not be maintained forever in a dynamic environment.

A number of actors and issues grew in importance during the fifties and sixties. The Soviet Union became militarily more powerful, and the Western European countries and Japan recovered economically and became competitive with the United States. Most important was the rise of national liberation movements. Societies that had been directly dominated by Westerners through occupation and colonialization began to seek and fight for independent statehood. The United States became the global superpower, ironically, at a time when national independence movements were reaching their heights in Africa and Asia.

Following World War II, the British, French, and other Western empires were in a state of decline and collapse—new, politically independent states were being created. Nevertheless, as the cold war dominated the foreign policy agenda in the United States, its initial policies were one of support for the colonialists, and when the colonialists retreated the United States directly intervened to maintain the status quo. During the fifties the United States was basically successful in pursuing its policies: communism was contained and capitalism promoted. The United States was strong enough to promote success and prevent failure when it decided to make a major investment in policy. This changed with Vietnam.

By the 1960s the United States was no longer hegemonic. Much of the world was less dependent on the United States, and it was becoming more dependent on its environment—global pluralism and interdependence were increasing in all spheres of activity. Furthermore, America faced a Vietnemese enemy who had never been defeated in its efforts to politically unify the country—persevering in its struggle against first the French, then the Japanese, the French again, and finally the Americans.[36] Environmental changes notwithstanding, societal and state institutions and beliefs persevered, and U.S. foreign policy continued to pursue global security through the containment of communism and the expansion of capitalism. Thus, the war in Southeast Asia was Americanized.

The Vietnam War was the first major political-military failure in the history of the United States. Simply put, after investing as much as $30 billion dollars and over 500,000 troops per year during the height of U.S. involvement in a war that lasted more than fifteen years, the United States was unsuccessful in pursuing its policy of global security in Vietnam. This spectacular and cumulative set of events, reinforced by the turmoil over civil rights and Watergate, triggered increasing dissatisfaction among the public. The structures and beliefs of the society and the state were frustrating the satisfaction of needs of more and more individuals. Thus, Vietnam politicized a variety of issues, which resulted in the development of massive social movements within society. According to Holsti and Rosenau, "the war in Vietnam represented a major landmark in American history, comparable to what students of domestic politics call 'watershed' elections."[37] The net consequence, in the late sixties and early seventies, was a period of transition in which large segments of U.S. society went through an agonizing reappraisal of U.S. foreign policy that resulted in change.

Post-Vietnam Continuity in Contemporary U.S. Foreign Policy

The Vietnam War and the other events of the times resulted in moderate changes in U.S. foreign policy. The dominant structures and beliefs of the society and the state that were the basis of U.S. cold war policies were modified. The dominance of the foreign policy establishment and its public support collapsed, shattering the cold war consensus. The national security state and its societal infrastructure have been weakened. No new dominant elites and consensus have prevailed. The result has been a more decentralized set of structures and a greater diversity of beliefs within society resulting in a new period of continuity where the foreign policy of the state has varied slightly with each new administration.

The dominance of the foreign policy establishment was destroyed. No longer would power reside in the hands of a small social network of individuals operating primarily through the presidency in foreign policy.[38] The Vietnam War and Watergate shattered trust in the power of the president.

New institutions and actors became increasingly important in society and the state, thus affecting the conduct of foreign policy. Congress began to reassert its long dormant authority in a number of areas. Numerous interest groups were created with a dominant interest in international and foreign affairs. Private corporate activities were increasingly transnational resulting in greater independence in thought and action. The media became increasingly critical in its reporting of events. Overall, the established institutions of U.S. society and the state were modified towards greater decentralization in the area of foreign policy.[39]

It is important to point out that the national security state, under presidential direction, and the national security infrastructure, although weakened, remain powerful forces in the making of U.S. foreign policy. Therefore, although much change has occurred structurally, much has also remained the same.

A similar pattern of continuity and change can be seen in the impact of the sixties on the beliefs of the public. The lessons of the Vietnam War were different for different segments of society. The consensus and the bipartisan support of the mass public and, especially, U.S. elites that had been the basis of U.S. foreign policy throughout the cold war had collapsed.[40]

Many people—sometimes referred to as Cold War Internationalists—continued to subscribe to the beliefs that the global order and, therefore, security and way of life in the United States were threatened by the expansion of communism. They continued to support the policies of military containment and the promotion of global capitalism. However, other interpretations of the world and the necessary role of the United States within it competed for ascendancy.

The major competing school of thought had a more optimistic vision. Reform (or Post Cold War) Internationalists perceived a much more decentralized and interdependent international system. U.S.-Soviet relations was an important issue, but it was not the only one of consequence. Other issues such as international economic development, human rights, and basic human needs were important. This meant not only a focus on East-West but also West-West relations (U.S.-Europe-Japan), as well as North-South relations. Therefore, it was important to concentrate on a number of states as well as non-state actors. The goal of U.S. foreign policy should be the pursuit of global community and justice. Hence, it was believed that the militarization of U.S. foreign policy needed to be reformed to emphasize political, economic, and social instruments of the state.

Although most people were sympathetic to either Cold War Internationalism or Reform Internationalism, other schools of thought also proliferated. Some people argued for a Neo-Isolationist approach. The world had become so complex and unmanageable that the United States should reduce its global commitments and involvement to only those areas most vital (e.g., Europe, Japan), thus maximizing U.S. independence. Another group, Security Internationalists, concluded that Vietnam indicated the failure of containment and the success of communist expansion. Therefore, in order to prevent Soviet hegemony the United States needed to pursue a policy of rollback and liberation.[41]

This proliferation of diverse foreign policy views across the U.S. political landscape demonstrates that the cold war consensus had shattered. Where consensus or lack of fundamental disagreement was the norm during the time of the cold war, following the Vietnam War diversity and disagreement prevailed. The intensity and breadth of disagreement was particularly high in global security issues—for example, the threat of Soviet communism and the preferred U.S. military role; there was much more agreement over global economic issues—such as the promise of global capitalism and private enterprise.

During the fifties and sixties, changes in administration in terms of party and personnel had little effect on foreign policy because of the shared beliefs within society and the dominance of the foreign policy establishment—cold war internationalism was the result. However, the aftermath of the collapse of consensus and the foreign policy establishment, as well as the weakening of the national security state and infrastructure, have resulted in different social networks representing different beliefs competing for control of the state. Therefore, as the presidency changed from individual to individual and party to party through periodic elections, U.S. foreign policy has continually changed, particularly over security issues.

One of the major goals of every administration, especially since Vietnam, has been to forge a new consensus within society consistent with that administration's values and beliefs. However, given the decentralization of power, the diversity of thought within U.S. society, the decline of U.S. power and resources, and the growing interdependence and complexity of the environment, no group of societal and state leaders has been able to gain widespread support for its policies. Therefore, a new and "unique" period of stability has developed in which constant change in U.S. security policy has been the norm. U.S. foreign economic policy, on the other hand, has remained much more continuous. In terms of overall general patterns, U.S. foreign policy in the seventies and eighties can be characterized by three different orientations.

The Quest for Global Stability. The foreign policy under presidents Nixon and Ford and guided by Henry Kissinger had a different emphasis than under previous presidents during the cold war. The fundamental goal of the Nixon-Kissinger era was to promote global stability. The major threat to the stability of the world was not communist expansion but the adventuristic activities of the Soviet Union in its role as a traditional global power, as well as the deteriorating political-economic situation.

The Nixon administration's response to the state's declining economic position was to take the dollar off the gold standard and to place a surcharge on imports in 1971, resulting in the collapse of the Bretton Woods system of fixed exchange rates and free trade. U.S. foreign policy had a dual approach toward the Soviet Union: on the one hand, détente was promoted when the Soviet Union was acting in accord with U.S. desires; on the other hand, containment was exercised when the Soviets were expansionistic. The purpose of the "carrot and stick" approach was to move the Soviet Union away from being a revolutionary global actor to one which accepted the status-quo as legitimate.

For a while it appeared that the "linkage" approach might work. Détente appealed to the Reform Internationalists, and containment to the Cold War Internationalists. The inducements of prestige (e.g., summit meetings and arms control treaties), trade (e.g., Most Favored Nation status, loans), and the normalization of relations with China resulted in the height of détente in 1972. However, the promises created false expectations of a new age of cooperation. The passage of the Jackson-Vanick and Stevenson amendments in Congress eliminated economic trade as an instrument to stimulate Soviet cooperation, while the Congressional cut-off of CIA support for two Angolan independence groups prevented U.S. efforts to contain Soviet activities in that area. In the final analysis, the skepticism in which Cold War Internationalists held détente and the Reform Internationalists held containment prevented the efforts at promoting global stability from being fully implemented.

The Quest for Global Community. The Carter Administration represented a shift to a new set of policies. Most of the people who staffed the Carter administration and supported its foreign policy identified with the Reform Internationalist orientation.[42] The major goals were global cooperation, a liberal economic order, and the promotion of justice. Military instruments were devalued. Instead, normalization of relations with traditional enemies, negotiations and preventive diplomacy, economic development as well as free trade, and human rights advocacy were the dominant paths to global community.

The support which Carter's policies generated in the early years of his administration was shattered by the Iran hostage crisis and the Soviet invasion of Afghanistan. The national trauma forced the Carter administration to abandon many of its earlier optimistic policies. This policy reversal, however, was to no avail since the Carter administration was unable to maintain domestic support for its domestic and foreign policies.

The Quest for Global Security II. The election of Ronald Reagan resulted in a U.S. foreign policy reminiscent of the fifties and the sixties. The Reagan administration perceived a bipolar international system in which Soviet communist expansion was the overwhelming threat—the United

States needed to contain the threat as well as promote global capitalism.[43] The means emphasized were similar to the earlier cold war period, resulting in the remilitarization of U.S. foreign policy.

Although Reagan was reelected for a second four years, consensus has not been regained in U.S. foreign policy. Disagreement over policy is still prevalent, especially concerning the Reagan administration's policies toward the Soviet Union, Lebanon and the Middle East, and, most of all, Central America. In fact, the Iran-Contra scandal has shattered any remaining possibilities of regaining consensus behind the Reagan administration's policies.

Contemporary U.S. foreign policy is one of consistent change and flux within the legitimate parameters of Reform Internationalism and Cold War Internationalism within society. The Vietnam War shattered the dominance of the foreign policy establishment, the institution of the presidency, and the cold war consensus. The structure of U.S. society is more decentralized, allowing more individuals and actors a role in affecting the government's foreign policy. At the same time, there exist disagreement and conflict in values and beliefs. Each elected administration has attempted to pursue its own particular brand of foreign policy. However, no administration has been successful in restoring consensus within the state and throughout society behind their policies. Although the resources and environmental conditions have made it increasingly difficult for any administration to achieve successful policy outcomes, it has not resulted in any great and lasting failures that could trigger the possibility of change in society, the state, and foreign policy. As Holsti and Rosenau argue, "perhaps the only constancy in U.S. foreign policy since the Vietnam War has been the conspicuous lack of constancy in its conduct."[44] Therefore, the future will probably entail a continuation of moderate fluctuation in governmental policy over time until a new period of transition and change occurs.

CONCLUSION

The purpose of this chapter has been to develop a theory to explain continuity and change in U.S. foreign policy over time based on assumptions of the power of human needs. The model posits that states tend to produce continuous policy over time because of the dominant structures and beliefs that permeate society and the state. However, when a government's policies fail to reflect changes in its environment, a period of transition eventually is produced. This results in unsuccessful policy outcomes and critical negative events, greater politicization of elites and masses whose needs are not being satisfied, and, thus, the possibility of change. Societies and states go through periods of stability and transition, resulting in continuity and change in the foreign policy of the state.

This model was used to explain the evolution of U.S. foreign policy since World War II. United States foreign policy was relatively constant for twenty years as a result of the rise of the national security state, the foreign policy establishment, and a national security infrastructure—held together by a bipartisan consensus based on anti-communism and pro-capitalism abroad. Yet, the Vietnam War demonstrated that U.S. policies, reflecting the institutions and beliefs of the state and the society, were no longer successful. The global environment was changing and the United States was not as dominant as it once was. The increasing politicization at home, reflected in the civil rights and the anti-war movements, challenged the imperial presidency and cold war beliefs. The result was greater structural decentralization and diversity in foreign policy beliefs within society and the state, which has resulted in three different versions of U.S. foreign policy since Vietnam. The new period of stability has, in other words, produced moderate changes in foreign policy from administration to administration.

The dynamic model of foreign policy change developed in this chapter can offer significant improvement in our understanding of foreign policy. It demonstrates the need to look beyond the president and the government to broader underlying forces to explain U.S. foreign policy over time—the interaction of the state, society, and the environment is what is critical. In this manner it illustrates how one can develop theory and explain U.S. foreign policy based on assumptions of individual pursuit of human needs.

NOTES

1. The theoretical model developed has the potential to explain the evolution of any state's policy, especially states in highly developed and liberal societies. However, it needs to be pointed out that this model was specifically developed with the U.S. in mind.

2. See Robert A. Nisbet, *Social Change and History: Aspects of the Western Theory of Development* (Oxford University Press, 1969), pp. 274, 281. There exists a considerable body of literature on theories of social change, especially in anthropology and sociology. However, most of the literature tends to emphasize revolutionary change, rather than lesser gradations of change and, therefore, is of limited relevance.

3. Stephen Krasner, *Defending the National Interest* (Princeton University Press, 1978).

4. Robert R. Alford, "Paradigms of Relations Between State and Society" in Leon N. Lindberg, C. Crouch, and C. Offe, eds., *Stress and Confrontation in Modern Capitalism* (D.C. Heath, 1975).

5. Changes may occur in some policies in some areas. Policy continuity means that these modest changes do not translate into overall policy change at the macro-level.

6. See, for example, Robert A. Dahl, *Pluralist Democracy in the United States: Conflict and Consent* (McNally, 1967); Theodore J. Lowi, *The End of Liberalism: The Second Republic of the United States* (Norton, 1969); Ralph Miliband, *The State in Capitalist Society* (Quartet Books, 1969).

7. See, for example, Graham T. Allison, *Essence of Decision: Explaining the Cuban Missile Crisis* (Little, Brown, 1971); John D. Steinbruner, *The Cybernetic Theory of Decision* (Princeton University Press, 1974).

8. This usually varies due to the nature of the political system. The more open a society the greater the possibility for more heterogeneity of thought.

9. See John Burton, *Deviance, Terrorism, and War: The Process of Solving Unsolved Social and Political Problems* (Martin Robertson, 1979); Joe D. Hagan, "Regimes, Political Oppositions, and the Comparative Analysis of Foreign Policy," in Charles F. Hermann, Charles W. Kegley, Jr., and James N. Rosenau, eds., *New Directions in the Study of Foreign Policy* (Allen & Unwin, 1987), pp. 339–365.

10. Harold Sprout and Margaret Sprout, "Environmental Factors in the Study of International Politics" in James N. Rosenau, ed., *International Politics and Foreign Policy* (Free Press, 1969), p. 53. See also Harold Sprout and Margaret Sprout, *The Ecological Perspective on Human Affairs,* (Princeton University Press, 1965); Harold Sprout and Margaret Sprout, *Toward a Politics of the Planet Earth* (Van Nostrand Reinhold, 1971.

11. Karl Deutsch, *Politics and Government: How People Decide Their Fate* (Houghton Mifflin Co., 1974), p. 17.

12. Robert O. Keohane and Joseph S. Nye, *Power and Interdependence: World Politics in Transition* (Little, Brown, 1977).

13. Neil J. Smelser, *Theory of Collective Behavior* (Knopf, 1962).

14. Burton, *Deviance, Terrorism, and War,* p. 76.

15. Nisbet, *Social Change and History,* p. 282.

16. See Karl W. Deutsch and Richard L. Merritt, "Effects of Events on National and International Images" in Herbert C. Kelman, ed., *International Behavior* (Holt, Rineholt & Winston, 1965), pp. 132–187.

17. Theda Skocpol, *States and Social Revolutions* (Cambridge University Press, 1979).

18. Arthur A. Stein and Bruce M. Russett, "Evaluating War: Outcomes and Consequences" in Ted Robert Gurr, ed., *Handbook of Political Conflict: Theory and Research* (Free Press, 1980), pp. 399–422. They point out that "though war has been studied in a variety of contexts, its role as an independent variable has been currently ignored. . . . War is a public policy with enormous effects. Yet it is the least evaluated of public policies, when it should be perhaps the most carefully assessed." pp. 399, 419.

19. Robert Jervis, *Perception and Misperception in International Politics* (Princeton University Press, 1976), p. 262.

20. As the popular saying goes, "if it ain't broke, why fix it?" In other words, people usually do not voluntarily change until they are forced to change. Alfred Stephen, in *The State and Society: Peru in Comparative Perspective* (Princeton University Press, 1978) emphasizes the responses of elites to crises, while James C. Scott, in *The Moral Economy of the Peasant: Rebellion and Subsistence in Southeast Asia* (Yale University Press, 1974), and Joel S. Midgal, in *Peasants, Politics, and*

Revolution: Pressures Toward Political and Social Change in the Third World (Princeton University Press, 1974), focus on the response of non-elites to crises. Critical events may not only effect the political beliefs and participation of elites and masses, they also are significant in the formulation of beliefs by the youngest members of society, thus explaining the importance of different generations on policy continuity and change. See Ronald Inglehart, *The Silent Revolution: Changing Values and Political Styles Among Western Publics* (Princeton University Press, 1977); V.O. Key, Jr. and Milton C. Cummings, Jr., *The Responsible Electorate: Rationality in Presidential Voting* (Harvard University Press, 1965).

21. See, for example, Ted Robert Gurr, *Why Men Rebel* (Princeton University Press, 1970); Stanley A. Renshon, *Psychological Needs and Political Behavior* (Free Press, 1974).

22. James N. Rosenau, "A Pre-theory Revisited: World Politics in an Era of Cascading Interdependence," *International Studies Quarterly* 28 (September 1984), p. 259.

23. The concept of "fortune" or "luck" has been ignored by modern social scientists, although more classical theorists have argued it is an important factor in human behavior and outcomes. See, for example, Carl Von Clausewitz, *On War* (Penguin, 1968)). This is probably due to the contemporary emphasis in the social sciences on the scientific method and post hoc explanatory research studies.

24. See, for example, William A. Gamson, *The Strategy of Social Protest* (Dorsey Press, 1975).

25. As Rosenau, in "A Pre-Theory Revisited," states, "it is hard to imagine how any theory of any polity, or any class of polities, can be viable without propositions that specify the values, processes, and institutions through which the internal-external balance is maintained (p. 288)."

26. See, for example, Seyom Brown, *The Faces of Power: Constancy and Change in United States Foreign Policy from Truman to Reagan* (Columbia University Press, 1983); John Lewis Gaddis, *Strategies of Containment: A Critical Appraisal of Postwar American National Security Policy* (Oxford University Press, 1982); Charles W. Kegley, Jr. and Eugene R. Wittkopf, *American Foreign Policy: Pattern and Process* (St. Martin's Press, 1982); John Spanier, *American Foreign Policy Since World War II* (Holt, Rinehart & Winston, 1983).

27. See, for example, Morton Berkowitz, P.G. Bock, and Vincent J. Fuccillo, *The Politics of American Foreign Policy: The Social Context of Decisions* (Prentice Hall, 1977).

28. See Ole R. Holsti, "The Study of International Politics Makes Strange Bedfellows: Theories of the Radical Left and Right," *American Political Science Review* 68 (1974), pp. 217-242 for a discussion of the similarities and differences between the revisionist literature of the left and the right.

29. See, for example, Gary Allen, *None Dare Call It Conspiracy* (Concord Press, 1971).

30. Democracy was primarily promoted in Western Europe and Japan, whereas capitalism was of greater global importance.

31. Richard Barnet, *Roots of War: The Men and Institutions Behind U.S. Foreign Policy* (Penguin, 1972); Godfrey Hodgson, "The Establishment," *Foreign Policy* 10 (1973), pp. 3–40.

32. According to Ole R. Holsti and James N. Rosenau, in *American Leadership in World Affairs* (Allen & Unwin, 1984), "Whether or not there was a foreign policy consensus in this country for about two decades after World War II is itself a point on which there is less than full agreement (p. 28)." In fact, a major challenge from the political far right occurred during the 1950s represented by the rise of McCarthyism. Nevertheless, the dominant interpretation has been to assume consensus.

33. In fact, World War II, beginning with the Japanese attack on Pearl Harbor, was a set of critical, negative events upon American society which triggered a period of transition in which U.S. foreign policy changed from its previous semi-isolationist orientation.

34. See Godfrey Hodgson, *America in Our Time: From World War II to Nixon, What Happened and Why* (Vintage, 1976).

35. Robert Gilpin, *War and Change in World Politics* (Cambridge University Press, 1981); Stephen D. Krasner, "American Policy and Global Economic Stability" in William P. Avery and David P. Rapkin, eds., *America in a Changing World Economy* (Longman, 1982); George Modelski, "The Long Cycle of Global Politics and the Nation-State," *Comparative Studies in Society and History* 20 (1978), pp. 214-215.

36. John E. Mueller, in "The Search for the 'Breaking Point' in Vietnam: The Statistics of a Deadly Quarrel," *International Studies Quarterly* 24 (1980), pp. 497-519, empirically demonstrates the exceptional will power of the North Vietnamese through an analysis of the high percentage of fatalities they suffered in historical comparison to other societies involved in war.

37. Holsti and Rosenau, *American Leadership in World Affairs*, p. 249.

38. See Hodgson, "The Establishment."

39. See Daniel Yankelovitch, "Farewell to 'President Knows Best'," *Foreign Policy* 59 (1978), pp. 670-693, for the decline of trust in the power of the president; Thomas M. Franck and Edward Weisband, *Foreign Policy by Congress* (Oxford University Press, 1979), for the increasing role of Congress; U.S., House, Committee on Foreign Affairs, *Executive-Legislative Consultation on Foreign Policy* (Committee Print, 97th Congress, 2d Session, 1982), on the rise of interest groups; Richard J. Barnet and Ronald E. Muller, *Global Reach: The Power of the Multinational Corporation* (Simon & Schuster, 1974), on the role of MNCs; Doris A. Graber, *Mass Media and American Politics* (Congressional Quarterly Press, 1984), on the role of the media. James A. Nathan and James K. Oliver, in *Foreign Policy Making and the American Political System* (Little, Brown, 1987), provide a brief overview of some of the major changes in the conduct of U.S. foreign policy.

40. Holsti and Rosenau, *American Leadership in World Affairs*.

41. Another school of thought, limited to intellectual and academic circles, believed that the United States and the world needed to be transformed. Transform Internationalists, who emphasized the role of economic factors, argue for the need to eradicate capitalism in favor of socialism; those emphasizing political factors want to eliminate the nation-state system in favor of, for example, regional and world federation.

42. Carl Gershman, "The Rise and Fall of the New Foreign Policy Establishment," *Commentary* 70 (July 1980): pp. 13–24; Jerel A. Rosati, *The Carter Administration's Quest for Global Community: Beliefs and Their Impact on*

Behavior (University of South Carolina Press, 1987).

43. Many of the members of the Reagan Administration adhere to the beliefs of the Security Internationalists. Consequently, the rhetoric at times has emphasized the need for liberation and rollback of communist gains. Likewise, some U.S. actions—such as the invasion of Grenada and the support for the anti-Sandinista contras in Nicaragua—could be interpreted along these lines. Therefore, it appears that the Reagan Administration represents an uneven mixture of Cold War Internationalism and Security Internationalism.

44. Holsti and Rosenau, *American Leadership in World Affairs,* p. 1

CHAPTER NINE

Conflict Resolution
as a Function of Human Needs

JOHN W. BURTON

In this chapter, as in much of his contemporary work, John Burton focuses on applying the assumptions of a human needs approach to questions of conflict resolution. He argues that traditional approaches to resolving conflicts are largely unsuccessful because they concentrate narrowly on state power and the interests of authority, ignoring the underlying sources of conflict—the deprivation of fundamental human needs. As a result, Burton argues, traditional methods only lead to temporary "conflict settlement," at best.

Long-term conflict resolution rests on distinguishing between interests and needs, and on creating institutions and practices that serve the needs of individuals and legitimize authority. In other words, the resolution of conflict in the final analysis rests on creating and maintaining valued, not coerced or socialized, relationships. Burton concludes with an extended discussion of examples from his efforts at "facilitated conflict resolution."

The political and social problems humanity faces are more complex than any others in human experience. Getting to the moon and inventing defensive space strategies are simple tasks in comparison. Yet it is simplistic explanations and solutions of human problems that are most popular and readily accepted. This trivializes complex and vital issues, the exposition of which cannot be simple.

Indeed, this trivialization of political and social issues is a major part of humanity's problem. Conserving and promoting values that are the essence of quality of life for humanity or for particular cultures, and, to this end, resolving political and social problems, are complex and political tasks. These tasks cannot be performed by acting on intuition and simplistic faiths that focus on selected aspects of the total political condition. Instead, new approaches must be developed, which can take a more comprehensive view of the nature of such problems. Efforts along these lines have been made to discover a common explanatory approach to sociopolitical problems. And, as a result, some positive changes in the study of conflict resolution have occurred.

THE FRUITS OF FAILURE

In both the research and practical application of conflict resolution processes we are currently experiencing a shift from one conceptual framework to another. We are moving from the traditional theory of power bargaining, negotiation, and the *settlement* of disputes to a new theory of problem solving which involves analysis of needs and interests. This analysis leads to the discovery of agreed options so that the *resolution* of conflicts can be achieved.

In significance this shift is as dramatic as the realization that the earth was not flat but round. There is now a new science of conflict resolution. Persons engaged in family, small group, and even industrial disputes have become accustomed to the resolution of disputes by analytical and interactive processes. In the international relations area, however, the shift is disturbing and challenging to decisionmakers and their advisors, both within states and within international institutions. Traditional international relations theory and practice have continued to take the state and state power as the unit of analysis and explanation of events; the state and its institutions have been regarded as supreme. As a consequence, over the years we have developed notions of majority government, and we define democracy in these terms. Law and order has been sanctified along with the state.

There are two connected reasons why the shift to a problem-solving conflict resolution approach is now occurring. The first is that traditional normative processes have failed. Power bargaining, where important values are at stake, in relation to which there can be no compromises, leads only to escalation of conflict (Cyprus, as one illustration, is witness to this); the adversary processes of diplomacy have been shown to be dysfunctional; arms control negotiations would be better termed arms race negotiations; mediation has been rejected as a process that commits parties in advance, and its modern form of shuttle diplomacy has a poor track record. International institutions have been shown to be as irrelevant as governments in the resolution of interstate and international conflicts, as United Nations, Organization of African Unity, and Organization of American States failures in mediation have demonstrated.

The second reason for this shift in thinking is that a complacent view is no longer acceptable in the thermonuclear age. It was once argued that mediation is "the art of the possible." The absence of apparent success was merely evidence that nothing better was possible. Yet, the threat of nuclear destruction has reinforced the search for alternatives, giving rise to challenges to traditional thinking and the emergence of alternative conceptual frameworks.[1] By the early 1960s perceived failure led to fundamental rethinking of classical and traditional political philosophy and its underlying assumptions.[2]

THE LAW AND ORDER MODEL: AN EXPLANATION OF FAILURE

In 1945, when the Charter of the United Nations was drafted at San Francisco, conventional wisdom held that the global society should approximate a centralized federal system. There were certain international legal norms to be observed and a court to interpret and to apply them. The Charter provided for means of peaceful settlement, such as judicial settlement, mediation and negotiation. Subsumed were the twin notions of norms and relative power as the final controls of behaviour and the bases of conflict settlement. Also, there was to be an enforcement institution, the Security Council, whose member states were to contribute forces for the enforcement purpose.

When one reads the Charter today one can read into "peaceful settlement" almost any process. In fact, at that time, there was within the conventional wisdom no conception of conflict resolution as distinct from settlement. World society was to be constructed and administered along the lines of the nation-state. Law and order, majority rule, and the common good were among the conceptual notions that made up the political philosophy of the time.

This philosophy, however, represents a power philosophy. At both the domestic and international levels the concept of the common good was defined by the powerful. The belief was that if power were employed to enforce international norms, it would result in a stability that was in the common interest. However, such norms had evolved over the years and reflected the interests and the practices of powerful states. These influential states were in a position to take advantage of trade, employ military means to defend their boundaries, intervene in the affairs of smaller states, and defy or veto any decision by a central authority.

We know now from experience that even at the domestic level the model on which the United Nations was based is falsely conceived. It posits legal authorities, that is, authorities recognized by the international society by dint of their effective control of persons within their territories. It assumes, however, that these legal authorities are also politically legitimized authorities; that is, authorities who derive their legitimacy from those persons over whom they exercise authority. In the absence of legitimization of this kind, the maintenance of law and order by a central authority through coercion is a source of domestic violence and protracted conflict.

There are few authorities in the world society who can claim such legitimization. At present there are some sixty or so overt domestic conflict situations in the world, and the use of internal and foreign military forces to maintain unpopular governments is widespread. Conflict may also occur because the legal norms of societies do not necessarily advance the development of their members. Notions of majority rule generally take little account of minority groups and the issues of ethnicity and distributive justice. The practice of dealing with conflicts by employing non-legitimized forces may be a form of conflict management, but it does not lead to conflict resolution.

The United Nations was flawed from the outset since many of its original members were, and still are, non-legitimized authorities. This created a situation where serious domestic conflicts were supported externally through interventions by great powers, and thus these domestic conflicts spilled over into the international system. The United Nations was powerless to intervene since its charter contains a domestic jurisdiction clause preventing it from dealing with these conflicts. The result is a global society plagued with serious domestic conflicts and no appropriate institution to which parties can turn for assistance. It is not an overstatement to say the United Nations is a body that affords protection to many state authorities who lack domestic legitimization and wish only to preserve the status quo by the use of violence. These authorities attract support from the great powers, which fear that domestic conflicts will result in altered ideological affiliations.

DISCOVERY IN INDUSTRIAL RELATIONS

It was not until the early 1960s that any effective challenge was made to the normative and authoritarian approach of classical conflict settlement theory. When it came, it came in the field of industrial relations. Scholars and consultants such as Blake, Shephard and Mouton[3] pointed to the need for interaction between management and workers if there were to be cooperation and increased productivity. This concept led to an interest in negotiation techniques and to the realization that to be effective, negotiation required some accommodation of the interests of the "weaker" side if stability were to be reached. As a result, techniques in such negotiating skills were studied and taught. Once there was a break from the authoritarian model of management and a realization that stability required accommodation to the needs of those concerned, it was a short step to interactive models of decisionmaking. In this mode decisions are made as a result of interaction among all parties concerned.

After a slow takeoff, there was an explosion of new thoughts and practices in all fields of behavioral relationships. They appeared in many areas—from family counseling to the handling of juveniles by courts. The extent of their influence was apparent at a second meeting of the U.S.-based National Conference on Peacemaking and Conflict Resolution held in St. Louis, Missouri, in September 1984, where five hundred young and older people were talking the same language of "problem solving." This ability to use a common language to talk about experiences of an interactive process at different social levels reflected a significant shift in the theory and practice of decisionmaking and conflict resolution.

At the international level, however, there has been little change. The original philosophical framework, leading to adversary diplomacy and politics, persists. For example, the United Nations, and its Secretariat in particular, still see the global society in the classical framework and rely on mediation or third party determinations. There is an almost total absence of any problem-solving endeavours, in the sense this term is employed in other fields. In his 1983 Report, the Secretary-General of the United Nations made it clear that change in the UN role was vital. Unfortunately, it seems that the only change he sought was to make the decisionmaking and coercive nature of the Security Council more effective. There was no suggestion of using, or even investigating, alternatives to the traditional mediation process. The traditional outlook of the United Nations was amply demonstrated in 1984 when the Secretary-General took an initiative in the twenty-year-old Cyprus dispute and attempted to mediate within the old bargaining-negotiating framework. Furthermore, he made a proposal that assumed acceptance of traditional notions of majority government and power sharing, which contemporary theory and practice have shown to be hollow.

A SHIFT IN THINKING

As in industrial relations, at the non-official level experiments have arisen out of a quite different philosophy of conflict resolution—a paradigm shift of a major order. This dramatic shift was perhaps too quick for many politicians and diplomatic practitioners to absorb and use.

In 1966, a group of lawyers in Britain published their considered view that the traditional conflict settlement institutions available to states were adequate.[4] They included judicial settlement, mediation, conciliation, negotiation, and the other means contemplated within the UN Charter, classical legal philosophy, and realpolitik international behavior. The lawyers, repeating the conventional wisdom of the time, came to the conclusion that only one trouble existed, an unwillingness on the part of states to use these instruments.

Working within their normative approach, these lawyers could not take into account two related phenomena. First, at the human level, they took no account of values and human aspirations that cannot be suppressed or made subject to societal control. Second, they had not come to terms with the fact that no responsible leader is in a position to hand over decisionmaking power on an important issue to a court or a mediator. Rather than argue that the existing institutions were adequate, it would have been reasonable to assume that there was something wrong with, or missing from, existing institutions and to search for what was relevant.

In response to this same issue, the academic community was sharply divided between those who adopted a traditional or power view and those who took into account the political consequences of human needs and behavior. The latter sought to determine, not how to settle conflict by the application of legal and power norms, but the nature of conflict and how promoting an understanding of it by the parties concerned might help to resolve it. Clearly, the latter process included the uncovering of data that would reveal the otherwise hidden motivations, goals, and interests of the parties to a conflict. By these means an accurate assessment of responses to conditions and policies and an accurate costing of their consequences can be made.

These considerations have led social scientists to rethink political theory and the assumptions on which it rests. One of the important contributors was Paul Sites.[5] He placed power in a realistic perspective by attributing effective power, not to governments, but to individuals and groups of individuals. Authorities in the state, management in industry, the teacher and the head of the family are no longer the locus of power. It is the individual, usually acting through an identity group of others with the same or compatible objectives, who is ultimately the controlling force. Not only do such identity groups constitute a binding force that brings individuals into social relations, these groups can also be the locus of conflict behavior in world society.

IDENTITY GROUPS

Of the 100 or so conflicts that are current in world society, the great majority occur in and between multi-ethnic societies that are a carry over from colonial expansions that separated tribes by state boundaries, and included different tribes within the one state boundary. Identity groups, however, are not confined to ethnic or cultural groups. They include class groups within societies, and underprivileged and underdeveloped nations in the wider society. There may have been a time when the nation-state was an identity group. In the modern world there are few, if any, nation-states. There are states that comprise several or many nations.

The implication of this observation is that there are needs of individual development and control that *will* be pursued, regardless of consequences. State manipulation, socialization, coercion and repression merely postpone the inevitable. The inevitable is foreseeable, given the universal availability of the means of violence. There is a historical continuity in protest against authoritative controls. The state has the means of repression and can survive for a long period of time at great cost; but finally suitably led peoples' power, reflecting human needs that *will* be pursued, prevails.

This may not seem to be the case for all societies at all times; but this is only because in some rare cases these higher valued human needs are to a large degree satisfied and are not, therefore, seen to be in competition with nationalism. Once altered circumstances threaten these more fundamental needs, however, loyalty is to the group that can preserve them, not to the state. This, for example, has been the response of Christians in Lebanon. In the majority of cases, underlying needs and values are submerged by reason of majority dominance and control, foreign interventions and a general apathy associated with abject poverty. Once altered conditions provide an opportunity to pursue these values, however, loyalty is to the relevant identity group, not to the state. This has been the case in Cyprus. Changes in population composition and migrations, changes in wealth distribution that create marked underprivilege and distributive injustice, and alterations in leadership and ideologies are amongst the many influences that give rise to protracted social conflicts where once there appeared to be political stability. Latin America, the Phillipines, Iran, Northern Ireland and Poland are but a few of the many places in which loyalty to the state has given way to loyalty to groups and movements.

Thus, we must give the term "nationalism" a different meaning—loyalty to the national group within the state. In many cases such national groups spill over into neighboring states. In some cases such national groups are present in many states. Muslims are demonstrating where their loyalty lies. In many instances Jews, Catholics, Blacks, Asians, Capitalists, and Communists have demonstrated loyalties that do not coincide with state "national interests." States are, for the most part, powerless to control this.

In the international and intercommunal fields we are dealing with issues for which men and women are prepared to fight and give their lives. We are dealing with conflicts that are protracted and even institutionalized, with no end in sight. Our task is not to find means of containment and suppression, as is done by traditional efforts of conflict settlement, but to determine the hidden data of motivation and intentions, and thus seek to resolve conflicts.

FROM POWER TO NEEDS

The sociological and international relations literature is now beginning to guide us in this search. On the basis of empirical evidence, Azar has argued that there are certain human needs, such as identity, recognition, security, participation, and control of the environment.[6] These same needs have been referred to by Sites as being at the root of the individual's allegiance to identity groups.[7] The next step is to make a clear distinction between ontological human needs and individual interests, such as commercial and role interests.

Azar has differentiated among interests, values and needs.[8] Interests are negotiable, can be bargained over, can be altered and traded. Values are cultural and are less subject to change and negotiation. Needs, however, are not for trading. No power bargaining, no judicial processes, no mediation, no negotiating techniques can alter the importance attached to them. It is needs that have been responsible over the ages for what freedoms have been acquired from serfdom in all its forms and from other institutions that deny full development of the individual. For Azar, this distinction among interests, values, and needs is a sufficient explanation—along with accompanying underdevelopment and external interventions—of conflicts in Lebanon and elsewhere, as well as of conflicts that appear to be conflicts of security and ideology.

Once a distinction is made between interests that can be negotiated, or even denied, and needs that are ontological to the human species and are not for trading and cannot be suppressed, we have differentiated two notions of conflict. Traditional means of settlement may be appropriate when only interests are at stake; but they are unlikely to be relevant or effective when values or needs are at issue.

This is a reconceptualization of conflict that has wide implications for conflict resolution. Classical thinking had led us to believe that conflict was only about interests and that there had to be winners and losers. As a result, it was thought the individual could be socialized and coerced into accepting certain social norms and means as a method to settle disputes. However, both theory and application reveal that protracted conflicts, the major concern in world politics, are primarily over nonnegotiable values. These values relate to human and identity needs such as those listed by Sites. As a result, it is impossible to socialize people into behaviors that run counter to their pursuit of security, identity, and other needs.

There is another distinction that we need to draw in making clearer the notion of conflict. Conflicts involve interests and needs. In addition, however, they also involve tactics. War is a tactic, a means to achieve the goal of interests or needs. Frequently conflicts are defined in terms of tactics, and the underlying interests or needs remain beneath the surface. In industrial relations, wage demands sometimes disguise underlying dissatisfaction with management. Wages are then negotiated instead of working conditions. In international relations, disputes over territory or boundaries sometimes relate to anxieties over security or values attached to ethnic identity, and are negotiated (or, give rise to wars) without the basic problems being addressed. In conflict resolution—as distinct from settlement—we are seeking processes that reveal the hidden data of motivation and intention, be they tactics, interests or needs. We seek some process whereby the underlying issues that do not come to the surface in power bargaining and adversary behavior are revealed.

It will be apparent that this view of conflict at the international level undermines the widespread belief that international conflict is a phenomenon different and separate from domestic conflict. We are discovering that domestic and international conflict are one and the same thing. Therefore, we will miss the explanation we seek if we have a narrow conception of global politics that is inter-state. We must seek the origins of what appears as international conflict in the failings of domestic systems to provide for the needs of people.

In *Global Conflict—The Domestic Sources of International Crisis*, I have argued that many conflicts (including the communist-capitalist conflict between the Soviet Union and its allies and the United States and its allies) reflect failings and insecurities in domestic systems, each side blaming the other for its own inadequacies.[9] In the United States there are increasing inequalities of income and opportunity, and the emergence of a poor underclass pushed even further down by cuts in welfare and support services. The possible establishment of welfare-type states on its borders is a challenge that the United States resists. Such innovations challenge U.S. authorities, their values and their institutions, thus threatening their legitimized status. Likewise, in the Soviet Union there are obvious signs of restlessness arising out of the nature of the controls that affect everyday life.

The legitimization of authorities is the focus of attention in the new paradigm, not their powers of coercion or defence. The separation of domestic from international that is a feature of traditional international relations studies has been misleading and has led to false notions of the nature of conflict. There is probably no phenomenon that can accurately be labelled international conflict that is not a spillover of domestic system failings and domestic politics.

These system failings and their political manifestations reflect failure to satisfy human needs, needs of identity, of participation and of distributive justice. Stated in political terms, these system failings that spill over into the world society reflect a lack of legitimization of government authority. In the world society many states are governed by elites that, while legal (that is, in control and internationally recognized), have little legitimized support. They rely on their own and on foreign military power to remain in control.

This continuing conflict between human demands and elite resistance has been embodied in Western political philosophy. Western party political systems of government are adversarial in their legal and political institutions. The underlying political-legal philosophy on which they are based is the classical one, that there are those who have a right to expect obedience and others who have a moral obligation to obey. Empirically, however, we have to conclude that the right of the elite to expect obedience is a right derived from possession of the power necessary to impose values and institutions on others. This applies at all social levels, from the family, the school, and the workplace to the highest political level. And now, because of a variety of historical and contemporary circumstances, which have played into the hands of individuals and identity groups, power elites are under fire in many countries.

The final goal of conflict resolution is the establishment of the legitimacy of authority, the creation of institutions that serve the needs of those over whom authority is exercised, and the promotion of values attached to relationships between authorities and people. Whether the authority be the parent, the manager, the community leader, the government, or the international institution, the avoidance and resolution of conflict finally rests on valued, not coerced or socialized, relationships.[10]

THE PROBLEM OF STRUCTURAL CHANGE

It follows that conflict resolution processes must be concerned with finding the political structures which promote the full development of the individual and the identity group to which the individual belongs. Structural change must be designed to explore options that satisfy needs, and to make clear to all parties the costs and consequences of resistance to change. Such structural and institutional changes might include the development of decentralized systems and forms of functional cooperation that avoid power and power sharing. This approach makes possible respect among identity groups and provides for effective cooperation between different cultures. Structures that are decentralized and rely on functional cooperation rather than elite power are the logical extension of certain trends now a part of social evolution. Such trends include the progressive movement from authoritative power control by a small elite (of which feudalism was a part) to forms of power sharing and nonpower forms of cooperative decisionmaking.

If the identity group is the locus of power, it is institutions that must adjust to it, not the other way around. This is not a condition of anarchy. To the contrary, constraints operate that ensure respect for appropriate institutions and social norms, since individuals and groups have needs for valued relationships with others. It is through these that security, identity and recognition ultimately are acquired. Social conformity or socialization is limited to that which contributes to valued relationships. Law and order imposed via the coercion of authorities can be maintained only to the extent that relationships with authorities are valued. It is this pursuit of valued relationships in order to satisfy needs that assures loyalty to the identity group: the state—in those rare cases in which the state is a nation-state—the nation, the community, the ethnic group, or if circumstances require, a deviant society.

Thus, in resolving a conflict situation we are led inevitably to a consideration of political structures and political institutions, and the degree to which they make possible the fulfillment of human needs. When the United States endeavored to impose a strong central government on Lebanon as the means whereby to achieve a stable regime, it was acting within a power or coercive framework that defined democracy and law and order in power terms. But it was confronting values that were attached to identity groups, and the need for the security and recognition of cultural differences. For this reason the U.S. policy could not succeed. In Cyprus, the government of the majority, acting within the traditions of Western political philosophy, sought a political structure that made second-class citizens of the Turkish minority, and it was doomed to fail. Appeals for settlements by those in power, based on normative notions of law and order, are mere bargaining ploys. Power negotiations within the framework of existing structures are unlikely to resolve conflicts. The structural issue has finally to be faced.

The boundaries that have resulted from colonial wars and the population changes that have resulted from migrations and uneven population increases, present us today with scores of other explosive situations, triggered by underdevelopment and underprivilege. In the Middle East, in Africa, and in the economically developed world, there will be increasing numbers of conflicts within states and across boundaries, as identity groups—which include class groups—seek means of pursuing their security and developmental needs.

A resolution process is, therefore, one through which status quo parties can make an accurate costing of the consequences of maintaining systems that are not accepted, and arrive at options that both preserve their needs and values, and also make possible their pursuit by others. In some circumstances and for limited periods of time, the assessment might be made that the existing situation can be maintained—an assessment, for example, white South Africans seem to have made in the past. What a conflict resolution process must be able to do is to provide those insights that enable accurate prediction, both in time and in costs, of allowing conflicts to be prolonged.

This places scholars and practitioners who pursue conflict resolution in an awkward position. They are concerned with change. To argue that there can be no stability in Central and South America—or in the United States itself—until there is distributive justice—until, that is, many of the demands of rebels are met, is not as easy politically as taking a normative power-bargaining approach. This is a challenge that anyone in the field of conflict resolution, theory or practice, must face.

RESEARCH IMPLICATIONS

The distinction that conflict resolution approaches draw between tactics, interests, and needs has important implications for those researching and practicing conflict settlement and resolution. Some scholars adopt a legal approach and seek to improve bargaining techniques. They believe these two can be combined in processes by which parties amend draft agreements, such drafts sometimes being prepared by a third party or mediator. There are those, on the other hand, who adopt a problem-solving approach which is analytical, in which the third party assists in analysis, but does not put proposals forward, and in which options that satisfy both parties are explored.

There are some distinctive assumptions underlying this approach. *First,* it holds that there is a distinction to be made between interests that are negotiable and needs that are not for trading. This is not an arbitrary or subjective distinction: certain needs exist that are ontological and not negotiable. Such needs are pursued regardless of human costs and consequences, and socialization processes and coercion do not seem to be able to stem the drive to achieve them. *Second,* it holds that the identity group, not the state, is both the appropriate unit of analysis and the source of conflict. In other words, the assertion is that effective political power rests finally with identity groups (ethnic, cultural, language, class, and other) and not with state authorities. Empirical evidence is supportive of both of these assertions.

Conflicts over material interests tend to lead to win-lose outcomes in which the gain of the one is the loss of the other, whereas conflicts over human needs have possible win-win outcomes. This is because basic needs, such as identity, security, recognition, justice, and political participation, can be met without depriving others. In fact, in most cases, the supply of the resource increases because of reciprocal behavior.

Facilitated international conflict resolution, as the problem-solving approach is sometimes referred to, has the following significant and related features:

1. It seeks to differentiate between interests that are negotiable and the underlying, basic motivations and values that cannot be bargained away.
2. It examines motives and values, perceptions of motives and values, and confusions between interests, tactics, and goals.
3. It provides an opportunity to assess the cost of ignoring, suppressing, or failing to promote revealed nonnegotiable needs.
4. It seeks to assist parties in dispute to deduce what alterations in structures, institutions, and policies are required if needs are to be fulfilled. Such fulfillment applies equally to the needs of persons previously deprived and to those whose interests are threatened by potential change.
5. It seeks to assist the parties involved in monitoring events and communications perceptively. It is also of assistance in anticipating responses and making the parties aware of important policy details as they move toward improved relationships. These activities are carried out both during the stage of conflict and during the transition to peace.

This approach to conflict resolution is not limited to ethnic, communal, class, or national conflicts within states. The same basic considerations affect international global relations, including the interactions of the great powers.

Some Cases

It is appropriate to refer briefly to two instances in which the nonbargaining, nonnegotiating, analytical process of interaction, assisted by facilitators, has been used recently by the Center for International Development at the University of Maryland.[11]

In September 1983 a meeting took place between a Tory and a Labour Member of the British House of Commons Foreign Affairs Committee, and members of the Argentine Council for Foreign Relations, and other members of the Council who were likely to be part of the new government then to be formed. There were present, also, appropriate scholars from Britain and Argentina. The purpose was to discuss the Falklands/Malvinas issue. The discussion was facilitated by a panel of five scholars drawn from different disciplines.

This preliminary meeting was followed by another in April 1984. This time, the five Argentine participants included members of the Congress Foreign Affairs Committee and of other congressional committees. These committees had refrained from formulating policies until they had the opportunity to meet with their British counterparts.

My colleagues at the center and I were impressed with two features of these meetings. First, there were discoveries made by the parties that could not possibly have been made within any formal, or even informal, bargaining and negotiating framework. The seminar format, including the third-party panel of scholars, was designed to ensure an analytical and exploratory discussion that would reveal the hidden data of motivation and intention.

Also impressive was the way in which what was discovered was typical of conflicts generally, and in accord with expectations based on the theoretical framework that took account of human-societal needs. For example, it became clear that the dispute over the islands was not exclusively, or even mainly, in relation to the islands as territory, or even sovereignty. The invasion was a liberating experience for Argentinians because of deeply-rooted feelings in relation to Britain, which clearly have to be tackled before there can be any lasting outcome on the islands issue.

There were, also, important payoffs for research. Here was an opportunity to consider the notion of sovereignty. In its legal form it is an all-or-nothing notion. Either there is sovereignty accorded or not. In practice this legal notion is a fiction. No small state is sovereign or in total control. Sovereignty is in reality a functional notion, not a legal notion. As a legal notion it is not negotiable. As a functional notion it invites cooperative interactions which are of mutual benefit. The same is true of other notions, such as majority government, democracy, and law and order, which are often at the root of conflict and made use of by the party that wishes to maintain the status quo, and to which we give little consideration.

In May 1984 the Center for International Development brought together eight Muslim and Christian Lebanese drawn from the various religious sects within the two major Lebanese communities. They were all closely associated with events there. This was followed in October of the same year by another meeting of persons directly representing leadership. Here again, it was impressive the way in which the discussions within this non-bargaining, facilitated, and exploratory framework led to discoveries that had not been made in the long years of violence and negotiation. Once again, there were discoveries that could be predicted within a needs-development conception. In particular, it came as no surprise to the panel, though it was a revelation to the Lebanese participants, to discover that there was a shared value attached to Lebanon as an entity, as the location of a special culture that was characteristically different from other Christian and Muslim cultures, and which all agreed must be preserved. This was not incompatible with the preservation of separate Christian and Islamic cultures as they had developed within Lebanon as a result of the interaction of the two. The final formula was that Lebanon was to be a united, independent, Arab state, a meeting ground of Christianity and Islam.

Experience had made clear some difficulties in the facilitated conflict resolution approach. First, there is an "entry" problem, that is, to persuade political leaders to risk the domestic repercussions in the event that these informal talks were to become known. Second, there is the "reentry" problem, that is, the problem participants have when they return with an agreed possible option and endeavour to communicate their findings to political leaders who have not had the experience of the facilitated process. Third, there is the "follow-up" problem, that is, keeping in touch with the parties and the parties keeping in touch with each other, sometimes during periods of actual fighting.

In addition to these three process problems, there are others that have been experienced. It sometimes takes two and three months to arrange meetings at times suited to all concerned. The work involved limits the number of cases that can be handled at the one time. There are very acute problems of finance as parties to disputes often cannot be seen to be financing these encounters, and minority parties in conflict with authorities frequently have no available finances.

All of these processes and administrative problems could possibly be solved, and certainly alleviated, by using modern communication technologies. "Official" interactions in the traditional power-negotiating model will not easily be transplanted. But analytical problem-solving processes or so-called "second track diplomacy" can run parallel with, and perhaps be a part of, official or first track diplomacy. The link between the two diplomacies is clearly important. It is a link that has not been explored in major negotiations: for example, arms negotiations. Clearly, an agreement on significant arms reductions is unlikely in the absence of some understanding of the underlying reasons for the perception of their need. An analytical problem-solving approach, facilitated by experienced persons, rather than a power-bargaining approach, would probably reveal unacknowledged or hidden common motivations and intentions, including domestic insecurities, that must be uncovered and tackled before there can be progress in arms negotiation.

PROTRACTED CONFLICTS

This analysis suggests why it is that almost all international conflicts are characterized by their continuity. There are attempts at negotiation, there are lulls in violent activity, but there are no permanent resolutions. It is understandable why conflicts are protracted in this way once we focus on the sources of conflict, sources such as security of identity communities, identity itself, accompanied by recognition of the identity, and other such universal needs and values.

A related reason for conflicts being protracted, emerging again after apparent settlement, lies in the very processes employed to obtain settlements. The diplomatic language of mediation and negotiation constantly makes reference to "leverage," "influence," and the role of major powers, which can exercise economic and other pressures on smaller states. Mediation itself carries with it some element of coercion insofar as there is an expectation that parties will accept the final proposals of the mediator. Stronger forms of intervention, such as judicial settlement, imply even greater coercion. Leverage, influence, persuasion, or any form of duress may result in a temporary settlement, but cannot resolve a conflict. As has been argued, there are needs that must be met, and over which there can be no compromise, if there is to be resolution rather than just a temporary solution.

Not only are traditional means of "peaceful settlement" characterized by "leverage," they are also devoid of analysis or means of analysis on which to base a resolution. Proposals from a mediator based on some external value system, external personal interpretation of events, some externally accepted international "norms", which do not reflect the basic needs and values of the parties, are unlikely to resolve conflicts. It is for this reason that conflicts are protracted by the processes employed to deal with them: the introduction of power diplomacy and the absence of an analysis of the conflict in question.

Such an analysis would help to explain the failure, not just of traditional diplomacy generally, but also of some of the specific techniques employed within it. When parties are confronted with a draft agreement, which they are then asked to amend in a negotiating framework, they are bound into the assumptions and philosophies that are implicit in the draft. An analytical approach would raise questions regarding the underlying needs and values. The settlements that U.S. officials are trying to manipulate in Central America will turn out to be temporary, at best, unless they fully take into account the needs for distributive justice and effective participation. For it is these needs that cannot be suppressed and are not for trading.

This analysis also suggests why it is that the record of the United Nations in conflict resolution is so poor. The UN can maintain "peace-keeping" operations, but it does not seem to be able to bring a conflict to the point of resolution. It has no analytical and non-coercive processes by which this can be done. There are some initiatives which are allowed to the Secretary-General. His interventions tend, however, to be the traditional mediatory ones in which the mediator makes proposals, which are then bargained over, rather than an analytical process through which new and acceptable options can be discovered. This must be expected as he has no staff that could conduct such a facilitated conflict-resolution process. The employment of consultants who could do this would raise all manner of problems within the decisionmaking processes of the organization. As a result, the conflicts handled by the United Nations, such as Cyprus, are protracted, to a large degree, by reason of the means employed to deal with them.

The requirement of conflict resolution is for processes that enable the parties concerned to be analytical and to arrive at agreements freely and outside any power framework. This means the finding of options that fully meet the needs of all parties, even though there is likely to be compromise on interests.[12]

CONCLUSION: THE PROBLEM OF CHANGE

At this time we can offer some hope to a world society that seems devoid of it. But it is restricted hope. The evolution of civilization has always required adjustment to change, yet "survival of the fittest" requires built-in mechanisms for resistance to change, until existing structures can no longer meet the challenge of competing ones. In the same way, leadership and elites seek to conserve existing roles and institutions by whatever power-means are at their disposal, until overcome by more powerful forces. Societies have always been in potential conflict because some factions drive toward change to fulfill their human needs, while others fear change and its threat to their interests. Change has traditionally been regarded as malign and antisocial. We have not developed a language for it, except a negative one—revolt, revolution, dissent, terrorism. Without a language and a conceptual framework we can have no theory of change, and, therefore, no processes of change except those of power and violence.

The shift from power to relationships as the explanation of events, the shift from the state to identity groups as the unit of analysis, and the shift in conflict resolution from power bargaining and normative processes to problem-solving ones based on human needs, are shifts that are paradigm shifts of a fundamental nature. They are challenging and offer a light of hope. Yet the full implications are not easy to grasp.

The evolving conflict-resolution processes are effective only to the extent that parties to disputes help to cost accurately the consequences of change and the resistance to change. In this sense, the processes of facilitated conflict resolution are designed to cut down the delays and upheavals that occur in change and to speed up the evolutionary process toward greater fulfillment of societal needs. Change can thus be more than the mere substitution of one ruling elite for another, who will pursue factional interests at the expense of human needs.

This is an important discovery when translated onto the global scene and the relations between the great powers, since both sides fear change lest it prejudice their relative power positions. Yet both sides know that change in many political systems is not merely inevitable, but also desirable. The United States does not particularly desire to defend repressive feudal systems in Central America and elsewhere throughout the globe, but it fears the consequences of unpredictable political change which could challenge its own system. The Soviet Union, if we can deduce its position from reactions by scholars there, was astonished and dismayed by the high level of violence that followed change in Ethiopia. If there were a reliable means of bringing about change with desired outcomes, many local situations would no longer attract great power interventions.

One dreams of great power agreements and an institutionalized means by which conflicts in any number of situations are subjected to an analytical problem-solving process before there is any transfer of arms or interventions by the great powers or by others. The dream includes each of the great powers giving the other the opportunity to change, helping the other to change, and not exploiting the existence of deformities that could finally lead one of the great powers to some desperate act of survival. Conflict resolution based on human needs is a step in the right direction.

NOTES

1. Edward E. Azar and John W. Burton, eds., *International Conflict Resolution, Theory and Practice* (Wheatsheaf and Lynne Rienner, 1986).

2. Michael Banks, ed., *Conflict in World Society: A New Perspective on International Relations* (St. Martin's, 1984); John Burton, *Conflict and Communication* (Macmillan, 1969).

3. R. R. Blake, H. A. Shepard and J. S. Mouton, *Managing Inter-Group Conflict in Industry* (Juef, 1964).

4. David Davis Memorial Institute, *Report of a Study Group on the Peaceful Settlement of International Disputes* (1966).

5. Paul Sites, *Control: The Basis of Social Order* (Dunellen, 1973).

6. Azar and Burton, *International Conflict Resolution.*

7. Sites, *Control.*

8. Azar and Burton, *International Conflict Resolution.*

9. John W. Burton, *Deviance, Terrorism and War: A Study of Process in the Solving of Unsolved Social and Political Problems* (St. Martin's, 1979); and Sites, *Control.*

10. John W. Burton, *Global Conflict: The Domestic Sources of International Crisis* (Wheatsheaf, 1984).

11. Christopher Mitchell, *The Structure of International Conflict* (Macmillan, 1981).

12. Ibid.; and Christopher Mitchell, *Peacemaking and the Consultants's Role* (Gower Press, 1981).

CHAPTER TEN

Global Institutions
and the Pursuit of Human Needs

CRAIG MURPHY

*Craig Murphy draws on the findings of a much larger research project on
the relationship between the history of industrialization and the evolution of
intergovernmental organizations (IGOs) to explore the extent to which IGOs
satisfy and promote individual human needs. Distinguishing between
"basic" human needs and "fundamental" human needs, Murphy reports that
IGOs have been more responsive to meeting individual human needs in
certain areas than in others. He closes by discussing the implications of
these activities by IGOs for future global stability and prosperity. Murphy,
an associate professor of political science at Wellesley College, is a
specialist on international organization, international political economy,
and international development. Among other works, he is the author of* The
Emergence of the NIEO Ideology *(Boulder, Colorado: Westview, 1984).*

A focus on needs is not new to the study and practice of international
organization (IO). Many studies of IO, as well as of development, have
taken a "basic human needs" approach, emphasizing the importance of
satisfying certain basic physical requirements for daily living (Johan
Galtung: ch. 7). However, here I want to distinguish between "basic" human
needs and "fundamental" human needs, the latter concept being consistent
with the definition and use of needs taken in this volume. Accordingly, this
chapter examines the extent to which large intergovernmental organizations,
especially those in the United Nations' system, satisfy and promote
individual human needs.

I argue that IGOs have not been responsive to fundamental human needs
in the conflict resolution area, where the traditional role of nation-states has
remained prominent (as demonstrated by John Burton). However, IGOs
have been much more important in contributing to the fulfillment of human

needs when dealing with dependent peoples, especially throughout the Third World: promoting decolonization, responding to the social welfare of refugees, furthering the modernization of societies and improving the overall standard of living of individuals. The things that IGOs do, which immediately benefit individuals, have always been determined by the activities of these organizations in issue areas other than conflict resolution.

THE PLACE OF MEETING BASIC NEEDS IN THE OVERALL IGO AGENDA

These observations have resulted from a much larger research project on the connections between the history of IGOs and the history of industrialization and provide some indication of just how important "basic-needs" policies and other IGO policies affecting individuals, are within the whole IGO agenda. Let me explain the basis for these conclusions.

I began this research by creating a list of global IGOs, adding autonomous secretariat divisions identified by Manley to Jacobson's standard list of such entities.[1] I also added organizations disbanded before 1980 but found on Wallace and Singer's historical list.[2] To identify sources covering the entire history of each organization I consulted standard IGO bibliographies and the subject catalogs of the New York Public Library, which has had a policy of collecting works on IGOs and has maintained a subject catalog, including citations to articles, throughout most of the 120-year history of global IGOs. Following procedures similar to coding events data, I read each of the sources and recorded what they reported were the ongoing activities of each organization, coding all of the active statements in which an IGO was the subject that referred to a repeated, externally directed action.

My unit of analysis was the "activity." Each record of an activity included the *decade* in which the organization carried out the activity, a standard *organization identity number,* the *verb* found in the source statement, and the rest of the source statement, which can be considered detailed description of the *issue area* of activity. In addition, I recorded the more general political-economic issue area the activity most immediately affects: 1) commerce; 2) labor; 3) economic development; 4) interstate relations; and, finally, the focus of this paper, 5) relations between individuals and government.[3] As a result of my investigations, some initial observations can be made with respect to the importance of human needs in IGOs in each of these areas.

Commerce

Over 50 percent of all the activities in the data set immediately affect commercial relations between firms and sectors. Most of these activities help liberalize the global economy—standardizing and lowering costs of shipping and communication, making trade restrictions transparent, and encouraging intergovernmental agreements to reduce trade barriers. National governments tend to give IGOs commercial responsibilities in response to demands from the world's most productive sectors, sectors which attract highly mobile capital. Those leading sectors find themselves in conflict with other, not as productive, often cartelized sectors. Leading sectors win their battles to give IGOs new responsabilities whenever they can mobilize many other sectors against specific protectionist interests. That is why the majority of IGO commercial activities affect transportation and communication, sectors whose services are used by all firms involved in the international economy, who together make a powerful bloc for liberalization.

IGO health activities, which affect individuals, arose along with commercial responsibilities to confine west Asian and tropical diseases so that international trade would be less subject to unpredictable quarantines and less suspect as a carrier of exotic disease. As medical science changed its primary way of controlling disease from quarantine, to treatment, to prevention, IGOs responded, becoming concerned with improving individual health.[4] When IGOs propose programs to free all individuals from an infectious disease, they find strong allies in those whose livelihood depends on the continuously increasing international flow of goods and people. Not surprisingly, IGO programs to limit or eradicate diseases probably have had more impact on more people than any other IGO activities that immediately affect individuals.

Labor

About 15 percent of the activities affect factor markets. The bulk involve IGOs promoting international standards for labor in highly productive sectors and promoting ways to shift the cost of maintaining those standards to national economies as a whole. In one sense, IGO activities in this issue area again favor the leading sectors in the global economy, but only to the extent that the increasing political power of organized labor in those sectors, which always triggers the development of these IGO responsibilities, is understood as inevitable.

International labor standards are not enforced by the International Labour Organisation's meager autonomous powers, but labor and employers in leading sectors have an interest in seing that standards are applied in all competing industrial economies. As a result, standards like maximum hours of work in factories and offices, and bans on child labor in factories are fairly uniformly enforced throughout the industrial world. Even in newly industrializing nations, few order-of-magnitude differences in labor standards tend to be imposed, largely as a result of a coalition of local, newly powerful, industrial workers, along with international pressure from older industrial nations. This is part of what has been happening recently in South Korea. Nonetheless, where local economies cannot compete with the world's most productive ones, a worker's basic needs can be ignored.

Development

Another 15 percent of the cases are development activities immediately affecting relationships between traditional and modern economies. IGOs help expand modern economies and, much less frequently, help maintain the coherence of traditional economies. The fundamental IGO role, the World Bank's original purpose, is to make the capital investment needed to transform traditional economies and make them less risky by identifying and aiding the process of modernization in places where existing economic conditions and government attitudes suggest that long-term capital investment can be made the most profitably. IGO activities in this issue area again can be said to favor highly mobile international capital. Yet, IGOs were given responsibilities in this issue area not only to protect capital, but also in reaction to demands by modernizing nationalists, first in eastern Europe and west Asia in the inter-war years, later in all parts of the world.

Responding to nationalist struggles, IGOs promulgated what might be called "modernization rights" of individuals that have become standard operational definitions of how some basic needs should be satisfied. These include rights to universal and compulsory modern primary education and access to advanced modern education. Many colonial governments granted those rights under pressure from local nationalist movements and from IGOs, but little IGO pressure on governments to assure those rights can be sustained after colonialism has ended.

Inter-State Relations

A number of IGO responsibilities immediately affecting relations between states also triggered IGO responsibilities toward individuals. IGOs have responsibilities to the living victims of past failures of the global "security" system—political refugees and some minorities. State systems have always created such victims, but IGOs were given responsibilities toward them only at a specific point in the history of the modern global political economy, the point at which opportunities for massive emigration of refugees and oppressed minorities to relatively unsettled lands became few. Since 1919 global IGOs have continuously been responsible for a shifting population of victims constituting about two-tenths of one percent of the world's total.[5]

IGOs overseeing the provision of an internationally agreed-upon set of minimum government services to refugees have a larger job than most national governm' .its undertake; the current refugee population of about eight million exceeds that of more than half of the state members of the international systems.

IGO responsibilities to the victims of international security systems immediately serve both states and the individuals involved. They also influence the development of IGO responsibilities to all individuals. IGOs establish standards of service for all refugees, minimum physical standards of nutrition and shelter that must be provided to all, and minimum political, social, and cultural rights that must be respected. The standards actually employed by global IGOs to judge the provision of services to the victims for whom they are responsible result in a major source of IGO-sponsored definitions of basic needs and human rights of all people.[6]

Of course, the IGO system has little ability to influence the satisfaction of basic needs and the maintenance of human rights outside refugee camps. IGO standards do serve as guides for aid programs oriented toward individuals, like the United Nations Children's Fund (UNICEF), which remains unusually free to choose its own goals because it obtains much of its funds in small donations from individuals rather from government grants. Otherwise, the most that global IGOs can do to promote comprehensive respect for basic needs and human rights is to engage in moral suasion based on information from a somewhat haphazard reporting system. National governments that are happy to let global IGOs provide minimum services to people who owe allegiance to no government are much less interested in having IGOs investigate the services provided to individuals over whom they claim authority. As a result, the material significance of almost all the IGO activities on behalf of individuals depends upon other forces in world society. What IGOs do to meet basic needs continues to depend on the forces that have given rise to IGO responsibilities in other issue areas.

GLOBAL INSTITUTIONS AND FUNDAMENTAL NEEDS: DEFINITIONS

People deprived of their basic physical needs and fundamental human rights find small comfort in IGO proclamations. In the world of concrete cases rather than abstract principles, IGOs rarely support individuals against any national government. The World Bank's former president, Robert McNamara, tried to establish the principle that the satisfaction of everyone's basic needs is in all of our interests by forcefully making the classical argument that the materially deprived *will* rebel. By responding to basic human needs, he and others in the area of development meant the necessity of satisfying certain basic physical requirements of individuals that guaranteed a minimal level of survival and standard of living. However, he found few new allies for the poor because the evidence was deemed to be too weak.

Yet, in order to see all the ways IGOs actually do affect individuals, it is useful to look at the connection between human needs and rebellion, as discussed by John Burton.[7] Instead of asking, "Will people fight when certain (already specified) needs are not met?" we ask, "For what needs (to be determined empirically) will people even fight?" We can call these "fundamental needs" to distinguish them from the sets of basic needs usually evaluated in studies of global IGOs. Fundamental needs are what people must have in order to survive, develop, and cope with change in their lives.

Fundamental needs can be defined as the key attributes of a cybernetic actor, as used by Karl Deutsch, identifying "memory" and its links to the environment through learning.[8] Or fundamental needs can be defined by focusing on the social psychology of learning itself, as in Burton, identifying an environment in which real changes can be distinguished from the unchanging background (thus, implicitly, identifying an image of the world that allows such distinctions to be made).[9] Thus, fundamental needs include the security and recognition needed to reinforce learning (by linking new information back to images that include a coherent and positive image of self), as well as the development of a sense of identity itself, including personal hopes and expectations. Here are two examples of how such needs, especially the need for identity, will be met come what may:

A Nigerian

An African university student, about to flunk out at the end of his second year, doubts his own abilities but is unsure of the source of his problems because of the seemingly random information coming at him from a university understaffed enough that overworked professors explain grades with the first thing that pops into their heads and may never have read a student's exam anyway. Some professors accept bribes. Assigned books fail to appear in the library. Supplies are scarce. Student stipends are paid months late in devalued currency, forcing the student to work long hours far from campus because he was told by one professor, who later failed him, that to work during a term was "unscholarly." ("Did he see me across town?") The student cuts through all the randomness by noticing that he is the only Northerner in his class, and the only classmate to have failed. He has failed because Northerners are not allowed to succeed. All the separately inexplicable, seemingly random insults he has experienced for two years now form a consistent background to this new "information."

An Assimilado

A "Portuguese" shopkeeper living on one of the Cape Verde islands in 1975, saving money to send his son to the university in Lisbon, learns from the radio that the government in Lisbon has decided to turn the island over to the revolutionaries who have been fighting the Portuguese army hundreds of miles away in Africa. Not only are these foreigners to take over, but Lisbon has declared that no one in Cape Verde is Portuguese. They are all African. Portuguese universities will be much more selective in letting these "foreigners" in. His son, who has never been the best in his class, will have no chance. Crushed, the shopkeeper tells his brother, visiting from America, "What is this! I am no poor black! I am no communist! I am no African! But they tell me I am no Portuguese, too!" "True," says his brother, "you are no Portuguese. In America we've known that all along. There the Portuguese treat us like dirt and the blacks want us to say we are black, too. But we say we are 'Cape Verdeans.' You are Cape Verdean. Your son is Cape Verdean. He shouldn't be going to university in Lisbon with Portuguese, or becoming an African communist; he should go to university with other Cape Verdeans, in Massachussetts or Rhode Island." Denied one part of a coherent identity, and denied recognition by an old government in which he put his faith and a new one that will completely deny his identity as he understands it, the shopkeeper accepts the recommendation of a brother who recognizes his most important dreams, and "becomes" a Cape Verdean.

So far I have discussed fundamental needs only as individual needs, but they have social implications and implications for governments as well. When individuals cannot continue to meet fundamental needs by maintaining relationships to existing institutions they will break those relationships and form new identity groups (in the term found in Deutsch's work, groups that can remember and learn together) in conflict with the existing social order. For example, as Deutsch's work shows, modern nationalism arose in large part as a way that people in modernizing societies, confronting great political and economic change, could meet their fundamental needs for identity and recognition.

In some cases the power of identity groups in conflict with the existing social order means civil war. Place the failing university student of the first example in Nigeria in 1965 and you have the makings of a staunch supporter of the anti-Ibo counter-coup and the crushing of Biafra.

Perhaps much less frequently, it can mean that governments have an incentive to join with the identity group itself, declaring itself the government of the disaffected and allowing enough participation by them that their personal hopes and expectations become bound up with the hopes and expectations of the government. By 1980 many of the revolutionaries who had returned to Cape Verde in 1975 had seen many of their comrades, born in the islands, kicked out of the "sister republics" on the African mainland that they had helped to liberate. The government stopped calling itself first and foremost an "African" or "liberation" government and started to call itself "Cape Verdean." It contacted people born in the islands and living abroad, especially in New England, set up a sort of "law of return" and opened channels for widespread participation and dissent. In a sense, the government was forced to find its own identity in the people it governed.

Relatively prosperous people who formed identity groups in conflict with their government usually need not either become partisans of civil war or rely upon the outside chance that their government will be forced to follow them. They often have the option of ignoring their government or leaving its jurisdiction.

At the other extreme, those who are the most deprived materially can find that death confronts them when they meet their fundamental needs. Hans Christian Andersen's "Little Match Girl," creating a fantasy of security and identity out of her last bits of consciousness as she froze to her death, is a powerful image of need satisfaction at the extreme. Fanon's clinical reports of the dreams of strength reported by the most victimized people in colonial Algeria are even more moving, because we cannot dismiss them as fiction.[10]

FUNDAMENTAL NEEDS, CONFLICT MANAGEMENT, AND CONFLICT RESOLUTION

What do global IGOs have to with meeting fundamental human needs? Surprisingly little. The vast majority of violent conflict since the Second World War can be traced to people attempting to meet fundamental needs through groups in conflicts with existing authorities in the Third World. Even though the "security" activities of global IGOs have been directed toward the same conflicts, IGOs do not address the problem of meeting fundamental needs.[11] Rather, the IGO goal is, as the title of one study puts it, *Moderation Through Management*.[12]

We can distinguish between *resolving* conflicts and *managing* them. Given our definition of fundamental human needs, "conflict resolution" is the process through which parties to a conflict work together to see how each can meet its fundamental needs without protracting the conflict; they treat their conflict as a joint problem arising out of the ways they have met fundamental needs in the past. "Conflict management" as practiced by global IGOs involves using all means *except* conflict resolution in order to moderate the effects of conflicts on the international order (the relations of dominance of government over the governed, the maintenance of boundaries of "sovereignty" between governments, and the maintenance of the global hierarchy of autonomous national governments). In addition, at times conflict management aims at moderating the effects that conflicts have in satisfying basic needs.

Historically, the range of means used by global IGOs to manage conflicts has been wide. They have intervened on the side of one party (usually that of a national government facing rebels) and helped physically subject the opposition. They have placed neutral troops between warring parties. Backed by regional powers or by superpower agreement, IGOs have invoked and enforced prior agreements between warring parties. Also, IGOs have facilitated direct bargaining between parties over scarce goods—land, mineral rights, etc.—at issue in global conflicts. IGOs even propose and help maintain cultural, economic, social, and political boundaries between states.[13]

None of these means of conflict management address the fundamental needs of the groups in conflict. Subject people can still maintain their identity, and through it, their conflict with those who have subjected them. People isolated from each other by troops or by international agreements, even if they have full autonomy within their own boundaries, can retain memories of past victimization by those from whom they are separated. And, unlike material things, fundamental needs cannot be divided; they cannot be met only partially; they cannot be bargained over.

Conflict resolution, as it is practiced in many labor-management settings and in international conflict resolution workshops, focuses on fundamental needs. The mutuality of working together itself helps meet the need for recognition. The act of focusing on the conflict as an identifiable problem makes it easier for all parties to learn from the past. And, of course, because the process treats human needs for security and identity as fundamental and nonnegotiable, conflict-protracting challenges to them can be avoided.

Before the global IGO system could promote conflict resolution, governments would have to shift their views about global conflicts as significantly as some employers and unions in industrial countries have had to shift their views about industrial conflict before adopting participatory means for resolving them.

To illustrate one key assumption of the traditional state-power paradigm that most officials would have to give up is that some decisionmakers act "irrationally." In the traditional paradigm the nemesis is the "revolutionary state," the state governed by decisionmakers so irrational as to believe that their worldview not only is correct, but that they can and must impose it upon the whole world.[14] Traditionalists grant that people can react violently when their sense of self is challenged and that a sense of self includes expectations for the future. These writers believe that the problem with the revolutionary state is that its leaders' sense of self is bound to be crushed.

Remembering that the international system arose when Europe was nearly pulled apart by Protestant Reformation and Catholic Counter-Reformation, traditionalists believe that an essential characteristic of modernity is that no all-encompassing worldview can be imposed on all people. What links Napoleon, Hitler, and Khomeini, in the traditionalist's view, is their denial of this "fact." Such leaders of revolutionary states are bound to be disappointed, but in the meantime they will wreak havoc if they are allowed to try to remake the world in their own image.

If such visions are "irrational," meaning only that they cannot be fulfilled, the traditional response is to moderate the horror such governments can wreak by forcibly stopping them, isolating them, forcing them to live up to international norms, or even bargaining with them by letting them carry out their projects as completely as they can, but only within a strictly contained realm.

Alternatively, as Burton argues, someone who believes in the possibility of global conflict resolution must believe that "parties to a conflict are responding to the situation in the ways that appear most beneficial to them in light of the knowledge that they have of the modifications of others and the option open: 'irrational' behavior is behavior not understood or approved by others."[15] To put the point both more concretely and more bluntly: to believe in the possibility of conflict resolution means to believe that those who follow the Hitlers and Khomeinis of the world, if given more information about their own motivations and those of others, and more possible ways to meet their fundamental needs, would not choose to do so through doomed movements that would deny the fundamental needs of others. At the very least, someone who entertains the assumptions that underlie this alternative approach to understanding global conflict would want to know what made Khomeini's followers identify with a messianic Shiism and what made Hitler's followers identify with Aryan imperialism.[16]

Such reflection takes us back to complex histories of what Azar and Farah call "structural victimization" which typifies rapidly changing societies in which people are forced to shift identities to meet fundamental needs.[17] Faced with limited options, people in rapidly changing societies often identify with groups whose "action scripts" turn the former victims of social change into victimizers of yet another group, whose subsequent search for new ways to meet their own needs continues the process. Perhaps the entire nineteenth and twentieth century histories of the center of international crises—east and central Europe, southwest Asia, and north Africa—can be told as that of a single chain of structural victimization.

Global IGOs are not equipped to consider that view history, or to trust in the long-term rationality of adherents to all-encompassing ideologies. The contemporary global IGO system for managing conflicts was created by the victors in a long struggle against revolutionary states whose behavior appeared to confirm every assumption of the traditional state-power paradigm. The genesis of the contemporary IGO system would be reason enough for its practice to affirm another key traditional assumption: "the interests of the greater powers and world society as a whole must sometimes be placed before the interests of the parties [in the conflict]."[18] In contrast, to resolve rather than manage conflicts we must assume that "in any conflict, the relations of the parties most directly concerned take precedence and are then subjected to the resolution of any conflict they have with interests at other levels."[19]

Yet, it may not be just the tragedy of the Second World War that has resulted in global IGOs that always concern themselves first with maintaining the structure of global society, and makes them suspicious of too much direct participation by conflict parties in any process of dealing with global conflicts. There may be economic reasons as well. The political economy of IGOs suggests that every aspect of the global IGO system develops to serve the current order, just as states (in the political economic sense defined above) help reproduce the geographic dominance of particular coalitions of sectors, classes, and modes of production. IGOs, arising out of states, can be understood as institutions that help maintain the state system, as well as (if my hypotheses are correct) help to maintain the importance of globally mobile capital and the current "class compromise" between labor and employers in the highly productive industries most attractive to such investment.

If the global IGO system is, inherently, a protector of the current order it must remain suspicious of challenges. It cannot be expected to grant an equal hearing to challengers. It cannot be expected to facilitate the participation of challengers in fundamental decisions about the future, even if that is what resolution of global conflicts would require.

Like most students of international relations, I am enough influenced by the state power tradition and its interpretation of history to be loath to see the conflict management role of IGOs abandoned. But I am realistic enough to see that conflict management may only perpetuate global conflict through chains of structural victimization, suggesting a need for institutions which can resolve conflicts since IGOs cannot.

An Important Exception: Global IGOs and Dependent People

The history of real institutions is never quite so straightforward as the necessary simplifications of even the most sophisticated social science models. The role of global IGOs in helping people meet fundamental needs is no exception. For a time parts of the UN system promoted conflict resolution—not the "the security" agencies, but the Trusteeship Council and other agencies dealing with dependent peoples.

For two decades after the Second World War a balance of power prevailed within the UN between those who refused to let colonizing states and colonists have any say in the process of decolonization and those who would refuse to let dependent people have any part. Disagreement extended down into the government of the most powerful state, the U.S., and even into the governments of some of the colonizers.

As a result, the global IGO system could act as a conflict resolver, bringing all parties into a process of solving the problem of decolonization. IGOs especially had this role in the decolonization of many African states that were lucky enough to be so poor and out of the way that IGOs focused on the needs of the parties involved rather than the interests of the superpowers.[20]

Now the superpowers find implications for their interests in conflicts in even the poorest parts of the globe. Even if they did not, the very sucess of decolonization removed the conditions that made it possible for the global IGO system to have a direct role in conflict resolution. By the time the former African colonies gained their independence, in the mid-1970s, wide agreement had developed within the UN about which parties in current world conflicts should be refused a hearing. Because almost all the world had been incorporated into nation-state members of the UN, few traditional anti-colonial nationalist movements remained. IGOs now rarely support the identity groups around the world that are fighting to assure their fundamental needs are met simply because now almost all these groups challenge the legitimacy of some state member much more fundamentally than did nationalists opposing a colonial state centered thousand of miles away.

In the few cases where true nationalist movements remain (e.g., SWAPO in Namibia), and in cases that are a bit more complex (e.g., the PLO and the liberation movements in South Africa), the influx of new nations into the IGO system assures that the consensus will be against current governments. Most would find it as difficult, on moral grounds, to fault the UN's treatment of South Africa as they would to praise the UN's ostracism of rebels fighting against repressive regimes. But the UN's ability to recognize internal challengers to the legitimacy of most members, assures that its role as a facilitator of conflict resolution has come to an end.[21]

THE FUTURE: GLOBAL IGOs AND BASIC NEEDS

Global institutions have played a larger role in satisfying basic human needs than in meeting fundamental human needs, in part, simply because they can do so without challenging the international status quo, either the state system itself or the interests of the great powers. At a government-to-government level, IGO commercial activities mean little diminution of sovereignty. They involve little more than collecting and providing information to governments and to business consumers, and also reducing transaction costs of intergovernmental cooperation by providing conference services and maintaining international accounts, in exactly the way that Keohane's theory of international institutions would predict.[22] Beyond providing information and reducing transaction costs of intergovernmental cooperation, IGO labor standard-setting is enforced by reporting procedures and retaliation. This is a somewhat larger use of enforcement powers than would be predicted by Keohane's theory, which otherwise would explain the pattern of IGO activities quite well. But again, these powers imply little challenge to the contemporary balance of power or to the governments of any nation, except, perhaps, the few newly industrializing countries where international labor standards are just beginning to be enforced. But even there, the power behind such enforcement is local labor unions and the lead sectors in the "graduating" economy; IGOs are only standard-setting allies. And, once again, the interests of the major powers are not challenged.

The development area is only a little different. Beyond providing information and reducing transaction costs of intergovernmental cooperation, activities in this issue area are enforced by empowering modern economies within modernizing countries against the government and against traditional economies. Development IGOs "tilt" toward development elites. In time perhaps more of these organizations than UNICEF will also find that they need to "tilt" toward meeting basic needs as well, that is, if IGOs discover they cannot fulfill their aims without having programs to meet basic needs. We already have seen some signs of this in the 1970s. The World Bank under Robert McNamara provided a forum for those who argued that development could only be achieved by alleviating poverty or meeting basic needs.[23] Its program even moved in the direction of focusing on poverty, although that never became its central thrust.[24]

Mahbub ul Haq, the Bank's vice president under McNamara, suggests that the international system may be evolving toward a global system of basic needs fulfillment.[25] He sees a parallel between internal and international economic structures. While at the national level a number of measures have been taken to meet basic needs—public ownership, redistributive income taxes, welfare schemes, social insurance, etc.—nothing of this kind has yet to happen in the international community, but the possibility of an evolution such as the one which has taken place at the national level exists. Perhaps, he argues, we will live to see the creation of mechanisms of international redistributive taxation.

Perhaps, but to the extent to which such a development would hurt the self-defined interests of the great powers, I think it unlikely. We cannot expect any act of intergovernmental will to transform the global IGO system into a rational, efficient system for assuring that individual basic needs are met—with the Food and Agricultural Organization (FAO) assuring we all have enough to eat, the World Health Organization (WHO) assuring we are all healthy, the International Labor Organization (ILO) assuring we all have good jobs, etc.

On the other hand, we have every reason to believe that as long as pressures for the integrated expansion of international economy increase along with the power of labor in leading sectors, and as long as whatever the dynamic is that underlies the rise of modern nationalism continues, IGOs will develop new responsibilities toward individuals, even if they do so incoherently and haphazardly. Moreover, as long as the international system creates stateless people for whom IGOs are given responsibility, IGOs will have to continue to define individual basic needs and minimal human rights, even if every national government has a vested interest in preventing articulation of any universal definition of what individuals should be able to expect from their governments.

NEW ROLES FOR IGOS IN MEETING FUNDAMENTAL NEEDS: MODERNIZATION AND REBELLION

As we look to future IGO roles in meeting fundamental needs we need to consider more than IGO activities relative to global conflicts. IGOs help meet fundamental needs in other ways as well. Whenever they help individuals cope with change, IGOs help meet fundamental needs, even if they only do so to help their state members.

To illustrate, we must go back to the question of rebellion that McNamara used to raise as a justification for anti-poverty development aid. What little we know about rebellion suggests that the best way to avoid it is to make the governed as active and equal participants in government as possible.[26] When their fundamental needs are not met people rebel by identifying with a group in conflict with a government that claims authority over them. People cannot rebel if their identity requires continuation of the government as it is, and a government can only assure that its continuation is fundamental to the identity of those it governs by ceasing to be separate from them.

Just because governments do not allow much participation by the governed does not mean that they *will* rebel. People can meet their fundamental needs yet treat demands from government only as one aspect of their environment. The people—Goran Hyden says the "uncaptured" peasantry—of Tanzania are a case in point.[27] Living within a "premodern" mode of production, an "economy of affection," where production relies on human energy and distribution is based on non-market expectations within a local, extended family-like community, Tanzanian farmers have a culture resilient enough to have thwarted government modernization efforts. Yet they do not rebel, even when the government violates what the global IGO community would say are basic human rights: the most notorious example being the program of forced relocation in the 1970s. Many Tanzanian farmers even have a certain affection for their government. Most treat it like a natural phenomenon, as if bureaucrats and floods that dislocate villages were much the same thing.

Nonparticipatory governments need only worry about rebellion when any one (or any combination) of the following four factors make it more likely that the governed will meet their fundamental needs through groups in conflict with the government:

1. When government actions thwart the reasonable hopes of the governed, forcing them to change that part of their sense of self that relates to who they will be in the future: for example, if the Tanzanian government succeeded, farmers would no longer be able to expect the material relief from any disaster that the local traditions of reciprocity assure them. At the next drought, faced with deprivation of food below long-standing expectations, they might organize against the government in new identity groups formed to meet their fundamental needs to make sense out of this unexpected distress, and point to the government as the cause.[28]

Nonparticipatory governments need not actually be the agents that thwart the governed's reasonable expectations. The probability that people will meet fundamental needs though identity groups in conflict with their government increase:

2. When hopes are thwarted by any cause

3. When a country contains conflicting identity groups opposed to the government[29]

4. When the government stands out as the only differentiated, easily identifiable institution in the country

In countries where people have little information about other institutions, nonparticipatory governments become lightning rods for criticism. People *will* make sense out of their world. If government appears to be the only powerful institution when hopes are dashed, people in government should not be surprised to be blamed.

Each of these four conditions is more likely to occcur in the Third World than in developed countries. In theory, the global IGO system helps its Third World members avoid rebellion whenever it helps assure that the reasonable hopes of Third World people will be fulfilled. Yet, empirical indicators of the degree to which IGOs have helped prevent the dashing of reasonable hopes may be difficult to construct. In addition to knowing what IGOs do, we would have to know people's hopes. Few people in the world are ever asked about their aspirations, by their governments or by anyone else.

But we can posit one set of aspirations that are shared worldwide because of the penetration of modern market economies into the traditional economies of affection. Our closest family relations have great meaning for us, in part because they remain divorced from the challenges of the impersonal market. As Christopher Lasch puts it, the nuclear family becomes the individual's haven in the heartless, modern world.[30] As a result, everywhere, people hope that relatives in the next generation (the people in our remaining economy of affection) gain more material advantages (from the modern market economy) than we did. We work so that our children (or godchildren, or nieces and nephews, depending on how our local culture defines an immediate family) will live longer, eat better, have better homes and jobs, and more leisure than we had.

With surprisingly few exceptions, around the world, our lives are better than those of our most immediate relatives in the last generation, and our children can expect still better lives than ours.[31] Have IGOs contributed to this? I would be reluctant to argue they have no significant role in helping individuals fulfill material aspirations, and, thus, helping them meet a fundamental identity need much more easily than would have been possible had the outlook for the next generation become bleak.

On the other hand, IGOs sometimes appear to force governments to thwart the material aspirations of the governed: for example, when the IMF requires austerity programs in exchange for help with balance of payments problems. IGO development programs, by themselves, can crush personal identities when they are bound up with traditional economies that must be changed. Thus, Third World governments which are successful in promoting development may still face rebellion.

Even at the very margins of human existence, when IGO relief efforts allow people to meet their fundamental needs through something other than fantasy, the result can be the unification of the destitute into an identity group actively opposed to those who claim authority over them. As Al-Mashat argues in his extensive cross-national study of basic needs fulfillment and the security of national governments, some of the most secure governments are those in states where people are the poorest.[32] He concludes that when those governments come under pressure to institute policies for basic needs development, governmental security requires that they grant the public an increasing voice in government, too; the inevitable logic of meeting fundamental needs will, otherwise, produce revolution.

Most people who work for the global IGO system, operating as they do on the basis of the traditional state-power system paradigm, would not see the logic of this argument. Instead, they give national governments in countries where people are most deprived McNamara's advice: Give bread to avoid civil war, but do not worry about continuing political repression. If the hypothesis of fundamental needs is correct, IGOs promoting McNamara's advice may, paradoxically, undercut the security of their members.

CONCLUSIONS

What do global institutions do for individuals? They mediate the influence of other forces in world society (the powers of mobile capital, industrial labor, and social movements in the Third World), and as a result of the emergence of IGO responsibilities in other issue areas, global IGOs have developed a comprehensive view of individual basic needs and rights. The IGO system can only secure those rights to the extent that they are promoted by the forces which gave rise to the IGO responsibility in the first place, or to the extent that an IGO dedicated to promoting a specific right has its own autonomous powers. Despite the fact that global IGOs are creatures of their state members, the non-fulfillment of the basic human needs that IGOs identify can be read as giving individuals the right to rebel. Yet, IGOs rarely support rebellion. In their role as conflict managers, IGOs are more likely to defend the security of governments against the governed.

In the broader sense of a fundamental *individual* need for security, IGO "security" activities play no role. Since the end of the unusual period when the UN trusteeship system had a major role, the only set of IGO activities which may have contributed to *both* the security of governments and individuals are some development programs. In fact, to assess the real contribution of global IGOs to global security, we should begin by looking at "non-security" functions instead of conflict-managing activities, which only shift and relocate the security problems of individuals, and, ultimately, of governments, perhaps even contributing to the chains of structural victimization that lead to protracted global conflicts.

We should not expect global IGOs to become institutions designed to solve the security problems of individuals because IGOs help reproduce the structure of world society as it is. They cannot be expected to encourage the participation of those opposed to world society as it is, a requirement of real conflict resolution. For the same reason, neither national governments nor even international political parties (whose aim, after all, is to gain control of the instruments of state) are likely to contribute to real conflict resolution.

Surprisingly, scholars may be most able to contribute more to resolving global conflicts. We have a professional interest in facilitating global conflict resolution simply because it is one of the best ways to learn about what we study.[33] In the thirties, E.H. Carr argued that the increasing demands for participation in government that gave rise to modern nationalism (and continue in contemporary identity-based movements for social change) made it impossible for European statesmen to avoid total war through time-tested balance-of-power politics.[34] But, Carr added, this problem would create its own solution through the development of a science of international relations responding to the changing public demands for information about the affairs of state. Perhaps he was right.

NOTES

1. Robert H. Manley, "The World Policy System: An Analysis," *International and Comparative Public Policy* 2: 35–141. Harold K. Jacobson, "WHO: Medicine, Regionalism, and Managed Politics," in Robert W. Cox and Harold K. Jacobson, eds.

The Anatomy of Influence: Decision Making in International Organizations (Yale University, 1981), pp. 175–215.

2. Michael D. Wallace and James David Singer, "Intergovernmental Organization in the Global System 1815–1964," *International Organization* 24 (Spring 1970), pp. 239–71.

3. See, cf., Douglas Nelson's (1983) work on the political economy of the non-security activities of domestic governments. These categories are designed to capture distinctions made by theories grounded in classical political economy.

4. Jacobson, "WHO".

5. Calculated on the basis of information in Louise Holborn, *Refugees: A Problem of Our Times*, 2 vols. (Scarecrow, 1973).

6. Ibid., pp. 32–36.

7. John Burton, *Deviance, Terrorism and War* (St. Martins, 1979).

8. Karl Deutsch, *Nationalism and Social Communication* (MIT, 1966).

9. Burton, *Deviance, Terrorism and War*, pp. 78–80.

10. Franz Fanon, *The Wretched of the Earth* (Grove, 1961).

11. William Eckhardt and Edward E. Azar, "Major World Conflicts and Interventions, 1945 to 1975," *International Organization* 37 (Spring 1978), pp. 189–356. Robert L. Butterworth, *Moderation Through Management* (Univ. of Pittsburgh Center for International Studies, 1978). Linda B. Miller, *World Order and Local Disorder: The United Nations and International Conflict* (Princeton University, 1967). Mark W. Zacher, *International Conflict and Collective Security, 1946–1977* (Praeger, 1979).

12. Butterworth, *Moderation Through Management*.

13. Manfred Halpern proposes that there are only eight archetypal ways that people relate to each other. In managing conflict, global IGOs promote four of these ways, what Halpern calls *subjection, isolation, buffering* (e.g., through international law), *boundary management* (consciously identifying and maintaining realms in which the relating parties recognize and foster each other's autonomy).

A sixth one of these relationships, *incoherence*, or the inability of parties to agree to relate to each other in one of the other seven ways, can be understood as the relationship of conflict that IGOs help manage.

Halpern's name for the relationship IGOs do not promote is *transformation*. He defines it in much the same way that we define "conflict resolution." Transformation involves the mutual and equal participation of all parties in newly choosing how to relate to each other, from among all options, whenever they confront a new problem. Transformation involves fulfilling fundamental needs. In order to engage in transformation we must have a secure sense of self, which is then reinforced by the mutuality of the relationship itself. Moreover, the conscious choice which is at the core of the relationship involves mutually making sense out of the environment affecting all parties.

The traditional state-power paradigm makes no distinction between transformation and Halpern's eighth archetypal relationship, *emanation*, in which parties relate as if one were embodied in the other, the way an infant relates to her mother or the relationship that can exist to a leader among people sharing an all-encompassing identity. Statesmen guided by the traditional paradigm know, as Halpern argues, that in the modern world all emanations easily break down into incoherence. Seeing the security of identity that typifies both transformation and emanation, traditionalists mistake one for the other, and fight against both, even to the point of forcing groups engaged in transformation to become groups centered on a tenuous, and destructive, emanation, by denying opportunities for mutuality and participation and the continuing, conscious collective choices that real transformation demands. Manfred Halpern, "Changing Connections to Multiple Worlds" in Helen Kitchen, ed. *Africa: From Mystery to Maze* (Lexington Books, 1976) and "Four Contrasting Repertories of Human Relations in Islam," in L. Carl Brown, ed. *Psychological Dimensions of Near East Studies* (Darwin Books, 1977).

14. See, for example, Graubard's lucid discussion of Henry Kissinger's views. The book highlights all of the themes that follow. Stephen Graubard, *Kissinger: Portrait of a Mind* (Norton, 1974).

15. Burton, *Deviance, Terrorism and War*, p. 121.

16. Many scholars argue that the range of responsibilities given to post-Second World War economic institutions was strongly influenced by reflection on the political economic sources of fascism's appeal to its followers, which was a major topic of interwar economists, including Keynes. If the founders of the UN system had been sensitive to not only the *political economy* of the structural victimization that linked the First and Second World Wars, but had also paid as much attention to contemporary work on the *social psychology* of that linkage (e.g., the work of Wilhelm Reich and that of psychologists of the Frankfurt School), the postwar IGO security system might have been different.

17. Edward E. Azar and Nadia Farah, "The Structure of Inequalities and Protracted Social Conflict: A Theoretical Framework," *International Interactions* vol. 7, no. 4 (1981), pp. 317–35.

18. Burton, *Deviance, Terrorism and War*, p. 121.

19. For a more detailed justification and empirical documentation of the importance of superpowers and their interests see Linda Miller, *World Order and Local Disorder: The United Nations and International Conflict* (Princeton University Press, 1967) and Mark Zacher, *International Conflict and Collective Security, 1946–1977* (Praeger, 1979).

20. Of the many works on postwar UN actions affecting dependent people, Mason Sear's autobiographical account stands out because it gives a clear picture of how the U.N.'s politically divided visiting missions could act to facilitate conflict resolution among nationalists, settlers, and colonial governments in Africa. Julius Nyerere's long introduction links together the actions of the visiting missions with the U.N.'s role, until the seventies, of providing a forum for both nationalists and colonial governments. Mason Sears, *Years of High Purpose* (University Press of America, 1980).

21. Ernest Haas, "Regime Decay: Conflict Management and International Organization, 1945–1981," *International Organization* 37 (Spring 1983), pp. 189–356.

22. Robert Keohane, *After Hegemony: Cooperation and Discord in the World Political Economy* (Princeton University, 1984).

23. Hollis Chenery, et al., *Redistribution With Growth* (MIT, 1973). Paul Streeten et al., *First Things First* (Oxford University, 1981).

24. Robert L. Ayres, *Banking on the World's Poor* (MIT, 1983).

25. Mahbub ul Haq, *The Poverty Curtain* (Columbia University, 1976).

26. The following discussion relies on Tilly's critical survey of empirical research on revolution. Charles Tilly, *From Mobilization to Revolution* (Addison-Wesley, 1978).

27. Goran Hyden, *Beyond Ujamaa in Tanzania* (University of California, 1980).

28. Because Nyerere's government is one of the most participatory in Africa it may be inoculated against such effects.

29. This point relates to one of most frequent ways that superpowers protract social conflicts in the Third World: encouraging the developmentt of competing oppositions to nonparticipatory governments (cf. Tilly, *From Mobilization to Revolution*).

30. Christopher Lasch, *Haven in a Heartless World* (Basic Books, 1977).

31. This is an important point Krasner makes in his argument that NIEO demands reflect governmental aspirations rather than popular aspirations in the Third World. Stephen Krasner, "Transforming International Regimes: What the Third World Wants and Why," *International Studies Quarterly* 25 (1981), pp. 119–48.

32. Abdel Monheim Al-Mashat, *National Security in the Third World* (Westview, 1985).

33. Herbert Kelman, "An Interaction Approach to Conflict Resolution and Its Application to Israeli-Palestinian Relations," *International Interactions* 6 (1979), pp. 99–122.

34. E.H. Carr, *The Twenty Years' Crisis* (Harper and Row, 1939).

CHAPTER ELEVEN

The Micro Foundations
of International Governance:
The Case of U.S./UNESCO Relations

ROGER A. COATE

In this chapter Roger Coate uses a needs-based approach to help bridge the gap between the micro (that is, individual) level and the macro (that is, global institutional) level in studies of international governance. Coate begins by discussing the human needs foundations of networks of social relationships and the various forces and tensions that give social systems their dynamic character. On this base he builds a theoretical framework for explaining the formation, maintenance, and decay of institutional relationships at all levels, including international governance. He then analyzes the breakdown in international cooperation between the U.S. government and the United Nations Educational, Scientific and Cultural Organization (UNESCO) by using such a needs-based approach. Coate's analysis yields conclusions that contradict the official (that is, U.S. governmental) justification for the U.S. withdrawal from UNESCO and, in so doing, illustrates the usefulness of a needs-based approach for understanding important dynamic aspects of international governance.

The past decade of research in international organization (IO) has witnessed a resurgence of interest in international governance—that is, in explaining "who-gets-what: how and why" in world society. This tendency has been most clearly reflected in the proliferation of empirical research and theorizing about the formation and maintenance of international regimes.[1] Yet it is not clear that we have learned much that is new about the dynamics of international governance or about politics in international institutions. While scholars have been "fiddling" with academic debates over international regimes and hegemonic global orders, conditions in many international institutions have reached crisis proportions. IO officials and representatives of member states have found their time increasingly occupied with crisis management.

At the center of this evolving "crisis in multilateralism" has been the deteriorating relationship between these international governmental organizations (especially those in the United Nations system) and their largest contributor, the United States. Not only has the U.S. government fallen behind in the payment of its assessed budgetary contributions to the United Nations and UN agencies, but in addition, the Reagan administration has raised challenges to the international legal order which threaten its viability. In this regard, U.S. officials have disassociated the United States from the UN Convention on the Law of the Sea as well as the legal jurisdiction of the International Court of Justice. Moreover, the U.S. government has withdrawn from the United Nations Educational, Scientific and Cultural Organization (UNESCO), and U.S. officials have hinted that similar actions might be taken against other international agencies. It would seem to be more appropriate to describe this overall situation as a crisis of U.S. participation in multilateral relations, rather than as a global crisis of multilateralism.

These and other events have enlivened an ongoing policy debate over the future of multilateralism and of U.S. participation in institutions of international cooperation.[2] As Ruggie has astutely pointed out, however, "the academic community, from which one would hope for the dispassionate analyses that should inform policy debates, has barely been heard from at all."[3] Relatively little systematic analysis has been conducted into the nature and causes of the evolving breakdown in multilateral cooperation. We are hard pressed when asked to explain such phenomena. Moreover, the academic community does not appear to have established a sound foundation in empirical research with which to explain such phenomena and from which to provide the kind of policy-relevant assistance suggested by Ruggie.

A major barrier to doing so has been the tendency to treat international organization as an almost exclusively interstate phenomenon. The human individual and the humanness of social institutions have generally been assumed away or otherwise disregarded. In doing so the ability to identify and analyze important forces underlying the dynamic character of international organization has been obscured.

Susan Strange has touched on an important dimension of this problem in her critique of international regime scholarship. She argues that "the *dynamic* character of the 'who-gets-what' of the international economy . . . is more likely to be captured by looking not at the regime that emerges on the surface but underneath, at the bargains on which it is based."[4] Moreover, many such bargaining relationships may not be meaningfully understood as relations among egoist nation-states.

We need to develop models that permit us to focus directly on the bargaining relationships among participants, if we are to understand the nature and causes of the current crisis in multilateralism. Also, we need the flexibility in our analyses to be able to include simultaneously individuals and more or less formally organized groups of individuals. In order to do so, however, the gap in international relations theorizing between the micro and the macro must be bridged.

The main purpose of this chapter is to explore the nature and contributions of a needs-based approach for building such conceptual bridges. After identifying the micro foundations of networks of social relationships, the forces and tensions that give these social systems their dynamic character are examined. Next, the implications of these and other factors for the formation and maintenance of formalized organizations are explored, as are the interfaces between organizations and their environments. These considerations give rise to a more general discussion of the micro foundations of international governance. Finally, the breakdown in international cooperation between the United States government and UNESCO is examined by using a needs-based approach, in an attempt to explain more fully the dynamics of who-gets-what: how and why in one specific institutional setting in world society.

BRIDGING THE MICRO-MACRO GAP

At the core of international governance lies human social interaction. Individuals and groups interact with one another in both cooperative and conflictual ways as they go about the pursuit of needs and values.[5] Analyses of social processes at the macro level need to be based on working assumptions which account for the motivations, beliefs, and other forces which underlie this interaction.[6] Doing so focuses our attention on the emergence and evolution of social networks through which the needs and values of individuals and groups are fulfilled or deprived.

These social networks tend to become characterized over time by persistent patterns of interaction and accompanying divisions of labor and influence among participants. Accordingly, participants' roles become institutionalized and social structures evolve. Contrary to assumptions frequently made by international relations scholars, the resulting institutions are characterized by functional relationships that may not depend either on coercion or on commonly shared values. These relationships are based primarily on the satisfaction of participants' needs and values and on role expectations which are related to them. The maintenance of these more or less formalized institutions is based largely on the values attached to them by participants, as they relate to the fulfillment of needs and values.

In complex social systems individuals tend to associate with a wide variety of these "identity groups." With respect to any particular issue, individuals may be involved in a wide array of relevant social relationships. Each particular relationship implies a specific role position and status relative to other participants. In order to move conceptually from the micro to the macro level, we must stop arbitrarily treating individuals and groups as unchangeable wholes. Participants need to be treated as complexes of roles and statuses that result from their participation in such multiple relationships.

An example, taken from UNESCO, might help to illustrate this point. During the reform process in UNESCO in 1984–1985, Ivo Margan occupied at least a half dozen relevant and often conflicting roles simultaneously. He was: (1) the Yugoslav ambassador to UNESCO; (2) a member of the organization's executive board, as an independent personality (designated by name, not state), representing simultaneously the government of Yugoslavia and UNESCO's general conference; (3) a member of the group of non-aligned countries at UNESCO; (4) a member of the East European electoral group; (5) chairman of UNESCO's temporary committee on reform; and (6) in late 1985 a candidate for chairman of the executive board (and later elected chairman). The role through which Margan appears to have made the most impact was that of chairman of the temporary committee—it was clearly not that of Yugoslav ambassador. His election in 1985 as chairman of the executive board—with Western support—underscores this important point. However, depending on the particular issue at hand, any one or more of these roles may have been important. Moreover, it should be noted that these were only Margan's formal institutional roles.

As Rosenau has suggested, conceiving individuals as "role composites provides an analytical context in which theorizing about world politics can systematically and meaningfully build in micro units expressive of needs, wants, orientations, and actions at the individual level."[7] Such a perspective on micro-macro relationships provides a foundation for building dynamic theories of social change.

One way to help forge a micro-macro perspective is to view international institutions, as well as world society more generally, as dynamic social fields comprised of forces and tensions. Generally speaking, a basic tension exists between centripetal forces, which tend to bind individuals together thus maintaining social institutions, and centrifugal forces, which tend to have the opposite effect. The value placed on the relationships through which individuals and groups attempt to satisfy their needs is perhaps the most important centripetal force.[8] The rules of the game which delimit such relationships normally evolve slowly out of practice, as do organizational ideologies which define the nature and scope of appropriate organizational activity and serve to legitimize such rules.[9] Those participants who benefit most from relationships will tend to resist significant changes in the status quo, further reinforcing cetripetal tendencies.

On the other hand, perceptions of distributive injustices, which may result from inherent inequities in who-gets-what, can be important centrifugal forces. Tensions are created within social institutions as changes occur in the relative positions, statuses, and perceived interests among participants as they interact and attempt to exert influence over allocational processes. Change may also be the product of environmental change more generally, especially when such change affects the availability of resources. These tensions exacerbate those which normally occur as individuals attempt to reconcile the conflicting requirements inherent in their various affiliations and positions.

Technological change and other environmental factors also can bring about challenges to the status quo. Technological innovation may alter the structure of participants' interdependencies as substitutes or alternative sources for needed resources become available. Analysis of these interrelationships can provide insight into the forces underlying the emergence and decay of international institutions.

Other centrifugal forces may result from changes which occur over time in the dominating ideology which defines the nature and scope of appropriate organizational activities. These changes may slowly create problems of legitimacy for institutions. Cox and Jacobson found this to be the case with a number of international organizations.[10] The dominance of functionalist objectives and activities, upon which these postwar international governmental organizations were founded, had given way to a predominant focus on development. As we will explore later with respect to UNESCO, in certain cases this gave rise to problems of legitimacy for these institutions among their primary support groups in rich Western societies. This directly affected these institutions that depended upon the governments of those societies for financial and other vital support.

Thus far, the discussion has focused primarily on those forces which cause individuals to aggregate into social units, as well as to disaggregate. Given such processes, social institutions develop and take on a coherence and structure quite distinct from the sum of their parts. In the discussion that follows we continue to explore micro and macro linkages by examining how formal organizations relate to the larger environments upon which organizational decisionmakers must depend for development and survival.

Organizations and Environments

Social groupings which are characterized by relatively high degrees of organization over time can be differentiated from their environments and treated as dynamic systems of action. "Formal organizations" can be defined as goal-directed, boundary-maintaining, activity systems.[11] Although abstract, this definition is instructive because it focuses on three of the most important functional characteristics of formal organizations.

Goal direction results from a continuous bargaining-learning process among participants within an organization as they relate to one another and to the external environment. Organizational goals represent the whole set of requirements and constraints that must be satisfied for any course of action to be deemed acceptable by organizational decisionmakers.[12] Simply stated, goals are a function of time and place. The above-mentioned shift in the dominant organizational ideology of numerous IOs from functionalism to development issues illustrates this point.

Boundary maintenance and satisfaction of performance requirements are also important organizational goal activities. In fulfilling these tasks, a crucial set of constraints arises from *uncertainty* regarding the acquisition of needed supports (that is, "resources," such as information, money, personnel) from the external environment.[13] In order to reduce such uncertainty, decisionmakers will attempt to exert control over those elements of the environment upon which the organization is dependent. In doing so they may lay claim to a certain domain within the organization's external environment. In this way, decision makers attempt to establish authoritative direction over individuals and organizations which pose threats to future acquisitions of vital resources. Also, decisionmakers strive for organizational autonomy and freedom from external control with respect to resource supports.[14] Thus, avoiding and exploiting dependence relationships become a central dynamic of interorganizational relations.

Organizations can also be characterized as bounded activity systems. Organizational participants must continuously engage in boundary interchanges with other participants in the environment. The individuals who are responsible for conducting such interchanges are susceptible to a relatively high degree of role conflict.

> They frequently get caught in the cross-fire between divergent role expectations, not only between those of their own organization and other organizations, but also between varying role conceptions among their own constituents. As 'activist brokers' between their own organization and its environment, boundary-role occupants must not only represent the organization to its environment, but also represent the environment to their constituents.[15]

Such role conflicts affect information processing and, therefore, organizational goals. Also, tensions resulting from these conflicts may intensify centrifugal forces. We must view organizations, then, as open systems comprised of individuals interacting in the context of larger interorganizational environments.

When organizational actors become involved in these boundary interchanges, they are interacting in exchange relationships with other participants. These exchange relationships tend to become regularized (patterned) over time as decisionmakers attempt to manage organizational resource dependence and establish some degree of control over vital resources. Thus, interorganizational relations present participants with constraints to, as well as opportunities for, resource dependence management. An important task for students of international organization, then, is to identify resource dependencies as they relate to interdependence among participants in interorganizational networks.[16]

The interdependence inherent in networks of exchange relationships can and often does lead them to become more or less institutionalized over time. The appearance of stability which results "comes about not through the discretionary interests and powers of exchange partners but through the formation of a stable interorganizational organization that regulates them."[17] The basis of this organization is found in interdependence, which is built on relations of concrete dependence.

This brings us to the essence of world politics. Social relations in world society are not fundamentally based in discretionary interests and powers of participants but in the formation and maintenance of interorganizational networks through which participants satisfy their needs and values—that is, through the formation and maintenance of international regimes. These interorganizational institutions are characterized by "sets of implicit and explicit principles, norms, rules, and decisionmaking procedures around which actors' expectations converge."[18] This focus on interorganizational relations enables us to look below the surface of that narrow band of interstate activities which has for so long dominated and obfuscated our visions and explanations of international governance. Of course, government units will continue to be important elements within our analyses; the mystical, mythical shroud surrounding such participants, however, can be stripped away.

Human Needs and International Governance

The emergence and continuation of international regimes and other global institutions do not necessarily depend on the purposive behavior of governmental units. Governmental entities might not even be active participants in some regimes at particular times, as was the case with respect to the population-development assistance regime during the 1950s.[19] Regimes emerge out of patterned behaviors among participants and are maintained in order that such relationships may be sustained. The resulting social processes and structures "exist primarily as participants' understandings, expectations or convictions about legitimate, appropriate or moral behavior."[20]

A needs-oriented approach refocuses our studies of world politics on the basic order which underlies social relationships at all levels, not on some abstracted notion of nation-states struggling for power within an anarchical world. Regardless of whether authoritative role structures in world society are highly centralized (e.g., an authoritative allocator) or substantially decentralized (e.g., based on reciprocity), participants give deference to role positions of others in exchange for perceived benefits expected or deprivations avoided. "Authority, whether it be coercive or based on relationships, is effective only to the degree that it is accepted and recognized as 'legitimized' by those over whom authority is exercised."[21] In such legitimized relationships it is the value placed on the relationship that matters.

In conclusion, social processes in international institutions are dynamic phenomena. On one side there are forces which tend toward stability and order. The values placed on relationships serve as a centripetal force in maintaining the regime structure or in allowing change only incrementally. Shared values and shared ideology also play important roles reinforcing such forces. On the other side, however, are strong forces for change or transformation. As Burton argues,

> the differentiation of power through social exchange does not result in a balanced or static condition. On the contrary, a differentiation of power is the stimulus to a reaction and to further differentiation of power. When imbalance occurs . . . the consequent compensatory processes do not return the system to the original state. On the contrary, system change is likely. The response to structures created by the differentiation of power by social exchange is organized opposition among those over whom power is exercised. . . . Hence there is a reactive or secondary differentiation of power that, far from creating a consensual society, seeks to establish alternative structures that provide alternative forms of privilege and elitist opportunities.[22]

These considerations indicate a need to move beyond a state-centered paradigm for the analysis of international governance. This is the case even if the researcher is primarily interested in analyzing intergovernmental relations. Little useful knowledge is likely to emerge from models of world politics which conceptualize the primary participants as homogeneous nation-state actors. Seldom is such a conceptualization warranted. Elites, representing governmental bureaucracies, other social units, and in some cases themselves, are the primary active participants in international regimes and other international institutions. A needs-based approach to the study of world society captures such realism and enables us to study more directly the inherent dynamic processes which underlie world politics and international governance. This is illustrated in the following section, where this approach is used to explain the evolution of the breakdown in U.S./UNESCO relations, which resulted in U.S. withdrawal from the organization.

A CRISIS IN U.S./UNESCO RELATIONS

On December 31, 1984 the U.S. government formally terminated its membership in the United Nations Educational, Scientific and Cultural Organization.[23] Three primary reasons were cited by Reagan administration officials as justification for the action: (1) excessive politicization of UNESCO's programs and personnel; (2) promotion by UNESCO of statist theories; and (3) unrestrained budgetary expansion and poor management practices. The administration's indictment was presented in detail in a State Department document entitled *U.S./UNESCO Policy Review.*[24] The "Executive Summary" of this report charged that extraneous political debate on contentious issues and other forms of politicization dominated UNESCO's activities. Statist theories were said to supersede Western ideals in the organization's activities in science, education, and culture. State control over free flows of information was claimed to dominate UNESCO's communications programs and activities. Also, it was said that concepts of collectivist rights (i.e., "rights of peoples") prevailed over Western notions of individual rights, which had been sanctioned in the Universal Declaration of Human Rights.

In transmitting this report to the House Committee on Foreign Affairs on February 29, 1984, the Assistant Secretary of State for International Organization Affairs, Gregory Newell, claimed that UNESCO's programs and personnel answered to an agenda that was often inimical to U.S. interests. When linked to the charges of uncontrolled and excessive budgetary expansion and poor management, U.S. officials argued that the situation had become unbearable and was not likely to improve. Thus, the U.S. had no alternative other than to withdraw.

Indeed, it does seem clear that a situation of severe proportions had been mounting for some time in UNESCO. However, the characterization of the situation provided by Mr. Newell and various other administration officials appears to have been misleading at best, especially when viewed in the context of the State Department's own documentation regarding the issue.

The February 1983 State Department *Report to Congress Required: in Sections 108 and 109 of Public Law 97–241* challenges the claim that the situation in UNESCO was so serious as to warrant withdrawal. This report conluded that: UNESCO's programs for the most part contributed to U.S. foreign policy goals and particular U.S. educational, scientific and cultural interests; vigorous, continued U.S. participation was essential to protect U.S. interests; and UNESCO was not implementing any policy or procedure that would justify withholding funds under the law.

With respect to the major U.S. concerns this report provided fairly unambiguous assessments. For example, the main problem related to anti-Israeli activities was said to have basically been resolved a decade before.

The anti-Western bias in UNESCO's communications debates was said to have ebbed since 1981, and much of the most controversial communications work of the organization was said to have been discarded or deemphasized. UNESCO secretariat officials were said to be increasingly supportive of such a new, more pragmatic approach. The Second Medium-Term Plan, which guides UNESCO's activities until the end of the decade, was said to have eliminated some of the most controversial program activities. Furthermore, this plan was said to provide a basis for programs which reflect U.S. and Western values.

In addition, excessive budgetary growth and mismanagement were not identified as being major problems from a U.S. perspective. While mentioning a perceived disregard of U.S. calls for greater budget stringency, the *Report* did not identify such a condition as a major problem; nor were UNESCO's management practices targeted as an item of major concern.

In the ten months that elapsed between the publication of this report in February and the announcement of withdrawal in December 1983, a major in-depth review of U.S./UNESCO relations was undertaken. Thirteen separate government departments and agencies with UNESCO-related mandates, eighty-three U.S. embassies and consulates, the U.S. National Commission for UNESCO, and numerous nongovernmental organizations were requested by the State Department to provide contributions to such a study. The *U.S./UNESCO Policy Review* was supposedly the product of this review process.

In contradiction to the "Executive Summary," analysis of the interagency contributions and other background materials upon which the *Policy Review* was claimed to have been based indicates that undue politicization, promotion of statist theories, and excessive budgetary expansion and mismanagement were not generally perceived to pose serious threats to important U.S. interests. Moreover, the conclusions presented in the *U.S./UNESCO Policy Review* itself bore only marginal resemblance to the recommendations from these bodies.

For example, where the "Executive Summary" of the *Policy Review* claimed that the situation in UNESCO had become unbearable, *none* of the reports from any contributing body viewed the situation in UNESCO as being so problematical as to warrant withdrawal. The recommendation of the interagency working group on science headed by the National Science Foundation stated that "the scientific benefits the United States derives from participation in UNESCO clearly warrant our continued participation."[25] The Department of Education's report on UNESCO's education sector stated that when the U.S. is well represented it usually prevails in negotiations that are considered to be fundamental to U.S. interests.[26] Most of UNESCO's education agenda was said not to be ideological, political or contentious. The most troublesome area, standard-setting, was said to represent only a small percentage of what UNESCO does. Moreover, UNESCO was viewed as a stabilizing institutional influence clearly in the United States' interests. This report claimed that "UNESCO virtually alone maintains the effort to develop effective methodologies for eradicating illiteracy."[27]

In the U.S. Agency for International Development's contribution to the Department of Education's report even stronger support for remaining in UNESCO was articulated: "UNESCO serves several functions in educational development unique to all other development agencies. . . . No other bilateral or multilateral development agency is equipped or willing to serve in these capacities. For those purposes alone, the U.S. should not cut off funding to UNESCO completely."[28]

The story is the same with respect to culture and communication. The Smithsonian Institution argued that it was essential to maintain access to UNESCO and that "UNESCO's essential programs not be crippled for want of U.S. financial support and leadership."[29] With respect to UNESCO's Communications Sector the U.S. AID report concluded, "In sum, basic U.S. interests in communications are reasonably well served. U.S. withdrawal would not enhance the achievement of those U.S. objectives."[30] If one is searching for support for withdrawal in these interagency assessments of UNESCO, it is very hard to find. Moreover, in the materials from the U.S. National Commission, which incorporate the views of a broad range of nongovernmental organizations, a similar lack of support can be noted.[31]

In addition to the in-depth UNESCO review, a second major event had occurred after February 1983 which could have potentially negated such positive assessments. The 22nd General Conference of UNESCO was held in Fall 1983 and had concluded just one month before the U.S. withdrawal announcement. Yet, the outcome of this General Conference also had been relatively positive from a U.S. perspective. Indeed, in his report to the National Commission in December 1983 the head of the U.S. delegation to the conference, Edmund Hennelly, concluded that his personal balance sheet showed that the conference had been a "clear plus for the U.S." He evaluated this General Conference to have been "among the least politicized and the most constructive from the U.S. point of view in recent memory."[32]

In light of this evidence, the official explanation of why the United States withdrew from UNESCO seems to have been strained at best. Given such positive assessments by U.S. agencies and institutions, it would appear as though the U.S. withdrawal action was either primarily based on reasons other than those officially stated in justification of the action or that White House and other high-level officials who initiated the decision were operating from an information base quite apart from the foreign policy bureaucracy knowledgeable about U.S./UNESCO relations. It appears that both these factors might have been at work.

Factors Behind Withdrawal

The litany of politicization, statist theories, and uncontrollable budgetary growth and mismanagement continued to be heard from Reagan administration officials throughout 1984 and beyond as justification of withdrawal. However, in mid-1984 these concerns were suddenly shifted to a subordinate status by the Assistant Secretary of State for International Organization Affairs, Gregory Newell. While still listed as problems, they were apparently no longer of fundamental importance; their exact status, however, was unclear.

A revised set of main concerns was presented by Newell in a July 13, 1984 letter to the UNESCO Director-General.[33] The administration's new official position specified three reforms that were said to be of "fundamental importance":

1. Creating mechanisms to assure that important UNESCO decisions and programs enjoy the support of all major groups, including the Western Group
2. A return by UNESCO to concentration upon its original purposes
3. The assumption by Member States of their rightful authority in the organization, through strengthening of the General Conference, and in particular, the Executive Board

This statement of fundamental concerns was accompanied by a number of proposed organizational changes. Yet, time and again in the months that followed, Mr. Newell made it clear that such recommendations should *not* be viewed as the list of reforms necessary to keep the U.S. in UNESCO. He consistently and quite adamantly refused to provide such a "laundry list," as he called it.[34]

This revised set of fundamental concerns had not been mentioned in Newell's December 1983 memorandum to Secretary of State Shultz recommending withdrawal. Yet, these concerns point to several general frustrations which appear to have underlain the administration's approach to UNESCO.

Substantial frustration seems to have been associated with a perceived inability to use UNESCO effectively as an instrument of foreign policy. In the words of one IO Bureau official: "there was a deep frustration, not just by administration officials but also by careerists who had grown weary from the struggle to persevere. U.S. officialdom is accustomed to seeing short-term wins or gains when, in point of fact, we are engaged in a long-term struggle for the minds of men in the UNESCO context. This is something this administration (ironically, given its ideological orientation) could never understand."[35]

While attempts to beat back Soviet and Third World challenges to the concept of free flow of information had been successful over the years, the perception among many high-level administration officials, as well as the American public at large, was to the contrary. UNESCO was seen as being controlled by an anti-Western/Third World majority that ran roughshod over minority interests. Biased reporting by American news media appears to have played a major role in this regard. The debates in UNESCO's delegate bodies over the establishment of a new world information order became an obsession with many American reporters covering UNESCO affairs. Focusing on certain member states' calls for actions to restrict the free flow of information, these reporters generally ignored the fact that no resolution regarding licensing of journalists, monitoring the press, or establishing journalistic codes of conduct had ever been adopted. Moreover, no top UNESCO official has ever called for such restrictive actions. To the contrary, both former U.S. Ambassador to UNESCO Esteban Torres and Ambassador Designate Edmund Hennelly have argued forcefully that M'Bow has been by and large effective in mobilizing the African delegations in ways that have assured that U.S. interests have been treated fairly.[36]

Such information, however, has generally become very confused in the United States. Self-interest dominated American news media coverage of UNESCO activities. As Leonard Sussman, Executive Director of Freedom House, has argued, "American press coverage has reflected the *possibilities* of press-controls, not actualities, and that important distinction has never been made clear."[37]

Such distorted press coverage has not been an isolated occurrence. For example, of 448 American press reports covering the 21st General Conference, all reported exclusively the communications issue, ignoring the overwhelming majority of UNESCO's activities.[38] Coverage of the 22nd General Conference in 1983 was equally misleading. As discussed earlier, the conference produced a number of positive results with respect to the U.S. government's perspective on the NWICO and other communications issues. However, nearly all news reports of the General Conference belied such changes.

Considerable frustration seems also to have existed over the general inability to control outcomes. Those member states who, in combination, contribute the overwhelming majority of UNESCO's budget were perceived not to have sufficient control over how the money was spent (i.e., over the program and budget). To overcome this condition, several sweeping actions were proposed that in combination would effectively give a handful of member states, including the United States, extensive control over UNESCO's program and budget.[39]

Administration officials also seemed to have been frustrated with the expansion of UNESCO's programs and activities to incorporate concerns they thought to be inappropriate. These officials wished to purge from

UNESCO all political debates that questioned the legitimacy of the established global economic and information orders. Thus, they called for a return to UNESCO's original principles. However, the nature of these calls revealed that these officials knew very little about UNESCO or the history of U.S./UNESCO relations.

These considerations and other events strongly suggest that withdrawal was a predetermined move against UNESCO on ideological grounds. Barely one week after Ronald Reagan had been sworn in as president in January 1981, David Stockman, Director-designate of the Office of Management and Budget (OMB), had proposed that United States officials might wish to consider withdrawing from UNESCO. Stockman urged such action in the context of an overall retrenchment in foreign aid, citing "UNESCO's pro-PLO policies and its support for measures limiting the free flow of information."[40] Furthermore, he discussed additional cost savings that could be made should the U.S. refuse to pay its legally binding assessments for 1981 and 1982.

Such early predilections were quite compatible with a broader ideological approach which was taking form in the White House and elsewhere, both inside and outside the United States government. According to a former high-level White House advisor who was actively engaged in the UNESCO issue, Stockman was merely attempting to exploit deep-seated anti-UN and anti-UNESCO attitudes among right-wing White House officials and advisors in order to slash the budget.[41]

A key element in solidifying the control by ideologues over the policy process with regard to U.S./UNESCO relations was the move in 1982 of a former Reagan campaign aide and White House employee, Gregory Newell, to the IO Bureau as the assistant secretary. Mr. Newell came on board just as the bureau was completing the 1983 Department of State *Reports to Congress* discussed earlier. Such timing helps to explain the discrepancy between those reports and Mr. Newell's claims about conditions in UNESCO. As one IO Bureau official has suggested, "the timing of his arrival in relation to these studies is important because it indicates that Newell came to IO loaded with a separate agenda and special mission."[42]

Events subsequent to 1983 indicate that a close link existed between the anti-UNESCO activities of the right-wing Heritage Foundation and U.S./UNESCO relations. Between 1982 and the end of 1984 Heritage writers produced eight anti-UNESCO tracts. Of these, the 1984 pamphlet on the then still classified General Accounting Office (GAO) report provided some clear evidence of Heritage influence. A European permanent delegate confided quite disapprovingly that during the GAO report controversy at the 120th Executive Board, the U.S. representative had provided him with a copy of this highly slanted Heritage brochure, leading him to assume that it was an accurate representation of the GAO report. He became quite disconcerted later, when the actual GAO Draft Report was made available to board members on a confidential basis.[43]

Also, it is important to note the similarity between the anti-UNESCO charges leveled by Assistant Secretary Newell and other administration spokespersons and those made by Heritage Foundation writers in their anti-UNESCO tracts. As part of his study of American press coverage of the U.S. withdrawal from UNESCO, C. Anthony Giffard conducted such a comparative analysis. He found that in news reports quoting administration spokespersons these spokespersons' views "echoed the Heritage position."[44] Such similarity might not have appeared so significant had these views not deviated so drastically from the historical record.

In addition, Jean Gerard, U.S. Ambassador to UNESCO, and Owen Harries, a senior fellow at Heritage, were jointly engaged actively in London in Fall 1984, lobbying for British withdrawal. A favorite theme of right-wing American supporters of such a British action was that U.K representatives in Paris had been "captured" by the UNESCO reform process. Thus, the Prime Minister should disregard British officials' advice to remain in UNESCO and should listen to Harries and those Americans who could see UNESCO more objectively. The transnational effort to get the United Kingdom out of UNESCO continued during 1985, and in November of that year Mrs. Gerard was back in London again meeting with British editors, columnists, and broadcasters.[45]

Back in the United States the relationship between the IO Bureau and the Heritage Foundation was brought further into public view in 1985, after the U.S. withdrawal. At that time Heritage President Edwin Feulner was appointed to the high-level U.S. Reform Observation Panel on UNESCO. It is interesting to note that this appointment was made following the wide circulation by Heritage of an ideologically charged anti-UNESCO fundraising appeal by Feulner.[46] Also, Heritage Fellow Roger A. Brooks was appointed to the position of policy planning coordinator in the state department's Bureau of International Organization Affairs (IO Bureau). In interviews with several IO Bureau careerists, great frustration was voiced that at least ten "Heritage types" had been brought in at the technical level of the bureau by then-Assistant Secretary Keyes, who had replaced Newell in 1985. Their function, it was charged, was to act as "ward captains" to monitor the behavior of the career professionals.[47]

It appears then that UNESCO was an immediate target of the Heritage Foundation and Reagan administration officials, while the United Nations more generally was the ultimate target. But why target UNESCO, an organization in which conditions had improved since the beginning of President Reagan's term in office? And how could UNESCO have been so vulnerable to a relatively small group of ideologues inside the U.S. government? As the analysis below demonstrates, a needs-based approach helps us to answer these questions and in so doing provides much insight into processes of international governance.

Origins of U.S./UNESCO Relations

While the roots of UNESCO can be traced to a tradition of transnational intellectual cooperation in education, science and culture that had evolved over two decades in Europe, the more immediate stimulus to establish such an agency was the outgrowth of British initiatives at the close of World War II.[48] Calls for the United Nations to establish an international organization for education were heard in London as early as 1941. By the end of 1943, national representatives in the London-based Conference of Allied Ministers of Education (CAME) had agreed that an international organization was needed to promote and facilitate the reconstruction of educational and scientific infrastructures that had been devastated by war.[49] The future of European and world peace and stability were held in the balance.

Similar ideas were being expressed in the United States. Yet, active United States involvement in the planning of UNESCO came relatively late. This action was taken only after it had become clear to U.S. observers that an intergovernmental organization in education would likely be established with or without U.S. participation. In November 1943 the U.S. observer in London, Ralph Turner, cabled the State Department that "we should enter the conference as quickly as possible if we are to affiliate with it at all, because the longer we stay out the less fluid it will become and the more difficult it will be to secure modifications in its organization or objectives."[50]

The U.S. response was a vigorous one: "Americans, wanting an originating role, tried the gambit of starting afresh. In April 1944, a U.S. delegation was sent to London for the announced purpose of opening up CAME deliberations and making of it 'an entirely new organization'."[51] The U.S. delegation brought before the conference a draft constitution for an international agency for educational and cultural reconstruction. U.S. officials endeavored to make certain that UNESCO would be consistent with a U.S. vision of an acceptable world order and that the organization would be open to U.S. influence and control.

The nature of this U.S. government initiative stood in marked contrast to the British government's more incrementalist approach. However, most of the CAME participants, including those from the United Kingdom, readily accommodated the U.S. suggestions. In fact, a small drafting committee, headed by the leader of the U.S. delegation, J. William Fulbright, soon drew up and circulated a modified draft constitution.

At U.S. insistence UNESCO's mandate was expanded beyond science, education and culture to encompass communications. Thus, Article I, Section 2 of the *Constitution* called on the organization to:

collaborate in the work of advancing the mutual knowledge and understanding of peoples through all means of mass communication and to that end, recommend such international agreements as may be necessary to promote the free flow of ideas by word or image.

Mass communication, as well as mass education, were to be basic pillars of this new world order. From the beginning the communications work of UNESCO was a predominant concern of U.S. policymakers.

Growing Problems of Identity

Yet, as so aptly stated by Sewell, "UNESCO was born plural."[52] A single institution had been mandated the task of dealing with an agenda that included global relations in science, education, culture, and communications. Moreover, such functional foci were to be used in the service of humankind to promote world peace. Thus, UNESCO was at the same time a functional agency mandated to promote collaboration in education, science, culture, and communications and a political body devoted to serving as a kind of world conscience. As Lengyel has astutely pointed out, such a "hybridization" of technical and ideologically normative roles has from the beginning created important difficulties in the organization. "UNESCO itself was, from the start, a sort of ideal type bound to run into trouble in a real world riven by ideological cleavages."[53]

The tensions created in attempting to balance these two roles intensified as the membership composition of UNESCO expanded and diversified. The liberal and rationalistic assumptions underlying the ideology expressed in the constitution were not universally shared. With the admission of the Soviet Union in 1954 it became clear to many participants, including those from the United States, that UNESCO could not function effectively with such a diverse focus. Thus, U.S. officials desired the organization to become primarily a technical agency. To be sure, however, UNESCO's ideologically normative role as world conscience did not die; it remained firmly embedded in the organization's constitutional foundation.

In general, UNESCO rapidly took on a more technical orientation. Early experiments with technical assistance activities expanded in scope as membership composition shifted toward the Third World. According to John E. Fobes, a former deputy-director general, "more self-examination of UNESCO's role in development took place in the years 1960–1962 than in all the years after 1946."[54]

President Kennedy's call for the establishment of a United Nations development decade had repercussions far beyond the halls of the general assembly. Soon, UNESCO secretariat officials were actively engaged with other multilateral agencies in an attempt to provide support to member states for operational activities related to educational and scientific development. With such cooperative efforts came substantial extra-budgetary funding. By the early 1970s approximately half of UNESCO's overall program resources were being channeled to development activities.

A shift in the dominant task orientation of UNESCO occurred; functionalism (i.e., intellectual cooperation for peace) rapidly gave way to a focus on social and economic development. Such a change, in turn, gave rise to problems of legitimacy both within and without the organization. A change in function of this kind cannot be done on an entirely value-free basis. The praxis of science, education and culture in advanced societies incorporates, reflects and is meant to perpetuate their value hierarchies; the transfer of these models, even in somewhat adapted forms, must therefore be accompanied by a transfer of values. That, in turn, means that conflicting ideologies or traditions cannot be avoided by a flight into technicity.[55] As discussed earlier, however, such a situation was not particular to UNESCO. As the political debate over development shifted in the 1970s away from an exclusive focus on national economic development to concentrate more generally on questions about global inequality as a factor in underdevelopment, legitimacy problems intensified.

In UNESCO these debates greatly aggravated identity problems. The essence of the liberal ideological foundations of the organization were being brought into question. In this regard, Lengyel has argued that the resulting Western countercharges that UNESCO was becoming increasingly politicized through excessive statism should be viewed in context for what they represent: a defense of private enterprise and the established liberal economic order.[56] There were attempts to rationalize the continuing conflict between functionalism and developmentalism by saying that UNESCO would utilize knowledge gained by its traditional intellectual role (i.e., research and exchange) "to inform" the planning of developing countries. However, the conflict between these two competing foci has persisted, and UNESCO's identity problems have not subsided.[57]

Early U.S./UNESCO Relations

These identity problems within UNESCO compounded the problems of U.S. participation in the organization. At the beginning, as well as later, Department of State officials found themselves forced to operate in substantive issue contexts about which they knew little and felt relatively uneasy. Unlike authorities in many other member states, they tended to be rather distrustful of national policies in education, science, culture, and communications. Lacking directly comparable sectoral ministries through which to conduct substantive participation in UNESCO, such participation was largely left to the State Department, whose officials generally felt uneasy about dealing in UNESCO's areas of competence. Given the predominant strategic geopolitical orientation in the State Department, U.S. participation in UNESCO came to be dominated more by a perceived need to

was largely left to the State Department, whose officials generally felt uneasy about dealing in UNESCO's areas of competence. Given the predominant strategic geopolitical orientation in the State Department, U.S. participation in UNESCO came to be dominated more by a perceived need to control the organization than by any conception of utility related to the satisfaction of needs and values in UNESCO's substantive areas of concern.

While there was relatively little conflict between the organization and its major funder regarding core programmatic tasks during these early years, problems did arise with respect to UNESCO's more ideologically charged role, as promoter of a liberal democratic world order. At a general political level frustration existed in the United States over what was perceived as UNESCO's uncooperative posture in the struggle against communism. Irritation grew over the unwillingness of the organization to assume a legitimizing role in a U.S.-sponsored initiative to establish a worldwide radio network to broadcast the "truth" to the peoples of Eastern Europe. From the beginning communications had been the primary focus of U.S. interest in UNESCO, and the organization was perceived to have faltered in regard to its communications mandate.

Irritation turned to outrage in some quarters in Washington as UNESCO was perceived again to have faltered over the Korean war issue. While UNESCO did actively become engaged in a worldwide educational campaign in support of the U.S./UN action in Korea, a number of important U.S. policy elites perceived such action as not having gone far enough.

Growing U.S. disillusionment with UNESCO was soon felt in Paris with respect to the organization's budget. In this regard UNESCO's second director-general (Torres-Bodet) and the U.S. delegation found themselves in substantial disagreement. Given the United Nations' "ability to pay" basis for establishing budget assessments, the U.S. delegation was in a position to threaten and, if needed, apply negative sanctions. The United States's share of the total assessed budget at this time was thirty-eight percent. UNESCO and its Director-General found themselves to be exceedingly vulnerable in this regard. In large part it was the U.S. delegation's exercise of such sanctions that led to Torres-Bodet's resignation at the Seventh General Conference in 1952.

The acting director-general, John Taylor, and his permanent replacement, Luther Evans, were both Americans. Yet, the U.S./UNESCO relationship remained strained. The conflict was related to questions of secretariat employees' national loyalty. In 1952–1953, U.S. Government agencies attempted to impose jurisdiction over U.S. citizens in the international civil service of UNESCO, as it related to questions of alleged disloyalty and anti-American activities.

The Director-General failed to respond as quickly and as completely as U.S. officials desired. Evans argued that the rules of procedure of the

seven American employees who had declined to appear before U.S. government loyalty boards. Regardless, the DG and UNESCO were denounced by the U.S. ambassador to the U.N., Henry Cabot Lodge, and others for not acting more quickly and more completely. Furthermore, UNESCO came under increased attack from various American civic groups, including the American Legion, the Daughters of the American Revolution, and the U.S. Chamber of Commerce.[58]

UNESCO's Growing Loss of Legitimacy

Despite such initial disappointments and frustrations, Americans remained actively engaged in UNESCO. While disenchantment grew, U.S. participation remained active and Americans who were engaged in UNESCO remained supportive. Such a posture was reflected in the quality of individuals appointed to represent the United States during these early years (e.g., Archibald MacLeish, William Benton, Milton Eisenhower).

However, the nature of U.S. objectives for the organization shifted in the mid-1950s. UNESCO's functional mandates were now the main focus of U.S. attention; the organization's role as a political force was to be minimized. However, the organization's mission in intellectual cooperation was being redefined in practice. There was a growing focus on technical assistance. As discussed earlier, UNESCO's functionalist programmatic orientation was rapidly giving way to a major concentration on development. Problems of identity grew.

An important problem of legitimacy for UNESCO slowly materialized in the United States. The nature of such legitimacy problems was rather complex. The State Department actively supported UNESCO's emerging technical assistance focus; the organization needed to get into the field, it was argued. In Paris a large staff was amassed to do so.[59]

Yet, with this increased focus on technical assistance came a desire in the United States to fund such activities through special funds (e.g., the United Nations Development Program [UNDP]) over which U.S. officials had relatively greater control than was the case with UNESCO's regular budget. With such a policy orientation came U.S. initiatives for greater budgetary stringency within UNESCO proper. The ongoing conflict over the budget intensified. Complaints were voiced in Washington over increased travel and other costs associated with such field activities. Funding levels proved insufficient for UNESCO to be effective in the field or to decentralize its activities further. The organization, thus, was left with a large staff in Paris, conducting activities which were largely only indirectly related to applied development. Paradoxically, this large imbalance between headquarters and field operations later became a symbol to Reagan administration officials of management problems in UNESCO.

Finkelstein and others have suggested such budgetary conflicts helped to

applied development. Paradoxically, this large imbalance between headquarters and field operations later became a symbol to Reagan administration officials of management problems in UNESCO.

Finkelstein and others have suggested such budgetary conflicts helped to fuel a growing sense of indifference in the early 1960s at the political level in Washington.[60] Also, the main governmental and nongovernmental agencies, which served as the organization's chief support groups, found UNESCO to be increasingly less central to their primary mandates. The U.S. National Commission continued to function but, after the late 1960s, less and less effectively.

A main turning point in U.S. participation in UNESCO appears to have coincided with the coming into office of the Nixon administration. A frequently told story alleges that the new president scrawled a pejorative note—"Let's gut this outfit"—on the corner of a UNESCO-related memorandum. While the validity of this tale is difficult to establish, it was about this time that U.S. participation became markedly more reactive and oriented toward damage limitation, rather than being positive and oriented toward projecting a leadership role.[61]

An indicator of such change can be found in the nature and tenure of appointees who have served as U.S. representatives to the Executive Board. There was a marked shift in the tenure of U.S. Board Members following the replacement in 1969 of Katie Louchheim, a Johnson appointee, with Louise Gore. In 1973 Gore was replaced by Edward Sullivan, a relative of Mrs. Nixon, who attended relatively few Board functions during 1973–1974. This period of U.S. participation in UNESCO was perhaps most notable for its inattention to issues of importance to U.S. officials and its ineffective-ness. It was during this time that Arab members were successful in pushing through their anti-Israeli resolutions.[62]

Beginning with Sullivan, the tenure of U.S. Board Members averaged only four Executive Board sessions. In contrast, between the 5th Executive Board in 1947, following the very brief tenures of Archibald MacLeish and Milton Eisenhower, and the election of Louchheim at the 15th General Conference in 1968, the average tenure of U.S. Board members was over twelve sessions. When viewed in the context of the substantial complexity of the organization's program and budget, the average tenure of less than two years per appointee since 1973 has likely inhibited U.S. delegates from assuming serious leadership roles. The manner in which the U.S. government has made its appointments to and used its seat on the Board in recent decades has undoubtedly limited U.S. effectiveness in UNESCO.

UNESCO's growing commitment during the 1970s to development and other Third World concerns brought a further channeling of organizational resources and energies away from intellectual cooperation. This, in turn, hastened a growing loss of interest. Those agencies with primary responsi-

organization declined. Lack of an active U.S. leadership role in program planning activities in UNESCO, in turn, greatly inhibited U.S. interests in these areas from being forcefully and effectively promoted.

Anti-Israeli resolutions and activities in UNESCO in 1974 led to further American alienation and disengagement. As discussed earlier, these actions almost brought an immediate response from Congress. Public Law 93-559 prohibited U.S. contributions until such a situation had been rectified. Although there was a speedy resolution to the situation, the ghost of these anti-Israeli activities continued to haunt U.S./UNESCO relations. One of the most significant long-term impacts was the change in attitude within the Jewish community toward UNESCO. While historically Jewish scientists and other Jewish intellectuals had been among the most active participants in U.S./UNESCO relations, many intellectually prominent Jews ceased to participate in UNESCO's work after these 1974 actions. Moreover, while Israeli officials in Paris in 1984 privately voiced trepidation over U.S. withdrawal, Jewish groups in the United States generally indicated strong support of President Reagan's decision.

As discussed earlier, U.S. officials were actively engaged during this period in the communications debate. Even in this area, though, such involvement tended to be dominated by a defensive and reactive policy posture. While U.S. officials were largely successful in fending off Soviet and other attacks on the Western media, a quite contrary perspective prevailed more generally in the United States.

Although the outcomes of UNESCO communications debates were relatively positive from a U.S. perspective after 1981, the impact of the issue on U.S. policy became increasingly negative. A notable example in this regard was Congressional passage in 1982 of the "Beard Amendment" (i.e., section 109 of the State Department Authorization Act for fiscal year 1982–83, PL 97–241), which prohibited U.S. contributions to UNESCO if it implemented any policy that licensed journalists or restricted the free flow of information and required the secretary of state to submit to Congress an annual report in that regard. Important policy successes in UNESCO, such as those in the communications and human rights areas, tended to be viewed by government officials and the public alike as having been failures. UNESCO's decline of legitimacy in the United States grew.

Thus, when UN Ambassador Kirkpatrick, Assistant Secretary Newell, and their associates targeted UNESCO for U.S. withdrawal, relatively few strong voices of protest were heard from American educational, scientific, cultural, or communications constituencies. Not only were most of UNESCO's activities viewed as being somewhat marginal to mainstream sectoral interests in these areas, but all but the most astute observers of the organization had been sensitized by the American media to view UNESCO with disregard.

CONCLUSION

One important lesson to be learned from the history of U.S./UNESCO relations is that the programmatic objectives and orientation, which serve to establish identity in any formal institution of multilateral cooperation, need to be continuously clarified and redefined as environmental conditions and the perceived needs and values of members change. Broad agreement among participants over such objectives and orientation is needed if the organization is to function effectively. Given the tremendous inequities, disparities and diversities that characterize a world society in rapid transition, there will always be tensions and conflicts over the exact nature of such identity and the appropriate means of translating it into action at the programmatic level. But the struggle for consensus in this regard helps clarify needs, values, and objectives; and to drive the issue-specific global value dialectic forward.

There will always be conflicts over identity in organizations like UNESCO, which deal in substantive issues that touch on the essence of ideologies (e.g., control over communications and information, culture, the substance of education and who should be educated, human rights), and one function of universal IGOs is to work through such ideologically sensitive matters of identity (i.e., these agencies' political forum function). At the same time, however, the maintenance of institutional legitimacy requires that multilateral programs and activities be based on the fulfillment of needs, as well as shared values, of participants and support groups.

There appears to have been much confusion in UNESCO. The organization and its members collectively had failed to deal effectively with competing demands for delimiting its organizational identity. UNESCO's base of legitimacy in regard to its major funders, especially the United States, had been allowed to erode.

The perceived decline in legitimacy of UNESCO appears to have been the single greatest problem in U.S./UNESCO relations. A retrenchment from active and constructive engagement in UNESCO accompanied this decline. When the largely political and ideologically driven decision was made to leave the organization, there was little overt opposition in the United States. While substantial needs for international cooperation in education, science, culture, and communications continued, the value of UNESCO in satisfying those needs was not perceived to be great. While UNESCO was perceived by many individuals as performing a number of important functions—some of which were performed by few other agencies—the organization was not viewed by high-level U.S. officials as being vital to the satisfaction of fundamental needs and values. Although a strong argument could be made that the organization did fulfill such needs, such perceptions of legitimacy were not widespread in the United States, and without them,

UNESCO was left vulnerable.

The organization was generally viewed as a Third World agency, devoted almost exclusively to providing development assistance. It should be made clear that many U.S. officials, including those who oversaw the withdrawal policy, seemed to prefer that UNESCO be just that: strictly a development agency. There appears to have been very little interest in the State Department—either by career diplomats and civil servants or political appointees (with a few notable exceptions)—to reorient UNESCO to deal more fully with intellectual concerns. Indeed, within the Reagan administration there seems to have been a great deal of suspicion about intellectuals, as well as substantial distrust of national policies in education, science, culture, and communications. At the same time, the nature and structure of the management of U.S. participation largely precluded any domestic functional agency from picking up such slack. At a time when U.S. preeminence was coming under increasing challenge in various of UNESCO's functional areas, the nature of U.S. policy processes inhibited an effective response.

The above analysis and conclusions about the breakdown of U.S./UNESCO relations illustrate how a needs-based approach helps us understand and explain various dynamic aspects of international governance. The U.S. withdrawal from UNESCO was not the product of some rational national policy response to a set of conditions in UNESCO which were wholly untolerable. The action resulted from the takeover of the U.S./UNESCO policy process by a small group of ideologues, who seemed bent on attacking the United Nations more generally. The key to their success was the loss of legitimacy by UNESCO among its support groups in the United States—the perceived value of maintaining the U.S./UNESCO relationship had eroded. Both identity problems within the organization and control in the United States over information resources about UNESCO by major wire services and other news media—which greatly distorted such information—made UNESCO a vulnerable target. While Reagan administration officials could not outright control the organization, they could damage or perhaps even destroy it.

A needs-based approach then is important for understanding the dynamics of international governance. Given the ideological, socio-economic, military-strategic, and cultural diversity that characterizes contemporary world society, we cannot assume that the existence and perpetuation of global institutions are based on common interests, shared values, or coercion. These institutions are maintained because they represent valued relationships related to the satisfaction of needs and values. Global institutions are characterized by a constant interplay of competing forces and tensions. But we must not mistake such tensions as representing anarchy. A substantial amount of order underlies world society. Theoretical approaches that deny or ignore the existence of this order are not likely to tell us much that is useful about the politics of international governance. While not a panacea, a needs approach is helpful in this regard.

NOTES

1. The various contributions to Stephen Krasner (ed.), *International Regimes* (Cornell University Press, 1983) are illustrative of such scholarship.

2. Traditional opponents of the United Nations had been intensifying their attacks. In the United States the Heritage Foundation and its "United Nations Assessment Project Study" continued to produce anti-UN essays, such as Burton Yale Pines' (ed.) *A World Without the U.N.: What Would Happen if the UN Shut Down* (1984), and Roger A. Brooks' "The United Nations at 40: Myth and Reality" (1985). From another perspective supporters of the UN, such as United Nations Association (UNA-USA) President Edward Luck (1984–85), were also taking a critical look at the organization and the future of U.S. multilateral relations. Even the Secretary-General of the UN, Javier Perez de Cuellar (1984), voiced concern over the mounting crises in multilateral cooperation.

3. John Ruggie, "The United States and the United Nations," *International Organization* 39(2)(Spring 1985):344.

4. Susan Strange, "Cave! Hic Dragones: A Critique of Regime Analysis," in Krasner, *International Regimes*, p. 354.

5. Paul Sites identifies eight human needs. These are the needs for: consistency of response; stimulation; security; recognition; distributive justice; meaning; rationality; and control. He argues that the first four emerge out of the dynamics of the socialization process. Suggesting that "the last four needs emerge because the first four . . . are not and cannot be immediately and consistently satisfied," he allows that the need for distributive justice, the need for meaning, the need to be seen as rational, and the need to control might more accurately be referred to as "desires." However, he continues to refer to them as needs, arguing that "in practice the motivational dynamics involved tend to be similar or the same as those of the first four needs." All relate to interaction within a social environment. Sites, *Control: The Basis of Social Order* (Dunellen, 1973).

6. Edward Azar, (ed.), *The Theory and Practice of International Conflict Resolution* (University of Maryland Press, 1985).

7. James N. Rosenau, "A Pre-Theory Revisited: World Politics in an Era of Cascading Interdependence," *International Studies Quarterly*, 28(3) (September 1984): 245–306.

8. Such a focus on needs can be seen in the writings of a few social and psychological field theorists, such as Lewin (1935, 1951), Tolman (1951), and Mey (1972).

9. In keeping with Cox and Jacobson's definition, organizational ideology refers to: (1) an interpretation of the environment as it relates to action by the organization; (2) specification of goals to be attained in the environment; and (3) a strategy of action for attaining these goals. Robert W. Cox and Harold Jacobson (eds.), *The Anatomy of Influence: Decision Making in International Organization*

(Yale University Press, 1973), p. 22. Also see: Kenneth J. Benson, "The Interorganizational Network as a Political Economy," *Administrative Science Quarterly*, 20 (1975):229–249.

10. Cox and Jacobson, *Anatomy of Influence*, p. 424.

11. Howard Aldrich, *Organizations and Environments* (Prentice-Hall, 1979), p. 4.

12. Richard Cyert and James March, *A Behavioral Theory of the Firm* (Prentice-Hall, 1963); James March, "Some Recent Substantive and Methodological Developments in the Theory of Organizational Decision-Making," in Austin Raney (ed.), *Essays on the Behavioral Study of Politics* (University of Illinois Press, 1962); and Herbert Simon, "On the Concept of Organizational Goal," *Administrative Science Quarterly*, 9(1) (1964), pp. 1–22.

13. Jeffrey Pfeffer and Gerald Salancik, *The External Control of Organizations: A Resource Dependence Perspective* (1978); and Sol Levine and Paul White, "Exchange as a Conceptual Framework for the Study of Interorganizational Relationships," *Administrative Science Quarterly* 4(1961):583–601. "A major consequence of competition for scarce resources is the development of dependencies of one organization on others in its environment, with resources sought on the basis of their relevance to the organization's task and technology" (Aldrich, *Organizations and Environments*, pp. 118–119).

14. Assumptions of egoistic self-interest should be used only with great caution. All interdependent relationships involve an element of reciprocity. As Crozier and Thoenig have argued:

> To analyze these relationships, one should not measure the resources as an accountant, but make a qualitative assessment of the actions open to the partners and of the dynamics of their games. It is equally indispensable to focus on the relationship as such and not on each partner's respective power. Even if one partner appears completely to dominate the other, the dependence remains reciprocal—no matter how absolute the right of life and death is held by masters over their slaves. Masters are dependent on their slaves' survival in order to retain lordship over them.

Michael Crozier and Jean-Claude Thoenig, "The Regulation of Complex Organized Systems," *Administrative Science Quarterly* 21(1976):547–570. Also see: Benson, "The Interorganizational Network," pp. 232–233.

15. Christer Jonsson, "Interorganization Theory and International Organization," *International Studies Quarterly* 30(1)(1986), pp. 41–42. Also see: William Evan, "The Organizational Set," in James D. Thompson (ed.), *Approaches to Organizational Design* (University of Pittsburgh Press, 1966).

16. In this regard it is important to distinguish among several interrelated aspects of resource dependence: sensitivity, vulnerability, essentiality, and substitutability. Sensitivity interdependence represents the speed and costliness with which changes in one participant's status or behavior bring about changes in another participant. Vulnerability is a focal organization's "liability to suffer costs imposed by external events even after policies have been altered" to deal with the disruption or change. These two concepts, of course, are not new to analyses of international regimes. Robert Keohane and Joseph Nye, *Power and Interdependence: World Politics in Transition* (Little, Brown, 1977).

The remaining two concepts, essentiality and substitutability, help to make more specific the nature of vulnerability. Essentiality refers to the degree to which a resource in question is crucial for the performance of vital organizational functions related to needs satisfaction and enhancement. Substitutability is the extent to which the particular resource(s) in question can be obtained elsewhere in the environment or can be substituted for by other resources. Thus, vulnerability is positively associated with essentiality, while being negatively associated with substitutability.

17. Huseyin Leblebici and Gerald R Salancik, "Stability in Interorganizational Exchanges: Rule Making Processes of the Chicago Board of Trade," *Administrative Science Quarterly* 27(1982), p. 227. They argue that "the very uncertainty of the exchange process itself forces upon exchange members a need to develop an interorganizational organization." Of course, such an "interorganizational organization" may be more or less formalized.

18. Krasner, *International Regimes.*

19. Roger Coate, *Global Issue Regimes* (Praeger, 1982).

20. Donald Puchala and Raymond Hopkins, "International Regimes: Lessons from Inductive Analysis," in Stephen Krasner (ed.), *International Regimes*, pp. 61–92; and Oran Young, "Regime Dynamics: The Rise and Fall of International Regimes," in Stephen Krasner (ed.), *International Regimes*, pp. 1–22.

21. John Burton, *Deviance, Terrorism and War: The Process of Solving Unsolved Social and Political Problems* (Martin Robertson, 1979).

22. Ibid., p. 127.

23. The material presented in this section has been taken from the author's book, *Unilateralism, Ideology, and United States Foreign Policy: The U.S. In and Out of UNESCO* (Boulder: Lynne Rienner Publishers, 1988).

24. U.S. Department of State, *U.S./UNESCO Policy Review,* Washington, D.C., February 27, 1984.

25. U.S. National Science Foundation, "Natural Sciences in UNESCO, A U.S. Interagency Perspective," Washington, D.C., 1983.

26. U.S. Department of Education, "U.S. Policy Review of UNESCO and U.S. Participation in UNESCO; Education Sector," Washington, D.C., 1983.

27. Ibid., pp. 6–7.

28. U.S. Agency for International Development, "AID Contribution to the Department of Education Statement of UNESCO," Washington, D.C., 1983, p. 2.

29. Smithsonian Institution, untitled report on the Smithsonian Institution's contribution to the U.S. policy review of UNESCO, Washington, D.C., 1983.

30. U.S. Agency for International Development, "UNESCO Communications Sector Evaluation: An AID Viewpoint," Washington, D.C., 1983, p. 2.

31. U.S. National Commission for UNESCO. *What Are the Issues Concerning the Decision of the United States to Withdraw from UNESCO?,* Washington, D.C., 1984.

32. Ibid.

33. Gregory Newell, letter to UNESCO Director-General M'Bow, July 13, 1984, in response to the DG's request (UNESCO Doc. CL–2989) for suggestions from member states for the 1985–1986 biennial program and budget.

34. If such a list were provided, it was argued, UNESCO and its member states might move to satisfy such demands in a minimally acceptable way. Then, if administration officials did not reverse the decision to withdraw, other member states,

252 ROGER A. COATE

who had negotiated in good faith, might become angry. Thus, no such list was to be provided. Personal interviews, Summer and Fall 1984.

35. Personal interviews, Summer 1987.

36. U.S. House of Representatives, "Summary," Joint Hearings of the Subcommittee on Human Rights and International Organizations and Subcommittee on International Operations, Washington, D.C., April 25, 1984; Nathan Weber, "UNESCO: Who Needs It?," *Across the Board,* 21(9) (1984), pp. 11–17.

37. Leonard Sussman, "A Review of the UNESCO Decision," Washington, D.C., May 17, 1984, p. 9.

38. Ibid., p. 2.

39. In addition, officials lamented the perceived loss of effective authority of UNESCO's delegate bodies to the Director-General. Administration officials viewed the resulting imbalance of authority as having worked against U.S. interests, as well as having led to flagrant management abuses.

40. John E. Fobes, "OMB Suggestion of U.S. Withdrawal from UNESCO," Memorandum to members of the executive committee and task force of the U.S. National Commission for UNESCO, February 1, 1981.

41. Personal interview, Spring 1987.

42. Personal interview, Summer 1987.

43. Personal interview, Fall 1984.

44. Anthony C. Giffard, *Through a Lens Darkly: Press Coverage of the U.S. Withdrawal from UNESCO* (Seattle: University of Washington, 1986).

45. Arthur Gavshon, "Washington Raises Pressure on Britain to leave UNESCO," *The Guardian,* November 22, 1985.

46. Edwin Feulner, letter, October 8, 1984.

47. Personal interviews, Winter and Summer 1987.

48. The historical material discussed in this chapter draws heavily on Walter H.C. Laves and Charles A. Thompson, *UNESCO: Purpose, Progress, Prospects* (Bloomington: Indiana University Press, 1957); and James P. Sewell, *UNESCO and World Politics* (Princeton: Princeton University Press, 1975), and "UNESCO: Pluralism Rampant," in Robert Cox and Harold Jacobson (eds.), *The Anatomy of Influence* (New Haven: Yale University Press, 1973); as well as on comments by John Fobes.

49. CAME, at this time, was comprised of the eight ministers of education of United Nations governments located in London plus British representatives.

50. Quoted in Sewell, *UNESCO and World Politics,* p. 6. This group included representatives of the education ministries of the governments of Belgium, Czechoslovakia, France, Greece, the Netherlands, Norway, Poland, and Yugoslavia.

51. Ibid., p. 63. This U.S. Delegation included: J. William Fulbright (Delegation Head); Grayson Kefauver; Archibald MacLeish; John Studebaker; C. Mildred Thompson; and Ralph Turner. An excellent discussion of the decisionmaking processes within the Department of State with respect to this issue is provided in Frank A. Ninkovich, *The Diplomacy of Ideas: U.S. Foreign Policy and Cultural Relations, 1938–1950.* (Cambridge: Cambridge University Press, 1981), pp. 76–86.

52. Ibid., p. 135.

53. Peter Lengyel, *International Social Science: The UNESCO Experience.*

(New Brunswick, NJ: Transaction Books, 1986), p. 99.

54. John E. Fobes, "UNESCO: Management of an International Institution," in Robert Jordan (ed.), *Multinational Cooperation* (New York: Oxford University Press, 1972), p. 113.

55. Lengyel, *International Social Science*, p. 7.

56. Ibid., p. 103.

57. I would like to thank Jack Fobes for clarifying this point for me.

58. T.V. Sathyamurthy, *The Politics of International Cooperation* (Geneva: Libraire Droz, 1964), pp. 159–161.

59. This discussion is based on interviews with former State Department officials.

60. Lawrence Finkelstein, "The Political Role of the Director-General of UNESCO," in Larry Finkelstein (ed.), *Politics in the United Nations System* (Durham: Duke University, 1988).

61. I wish to thank former Assistant Secretary of State for International Organization Affairs Samuel DePalma, as well as Jack Fobes, for their helpful clarifications on this point.

62. Also, it should be noted that Maheu was ill at this time and the Secretariat was in transition between Directors-General.

63. Even in respect to development activities, efforts to secure significant U.S. AID involvement were only minimally successful. Personal interview, summer 1987.

PART THREE

CONCLUSION

The concluding section is a self-critical evaluation of the potential of a human needs approach to the study of world society. The emphasis in this chapter is on the weaknesses and limitations of a human needs approach. Such a self-critical review (which is something most studies do not provide) helps to point toward future concerns, a future research agenda, and the potential of a human needs approach.

CHAPTER TWELVE

Human Needs Realism:
A Critical Assessment of the
Power of Human Needs in World Society

DAVID J. CARROLL
JEREL A. ROSATI
ROGER A. COATE

In this closing chapter, David Carroll and the editors conduct a self-critical assessment of the weaknesses and promises of a human needs approach. The authors address a series of epistemological problems involved in establishing empirically the existence of a concrete set of human needs and their relationship to human and social behavior. They acknowledge and discuss the major obstacles that lie in the path of inductive analysis in the human needs framework. At the same time, they stress that needs theory, deduced from the existence of individual human needs, provides a firm basis for theory and practice in international relations. Anchored in a greater awareness of the underlying sources of individual behavior, "human needs realism," based on inductive and deductive analysis, complements existing approaches while enriching our understanding of human behavior in world society.

Carroll is a Ph.D. candidate in International Studies at the University of South Carolina. His areas of specialization include international relations theory and the political economy of development.

In arguing that human needs are a fundamental underlying source of political and social interaction in world society, this book is engaged in an important, yet daunting task. A major aspect of the challenge, and a part to which most of this volume has been devoted, has been to gather together a coherent set of writings, each of which contributes to demonstrating the importance of human needs in explaining individual and group behavior across a range of applications. A related, but perhaps more difficult and enduring aspect of the task, is to critically examine the value of a human needs approach to the study of international relations. This chapter makes an initial effort in this regard by conducting a self-critical review of the weaknesses, promises, and future of the approach.   In order for a human needs perspective to be part of the study of world politics it is not enough to demonstrate the promise of its strengths. Its weaknesses also need to be highlighted and addressed in order to determine the potential contribution and future agenda of a human needs approach to the study of international relations.

HUMAN NEEDS REALISM

Clearly, there a number of problems and unanswered questions, both empirical and theoretical, concerning the viability of a human needs approach in international relations. Some of these deal with the difficulty of "proving" empirically the existence of human needs, and the link between these needs and actual behavior. Since these are very real concerns which must be addressed, we will consider them at some length. Perhaps an even greater obstacle to the process of establishing a human needs approach, however, is the prevalence of simple misconceptions about the term "human needs" itself: in the eyes of all too many theorists and practitioners of international relations, the concept of "human needs" smacks of idealism and of some kind of sentimental attachment to the worth of human beings— laudable as an idea, yet unworkable and impractical as a "scientific" or "realistic" approach to the study of international relations.

While some critics may likewise label the generalizations in this book as far-fetched and idealistic, we believe that to a large extent this type of reaction is due to preconceived (and misconceived) notions of the term "human needs," rather than because of any failings of the approach itself (which are undoubtedly numerous, as we will discuss). Certainly, the concept of human needs may appear at first glance to the unacquainted as overly simplistic and idealistic. But the inherent complexity of the concept and the range of applications found for it in the chapters in this volume should dispel many of these concerns.

It should be clear that, by and large, the authors in this volume harbor no idealistic illusions concerning the inherent goodness of human nature, nor about easy paths to harmony and peace in human social relations and international relations. On the contrary, the authors seek to underscore the very *complexity* of human nature as a fundamental source of human behavior. To the extent that attention is brought to this important yet complex source of human behavior an important goal of this work will have been achieved. More important, however, it generates a more realistic and comprehensive treatment of human behavior and social relations.

Thus, a major objective of the book has been to suggest simply that the concept of "human needs" provides social scientists with an important conceptual tool that will facilitate a more comprehensive and realistic understanding of the sources of motivation that underlie micro-level behavior. Moreover, the notion of human needs can serve to guide the development of empirical theory at the macro-level. By generating a set of deduced assumptions regarding micro-level human needs, the human needs approach builds a foundation upon which social scientists can formulate more powerful macro-level theoretical explanations.

This major strength of the human needs framework draws attention to the distinction between inductive and deductive analysis which we raised in Chapter 1. Inductive analysis derives theory on the basis of empirical observations of human behavior. Deductive analysis, on the other hand, develops theory based on a set of fundamental assumptions about human behavior (which are derived to a greater or lesser extent from empirical observations). As we will see below, inductive analysis in the human needs framework faces numerous epistemological problems due to the difficulty of directly linking human needs to observed individual behavior and patterns of social relations. Deductive analysis in the human needs approach, however, is much less problematic. Although questions of overall validity can be raised, the human needs approach to world politics allows for the development of a powerful theory that transcends the limits of conventional approaches to the study of international relations. In order to arrive at a thorough and well-balanced assessment of its value, the human needs approach should be evaluated in terms of its potential advantages and disadvantages for inductive as well as deductive analysis.

The major advantages of deductive analysis based on assumptions of human needs flow from the explicit attention that is thus drawn to the impact of human needs on human behavior. This is especially important, since questions about the linkages among human needs, human nature, and political behavior have been overlooked in much of the work in international relations. A large and respected corpus of theoretical and empirical literature in international relations scholarship has simply assumed, a priori, that human nature is evil and aggressive. The range of human needs is thus circumscribed to the pursuit of power, security, and prestige. This basically aggressive and egoistic characterization of the individual, when reified in the form of the nation-state, has served as a causal force underlying many of the "realist" writings in international politics.[1] The so-called "neo-realists" have tried to avoid these simplistic individual level assumptions by reifying the "international system" so that the forces flowing from the structural characteristics of this system account for state behavior.[2] Yet, here too, an atomistic view of nation-states as unitary, rational actors underlies the approach, so that ultimately the question reverts to reification of egoistic state actors.

The human needs perspective proposes, among other things, to replace this fundamental simplifying assumption of human nature used by "realists" (and so-called "neo-realists") with a more realistic set of assumptions and to open up these assumptions to detailed investigation and analysis. It suggests that examining human needs can actually help shed light into the "black box" that surrounds our understanding of state and international behavior. In this way the approach points toward a more comprehensive understanding of human behavior, both in terms of individuals and in terms of larger social aggregates, including various social and political groups and organizations as well as states. In this light, therefore, a strong current of realism—"human needs realism"—should be acknowledged. Focusing attention on the complex composition of human needs motivation, which leads individuals to join into various groups on the basis of needs and values satisfaction, should be recognized as a "realistic" and responsible approach to analyses of social and international relations.

Certainly such an approach is more realistic than simply assuming, a priori, that humans by their very nature are fundamentally evil and aggressive (or conversely that man by his nature is fundamentally good). Such assumptions are belied by everyday experiences which demonstrate mankind's complex and contradictory nature, combining at various times benevolence and altruism with evil and selfishness. Moreover, even the greatest philosophers have been unable over the ages to agree upon a single concept of human nature. It would thus seem both naive and pretentious for scholars of international relations to continue to rely on such singular and simplistic notions of human nature.

In order for the merits of the human needs approach to be fully exploited, however, a wider acceptance and utilization of the concept has first to be brought about. Only when a significant number of serious scholars and practitioners begin to accept the validity of the human needs concept, and utilize the insights it generates will the full potential of the approach be realized. Therefore, the reluctance of many analysts of international relations to even consider the potential importance of the concept and approach of human needs is clearly a problem. As suggested earlier, we believe that this hesitation is due in large part to the intellectual rigidity that pervades the field of international relations.[3] A major goal of this chapter, then, is to help dispel misperceptions about the realism and potential of a human needs perspective, as well as to reflect self-critically on such an approach.

At the same time, however, it is clear that at least part of the lukewarm reception given to the human needs approach can be traced to the inability of human needs theorists themselves, and others, to build an appealing and intellectually coherent paradigm, one that is clearly superior, in the Kuhnian sense, to existing ones. There is no question that a number of difficult issues need to be more thoroughly resolved before a new approach incorporating human needs assumptions be realistically considered as an addition to the predominant approaches. However, we believe that these problems, to a large extent, are confined to human needs approaches that rely on inductive analysis. In order to establish a firm empirical micro-level basis for inductive analysis, major progress will have to be made in addressing these concerns. Nevertheless, we are optimistic since we feel that the merits of the human needs perspective are compelling, especially in the case of deductively derived theory and research.

As a closing note to this volume, then, it would seem appropriate to step back and critically examine these weaknesses and limitations, focusing especially on the questions that were raised initially at the end of Chapter 1. An intentionally self-critical assessment of these problems, and the potential ways that they might be overcome, or circumvented, can help in clarifying the prospects for integrating human needs into international relations research. In fact, it is probably the best way to squarely confront the questions that loom regarding the practicality and likely success of research employing a human needs approach, both inductively and deductively.

WEAKNESSES AND LIMITATIONS

The crux of the human needs approach, as applied to international relations, can be found in the work of John Burton (see, for example, Chapters 3 and 9 in this volume). Burton claims that over time all societies experience conflicts between the institutional values and structures of society on the one hand, and human needs at the level of the individual on the other hand. Burton sees this dynamic 'historic process' by which societies evolve dialectically as driven by the tension between the existence of individual human needs, on the one hand, and the degree to which societies and social institutions are responsive to these needs on the other hand.[4] Individuals, in striving to meet their needs, will interact with other individuals. As a result of this interaction, individuals identify with, and join in various associations that might facilitate the satisfaction of their needs. The requirements of maintaining certain social institutions—that is, political structures—are often inconsistent with individual human needs, since social institutions tend over time to express and "legitimize" the bargaining power of elites and higher status groups.   Societies that thus fail to meet the needs of their members become unstable over time. If they are to survive and be seen as legitimate by the vast majority they will ultimately be forced to undergo change. As we suggested in Chapter 1, international relations, thus, are a function of the processes of legitimization and delegitimization in world society, which result from individuals and groups pursuing needs and values.

Seen in this human needs perspective, the social networks of relationships that individuals enter into, and that are salient in terms of important needs and values, become important objects of inquiry. It is at the level of such social networks that individual need satisfaction is determined. Intergovernmental networks have traditionally been the almost exclusive concern of scholars of international relations. Yet, with respect to political processes through which needs are satisfied or deprived, intergovernmental relations are but one type of relevant social relation in world society. Perhaps even more important for a substantial portion of the world's people are nongovernmental networks and institutions, including, for example, those involved with global trade, investment, and finance.

Assuming that one accepts the validity of this human needs approach on the face of these deductive arguments, a number of important questions arise, especially in so far as empirical analysis is concerned. Indeed, almost every strength in the theory of human needs pointed to by the supporters of the approach has a corresponding downside which raises problems that cast doubt on the practical utility of the approach. This represents a dilemma for those would-be adherents of the human needs perspective who allow immediate empirical problems to overshadow the richness of the theory's set of fundamental assumptions. The most immediate, and perhaps the most important question in this regard concerns the concept "human needs" itself.

The Concept of Human Needs

In trying to apply the abstract concepts in the previous discussion regarding human needs to real world situations, we are confronted immediately with the question of determining *exactly* what are human needs? As this volume has shown, no consensus exists at present regarding this crucial definitional question. Are human needs to be defined and understood as some minimum set of universal needs common to all individuals everywhere, as John Burton suggests? Or, are human needs better understood as culturally relative, varying across diverse cultural contexts?[5] This question is a vitally important one since the way human needs are defined will clearly affect our understanding of behavior: if the pursuit of human needs does in fact vary across cultures—due to the interaction of needs and values—then it should be expected that needs will in fact be "seen" differently by peoples of different cultures. That is, if values rooted in culturally relative contexts serve as "filters" through which underlying human needs are processed, then an expanded set of behavioral modes becomes possible. Different means might be employed in the pursuit of the same individual needs, and varying levels of need satisfaction and varying sorts of need-pursuing behavior could be recognized as "normal" or "legitimate," as one moves from culture to culture.

The need for identity that Burton and others have discussed, for example, might be radically different in Eastern or Native American cultures than the identity need as understood by Westerners. The former tend to stress the collectivity as a source of identity, whereas in the the latter, a greater emphasis is usually placed on the individual. A number of similar examples could be cited as evidence of the types of problems that arise in situations where cultural values have a strong imprint on the conception of human needs.

A related, and perhaps prior concern, is the question regarding the degree to which needs are determined by society and the process of socialization, as opposed to being ontological, universal needs that all individuals share because of the very fact of their human-ness. There are well-established schools of thought in psychology that believe that human behavior (and perhaps by extension, human needs as well) is largely a function of the environment in society with which individuals respond. This concern is only heightened if we conclude that needs, as related to human behavior, are culturally relative, since the socialization process will vary across cultural contexts as well.   Indeed, if needs are to a large extent a product of the socialization process, and thus not very different from "learned" values and desires, and if what is "learned" changes from one society to another, then what the concept "universal human needs" contains becomes very small, in effect merely a residual concept.

All of these concerns revolve around the key question of the degree to which human needs, as they interact with values, are changeable, both across time, as well as across space (both physical and cultural).   Although it would seem that the human needs approach requires us to assume a very limited degree of variability in human needs, this might not necessarily be the case. Ramashray Roy, for example, argues in Chapter 4 that industrialization and technological progress tend to produce over time a gradual proliferation and change in human needs.   He sees this as a negative, even dangerous, development since such a seemingly unending expansion of human needs threatens the long-term harmony and stabiltiy of man's relationship with society and nature.   Thus, Roy calls for Gandhian self-restraint, and for the "reform of man himself" to control and reshape human needs. Obviously, Roy's conception of human needs is dynamic and variable. But again, this is not necessarily inconsistent with the fundamental assumptions of the human needs perspective.   As long as it can safely be assumed that some set of fundamental universal human needs exists, such that changes in these only occur over very long periods of time (and over relatively great cultural-value distances), human needs theorists can still be credited with important and valid insights.

Yet even if these issues were somehow addressed at a general level, important underlying questions would then have to be resolved. Assume for example that it could be established that some set of universal human needs do in fact exist. Assume further, that beyond this it could also be established that socialization (varying in its form, content, and intensity across cultures) plays an important role in determining exactly how human needs are perceived, how these needs interact with cultural values, and consequently, how these needs are acted upon. At this point it becomes important to know a number of other things, such as: the precise nature of human needs, whether a hierarchy or priority of needs exists, and how human needs are different from, and related to, interests, values, and desires. Social scientists are thus impelled to conduct extensive empirical research aimed at answering these questions. But such research faces a number of obstacles that could prove insurmountable in the long run. In short, in order to fully develop a major strength of the human needs approach, a score of problems will inevitably arise. If inductive analysis in the human needs approach is to be fruitful these will have to be resolved in one manner or another. In the next several sections, we will briefly explore the kinds of problems that will almost certainly hound social scientists in their attempts to give empirical grounding to the concept of human needs.

What Is the Nature of Human Needs?

That some set of universal human needs does exist is something we can accept as self-evident, arising out of the very fact of mankind's human-ness. We can assert further that these ontological human needs contain both physical (minimum survival requirements) and psychological elements. This is not at all unreasonable, especially when one considers the store of empirical historical and experimental evidence, surveyed by James Davies in Chapter 2 (or, for example, compiled by Johan Galtung regarding development in Chapter 7). Yet, the *exact* mix of elements that make up these universal needs is something that may prove impossible to ever really determine, since social scientists cannot "see" human needs empirically.[6] Rather, the existence of needs is something that at present can only be hypothesized, and then "observed" via some sort of *indirect* means.

We can hypothesize, for example, that a given set of universal needs exists, and then deduce the extent to which these needs are being met on the basis of the types of behavior in which individuals engage.   In a similar vein, the absence or presence of what Galtung and Lederer call "need-satisfiers" could serve as indicator of human needs.[7] Nevertheless, the fact remains that at our present state of knowledge, these epistemological problems will preclude any *definitive* identification of human needs, or any consistent separation of human needs from interests, values, and desires.

These sorts of methodological limitations are admittedly troubling in light of the types of propositions that a human needs approach generates, which tend to focus on the degree of need satisfaction and on various kinds of needs-hierarchies and prioritizations.   In fact, a key insight into human behavior offered by the human needs perspective is based on the proposition that behavior is a function of the level to which human needs are satisfied as related to the relative priority placed on those needs. But, since the degree to which human needs are met cannot as yet be determined with any degree of confidence (let alone the fact that the concept itself is very difficult to ground empirically), it is not surprising that critics often question the practical utility of the approach.

Human Needs-Hierarchies

Obviously, these sorts of epistemological problems also undermine attempts to establish empirically the existence of needs-hierarchies. Yet, as we noted above, the distinctions that such needs-hierarchies reveal can be very important for building needs-based theories. James Davies, for example, points out in Chapter 2 that what is often considered "irrational" behavior might actually be better understood as completely rational once a prioritization of human needs is recognized. In essence, Davies is arguing here that "rational" behavior can only be defined in relation to individual behavior and to the level of human needs satisfaction. In Chapter 3, John Burton builds a similar argument about what is usually labelled "deviant" behavior.

It should be pointed out that the work along these lines by both Davies and Burton also stresses the fact that human needs theory inherently incorporates an element of purposive behavior and self-interest into its conception of human nature. Human nature is not seen merely as some abstract set of human needs. Instead, building on the work of Abraham Maslow, needs theorists often envision some sort of hierarchy of needs, which together with the degree of need-satisfaction and a variety of other intervening variables (interests, values, desires) set the parameters for the range of "rational" behavior that is ultimately decided upon. This emphasis on purposive behavior—within the context of a hierarchy of human needs —further underscores the "realism" of the human needs approach. In addition, it suggests that "human needs realism" is actually quite compatible with many existing approaches to international relations, including rational actor models and approaches that stress the role of perceptions in understanding "rational" behavior.

Assumptions about rationality as grounded in needs-hierarchies, however, can at times be confounded by situations in which behavior appears deviant, or "irrational," even in the context of a hierarchy of needs. Numerous examples of self-sacrificing and intentional need-deprivation could be cited as evidence of this possibility. Cases like Gandhi or Martin Luther King, Jr., in which certain needs are intentionally subordinated to the promotion of other needs, are clear examples of this type of situation. But, these cases do not necessarily contradict the basic importance of needs-hierarchies for explaining variations in what can be considered "rational," since individuals will generally tend to emphasize the satisfaction of certain (basic) needs more than others.   However, it is important to recognize that such "hierarchies" are not so rigid as to predetermine individuals' actions in all cases.

Moreover, it should be noted that needs-hierarchies are not a crucial element of all human needs approaches. Galtung's appeal in Chapter 7 for a human needs approach to international development, for example, is actually critical of current developmental approaches based on needs-hierarchies. Compatible with arguments by Burton in this regard, Galtung argues that such needs-hierarchies tend to emphasize a set of policies that are more oriented toward the needs of Western elites than the needs that must be promoted to further human development. Furthermore, he suggests that humanity in all its cultural manifestations is too diverse, so much so that constructing some universal hierarchy of human needs becomes almost impossible, and not all that useful.   Instead, Galtung favors a more modest research agenda that would encourage the investigation of a rich and diverse set of needs corresponding to the cultural diversity of mankind.   Galtung's approach, like that of several other chapters in this volume, highlights the fact that human needs based theory can generate interesting and provocative ideas, regardless of whether or not needs-hierarchies are considered important.

Human Needs vs. Values, Interests, and Desires

Besides trying to delineate the nature of human needs and needs-hierarchies, future empirical research must also attempt to distinguish these relatively unchanging phenomena from what Azar has suggested are the more time-bound notions of values, interests, and wants (or desires).[8] Values, interests, and desires, more so than needs, are closely tied to socialization and to the political, social, economic, and cultural environment. As such, they reflect the impact of social and cultural institutions and norms, as well as the influence of a multitude of more specific social groupings and relationships of which an individual may be a part. While the social relationships particular to certain individuals play a much larger role than the more general societal values, both will have an impact on determining how an individual acts upon his/her human needs.

At the same time, however, it must be remembered that in the long run of history there is a dialectic interplay between individual human needs and the larger societal values and interests that society promotes. This, again, is the 'historic process' to which Burton makes reference.[9] As was noted in Chapters 1 and 3, both Sites and Burton suggest that society itself, and hence societal values, only comes about as a result of the long term existence and pursuit of individual human needs.[10] Thus, the existence of human needs causes individuals to come together into various social groupings which aggregate at some level to create "society." Yet society itself, plus the myriad of lesser social relationships in turn shape and limit how individuals interpret and act on their needs.[11]

Distinguishing an individual's needs from values, interests, and desires, therefore, is a complicated task. Nevertheless, it is not a major barrier to working with the human needs approach. Since human needs are more enduring (even though some variability across social and cultural space might be recognized), these should be distinguishable from the more variable patterns of individual values, interests, and desires. And, since the latter are largely derived from the specific network of social relationships in which one interacts, research could examine how social relationships create and transmit values and interests, so as to help in the task of identifying individuals' values, interests, and desires. In a sense, research in this area should not be foreign ground to scholars of international relations and political science. On the contrary, the study of values, beliefs and opinions constitute major areas of traditional concern in these disciplines. Ronald Inglehart's analysis of value change in Western Europe (from materialism to post-materialism) is one good example of empirical political research that exploits the theory and concepts of human needs and needs-hierarchies.[12]

What is new is the emphasis placed on uncovering the links between the pursuit of human needs, especially in the context of social relationships, and the more conventional concepts of power, values, and interests. The human needs perspective recognizes the importance of power and the related concerns of traditional political realism. But it tries to treat these concepts within a larger framework that directs attention to the fundamental sources of human motivations. Thus, the focus is not on the attributes, capabilities, and interests of state actors. Rather, it is on the specific social relationships that give rise to influence, control, and authority. Furthermore, attention is also directed to the link between these various social and political relationships and the underlying individual human needs, which serve to motivate individuals to enter into these relationships in the first place. This, once more, points to the intellectual sophistication of "human needs realism".

Human Needs, Ideology, and the Processes of Legitimization

Examining the role of values, interests, and desires, which intervene between underlying human needs and actual human behavior also brings attention to the importance of ideology. Like values and interests, ideologies are related to the variety of social and economic forces that envelop the individual, especially those social relationships and economic forces that are salient to the individual in terms of satisfying needs. Similarly, ideologies occupy an intervening position in the chain that links fundamental human needs to individual behavior. But, determining the exact empirical relationships between individual needs, ideology, and behavior also remains problematical.

A matter of special interest to social scientists is the role ideologies have on an individual's awareness or perception of his/her level of need satisfaction. This in turn influences the degree to which individuals participate in sociopolitical relationships and the extent to which associated social and political structures are viewed as legitimate sources of authority (that is, to what extent they are valued because they satisfy needs).

Historically, ideologies have often served to reinforce the dominant social institutions and values developed by elites. In attempting to shift attention away from unmet needs within society, communist ideology, for example, focuses attention on certain unmet needs in capitalist societies, while liberal ideology directs attention to the neglected needs in communist or socialist societies. Furthermore, as Ashley notes, liberal "laissez-faire" ideology attempts to create an image in which the productive economy is a sphere of reality discrete from the political realm, so that no political responsibility is found for economic inequality and deprivation.[13] Thus, the political foundation of economic relationships highlighted by writers as diverse as Carr and Gramsci is obscured.[14] Alternatively, ideologies can dramatically alter an individual's awareness and perception of needs, possibly "awakening" individuals to the fact of need deprivation or to ways in which such a situation can be realistically countered.

It is also possible that ideologies might create "false" needs (false consciousness as it were), so that individuals perceive and act on "needs" that are not really needs ontologically. "Needs" in this light are often seen as created by various political and economic elites via their control over communications and advertising as a means of manipulating the masses (possibly to buttress sagging legitimacy). A case can be made, for example, that the television and radio media have fostered the development of the "need" to consume. In addition, a tendency to conform to the "legitimate" authorities and to be more passive and apathetic is condoned by these media, since the outside world seems to be overpowering, and yet at the same time distant.

Thus, ideology not only colors how individuals perceive their needs, in addition, it might help to explain why it is that needs can at various times change from "latent" to "active," or vice versa. This is important since we can point to scores of cases throughout history in which it would seem that individuals' needs were not being met, yet in which no significant challenge in the form of "deviant" behavior was mounted. Why is it, for example, that serfs in feudal societies, or slaves in a variety of other societies, did not always attempt to change the structure of society or the nature of the social and economic relationships that tied them to others in society? Although a complex range of factors are most likely at work in any single situation, one answer would be that serfs' basic needs were not being deprived to the extent to which it would be "rational," in terms of the anticipated costs and benefits and chance of "success," to actually attempt to undertake such actions.

Given the overwhelming power of lords and other elites who controlled social institutions, it would seem likely that there was often no real possibility to expect to bring about change.

Another possibility, however, is that such action or nonaction is more a function of the extent to which individuals are truly conscious of their socioeconomic and political situations, and the possibilities for participation or action these circumstances hold. Ideologies may work to alter individual's consciousness of needs deprivation and at times reveal the exploited power in their situations. They may even change the perceived costs and benefits associated with actions to change the status quo and delegitimize reigning sources of authority. These are topics of great importance, which, admittedly, are difficult to empirically link to the concept of human needs.

Human Needs, Participation, and Social Networks

In spite of the problems discussed above regarding the difficulty of empirically grounding the concept of human needs and the problem of differentiating needs from values, interests, and ideologies, the human needs approach is a critical navigation point for focusing on social relationships as important objects of inquiry. In a human needs approach, social networks of individuals and groups are the units of analysis, since it is through these networks that human needs are pursued and where values, interests, and power arise. Building theory with such a human needs approach does not require that we first achieve a comprehensive and problem-free empirical understanding of human needs.

Clearly, a human needs approach to the analysis of the nature and dynamics of social relationships will encounter difficulties similar to those discussed above. How, for instance, do we know that an individual's participation in a given social relationship or organization reflects an underlying human need? Similarly, how can it be determined whether or not participation in such a relationship has, or has not, served to satisfy the particular need that we assume gives rise to participation in the first place? How can we actually know, or somehow measure, the level and impact of needs deprivation and satisfaction? These, again, are empirical and epistemological problems to which no easy answer exists. Nonetheless, this should not stop creative and forceful minds from utilizing the insights that human needs assumptions offer to forge theoretical insights that improve our understanding of the human condition.

Theorizing about the nature of social networks and relationships based on a human needs approach does not require explicit and definitive empirical linkages. The development of theory and a research agenda is not dependent solely on inductive, empirical analysis, but is also heavily dependent on deduction. There is sufficient empirical evidence to allow one to conclude that individuals have human needs which motivate and affect human behavior. Although there is no consensus as to the specific nature of these needs and their specific relationship to values, ideology, interests, etc., there is a growing consensus as to their existence and their importance. Thus, one is on firm ground in deductively theorizing about human behavior based on assumptions about individual human needs.

An area where the human needs approach would seem to hold out special promise is in linking theory and research at the micro-level to that at the macro-level. As we argued in the first chapter, three key factors (or concepts)—groups, values, and social networks—can enable us to build up from the level of the individual to macro-level collectivities, via the groups and social networks of relationships in which individuals participate in order to pursue their needs and values. Each of these social networks can correspond analytically to a specific system of social relationships definable in relation to the particular issue or problem under investigation.

The work of Quincy Wright and others in social field theory some thirty years ago provides the basic conceptual and analytical tools for examining the characteristics of, and the relationships between, various social networks.[15] Thus, social networks, and the groups of which they are comprised, can be treated as systems of action within a social field consisting of various characteristics (such as capabilities, value orientations), which correspond to those factors important in the context of the issue at hand. As we aggregate the virtually infinite array of possible social networks of relationships into larger collectivities, the entire range of processes that relate to value allocation, as well as need satisfaction and deprivation, come into view. In effect, then, this framework could afford analysts the opportunity to look into any and *all* social relationships that make up the substance of politics in world society, in any of its forms or levels—local, governmental, international. And no reference is necessary to terms such as "states" or "power," which tend to blind us to much of what happens in world society.

This is reinforced by Rosenau's work on "roles" and his treatment of the individual "as a composite of identifiable and competing roles."[16] Focusing on roles expands the range of units that can be analyzed as existing in social fields by allowing scholars to break down the individual into analytic subparts, corresponding to the various roles an individual occupies within a set of groups, institutions, and social networks. Rosenau seems content to utilize the concept of "role" without dwelling on the question of what motivates individuals to assume these roles in the first place. The human needs perspective assumes that the entire set of roles that an individual occupies is largely a function of the individual's pursuit of needs and value satisfaction. This is entirely compatible with Rosenau's analysis, yet goes beyond it by delving into the underlying human needs that motivate individuals to assume the variety of roles that they do.

Thus, the study of human behavior at the macro-level by focusing on groups, values, and social networks due to assumptions of individual human needs comes close to reflecting the complexity of world society. Reliance on deduction for the development of theory, based on assumptions of human nature and behavior, is no different for needs theory than for so-called realist theory (or, for that matter, almost any body of thought). However, while realist assumptions about human nature go unexamined, the concept of human needs has received a considerable amount of study and analysis over time. Furthermore, not only is needs theory inductively and deductively derived, when applied to the study of world society through the concepts of groups, values, and social networks, the micro-macro gap is directly addressed and minimized.

RESTORING RELATIVITY OF THOUGHT TO REALIST ANALYSIS

An important idea in the writings of E. H. Carr suggests that international relations theory is not a static and absolute conceptualization of an unchanging world, but rather a dynamic and relative one, evolving over time in dialectic interplay with the real world circumstances that surround the theorist.[17] Theory, like all thought, is relative. It is historically conditioned by currents in the intellectual world and in the world of political and social relations in which it develops. As the world changes, and as our knowledge and understanding of our world develops, theory evolves.

In some ways, human needs theorists envision their efforts as a contribution to the progressive evolution of theory in international relations and related disciplines. In response to a range of developments in the twentieth century, which have placed a new emphasis on problems and actors that more traditional approaches to international relations cannot adequately comprehend, the disparate strains and long historical roots of a human needs approach are gradually coming together into a coherent whole. Human needs theorists' focus on the interaction between individual needs and culturally relative values in a group context sheds a different light on these problems and actors that are so intractable for traditional state-centric approaches.

As such, the insights and assumptions of a human needs approach complement a whole range of recent writings in international relations theory, ranging from the issue area and regime frameworks found in the writings of authors such as Mansbach and Vasquez, Keohane and Nye, and Keohane, to structural and world order approaches typical of Galtung, Mendlovitz, Falk and others.[18] Together with a score of other writings, such as the work of scholars like John Burton, Quincy Wright, and James Rosenau cited previously, the human needs approach is peeling away those overly rigid assumptions of traditional realism that now appear to many as unwarranted, outdated, and unworkable. As part of this effort, scholars are beginning to take note of the potential benefits of inter-paradigm borrowing as a mechanism to advance the evolution of international relations theory.[19] We believe that the central assumptions of the human needs approach can constitute a significant element in this interplay and development of international relations theory.

Fundamentally, it is individuals that drive world society. Thus, in order to analyze world society realistically, scholars must consider what are the underlying motivations that cause individuals to enter into social relationships, as well as the processes through which this occurs. A framework that proceeds from the assumption that one of the primary sources of human motivation is the existence of some set of human needs provides a realistic foundation for subsequent theoretical and empirical work. Indeed, we feel that this is the primary strength and contribution of the human needs approach.   Its set of fundamental assumptions, logically deduced from the existence of individual human needs, provides a firm basis for research and practice in international relations.

The preceding sections have shown that theory grounded in assumptions of human needs can both complement and enrich our understanding of the complex social problems and relationships of world society. Thus, critics who label the concept of human needs unworkable and who claim that this problem poses an insurmountable obstacle to practical research in international relations are quite premature in writing off the approach. Clearly, there are major epistemological problems and basic disagreements concerning the empirical content of human needs concepts. These are hurdles that cannot be dismissed lightly. On the other hand, it is only through basic research designed either to resolve such issues—or where required, to work around them—that real progress will be possible.

As was noted in Chapter 1, difficulties and debate over the problem of how to define one of the core concepts of political science—power—has not prevented political scientists from utilizing it as a basic guidepost in their work. Scholars of international relations would be well-advised to take clearer notice of this. More scholars need to acquaint themselves with the human needs perspective, and make use of its set of assumptions in building theory and conducting empirical analysis. This should be especially useful since many of them rely on implicit, but unexamined, assumptions concerning the same general motivational phenomena.

As we have seen, numerous problems will doubtlessly confront empirical research guided by a human needs orientation, especially when such research emphasizes an inductive approach. Empirical investigations directed specifically at discerning the nature and content of human needs may ultimately reveal crucial limitations of the human needs concept. Nevertheless, such analysis could point the way to a dramatically improved understanding of international relations, and social relations in general.

Deductive theory, however, founded on the assumptions of human needs, such as the working propositions summarized in Table 1.1, can proceed in spite of epistemological questions. "Human needs realism" can enrich our understanding of the world around us by forcing analysts to investigate, both theoretically as well as empirically, what are often unexamined assumptions. In this light, the assumptions of "human needs realism," which are anchored in a heightened awareness of the sources of individual behavior, are a response to the need for theory to adjust to the social and political problems of the day.

Indeed, the more "realistic" world view provided by a needs approach is perhaps its most important contribution to the study of world politics. Political processes and outcomes in world society are not based fundamentally on the anarchic relations of state actors; they are based in an inherent entropic order, created by the complex interdependence which results as individuals and groups go about the day-to-day process of satisfying needs and values. This resulting order not only severely constrains the range of options for all participants interacting in world society (including those individuals and groups who are acting in the name of states), but, more importantly, provides, in varying degrees, systems of governance over these relationships. Thus, a human needs approach moves us much closer to the realism of world society toward which students of international relations have long been striving.

NOTES

1. See, for example, Hans Morgenthau, *Politics Among Nations: The Struggle for Power and Peace* (Alfred A. Knopf, 1978); and Raymond Aron, *War and Peace: A Theory of International Relations* (Praeger, 1966).

2. See Kenneth N. Waltz, *Theory of International Relations* (Addison Wesley, 1979); Robert Gilpin, *War and Change in World Politics* (Cambridge University Press, 1981); and Stephen Krasner, *Structural Conflict: The Third World against Global Liberalism* (University of California Press, 1985).

3. Perhaps, a part of this rigidity can even be traced, as Ashley suggests, to the desire of some analysts of international relations to serve as advisors to state elites who are mainly concerned with maintaining the status quo. Richard K. Ashley, "Three Modes of Economism," *International Studies Quarterly*, 27, 4 (December):463–496.

4. John Burton, *Deviance, Terrorism and War: The Process of Solving Unsolved Social and Political Problems* (Martin Robertson, 1979), pp. 83–84.

5. See Katrin Lederer, "Introduction," in Lederer, ed., *Human Needs* (Oelgeschlager, Gunn & Hain, 1980), pp. 1–14 for a discussion of this issue.

6. Christian Bay, chapter 5.

7. See Galtung, Chapter 7, and Lederer, "Introduction," p. 3. for discussions

need "satisfiers."

   8. Edward E. Azar, ed. *The Theory and Practice of International Conflict Resolution* (University of Maryland Press, 1985).

   9. John Burton, *Deviance, Terrorism and War,* pp. 64–65.

   10. Paul Sites, *Control: The Basis of Social Order* (Dunellen, 1973), p. 15; and Burton, *Deviance, Terrorism and War,* pp. 64–65.

   11. See Burton, *Deviance, Terrorism and War.*

   12. Ronald Inglehart, "The Silent Revolution in Europe: Intergenerational Change in Post-Industrial Societies," *American Political Science Review* 65:991–1017.

   13. Richard K. Ashley, "Three Modes of Economism."

   14. E. H. Carr, *The Twenty Year's Crisis* (Harper and Row, 1939), and Antonio Gramsci, *Selections from the Prison Notebooks of Antonio Gramsci* (International Publishers, 1971).

   15. Quincy Wright, *The Study of International Relations* (Appleton-Century-Crofts, 1955).

   16. James N. Rosenau, "A Pre-Theory Revisited: World Politics in an Era of Cascading Interdependence," *International Studies Quarterly* 28, (September 1984): 269.

   17. E. H. Carr, *Twenty Years' Crisis.*

   18. Richard W. Mansbach and John A. Vasquez, *In Search of Theory: A New Paradigm for Global Politics* (Columbia University Press, 1981); Robert Keohane and Joseph Nye, *Power and Interdependence: World Politics in Transition* (Little, Brown and Company, 1977); Robert Keohane, *After Hegemony: Cooperation and Discord in the World Political Economy* (Princeton University Press, 1984); Johan Galtung, *The True Worlds: A Transnational Perspective* (The Free Press, 1979); Saul Mendlovitz, "On the Creation of a Just World Order: An Agenda for a Program of Inquiry and Praxis," *Alternatives,* 7, (Winter 1981): 355-373; and Richard A. Falk, et al. (eds.), *Studies on a Just World Order* (Westview Press, 1982).

   19. See Hayward Alker and Thomas Biersteker, "The Dialectics of World Order: Notes for a Future Archeologist of International Savoir Faire," *International Studies Quarterly* 28 (2) (1984): 121–142.

Index

INDEX OF NAMES

INDEX OF SUBJECTS

160, 250; definition, 4, 6, 7, 14, 16, 17, 27,
39, 48-52, 62, 132, 263; hierarchy, 19, 25-
27, 31-32, 38, 62, 81-85, 89, 138-140, 148-
149, 154, 156, 157, 266, 267; in political
philosophy, 59-76; nature of, 24-32, 38-53,
56, 62-63, 66, 69-71, 74, 75, 79, 81, 89, 90,
133-150, 156-159, 194, 195, 199, 206, 210-
212, 215, 263-265; satisfaction, 5-17, 25-
32, 37-43, 46-47, 49-57, 61, 69-75, 132-
135, 138-141, 150, 170, 171, 198, 262, 263;
theory, 3-7, 13-17, 21, 27, 39-47, 50, 51,
54-57, 90, 107-109, 136, 138-156, 158,
204, 228, 249, 270-274; versus societal
needs, 34-57 (*see also* human rights; power,
of human needs; realism, human needs; and
theory, social control)
Networks: international, 232-233; social, 9-
15, 20, 164, 166, 175, 178, 180, 228, 232,
262-263, 270-272
Nixon administration, 180, 181

Paradigms, 4-8, 10, 12, 13, 15, 54, 61, 104-
107, 153, 155, 192, 214, 261 (*see also*
Gandhism, ideology, liberalism, Marxism,
realism, socialism, and state system
ideology)
Participants, 3, 10-16, 105-107, 115, 118, 166,
228; passive, 12, 15; roles, 12, 20, 37, 44,
49, 50, 229, 231, 271, 272 (*see also*
individuals and groups; role defence)
Participation, 20, 37, 38, 48, 53, 56, 57, 94,
99, 103, 171, 270
Personification, 5
Political: philosophy, 36, 156; process, 6, 12;
theory, 4-6, 193
Politics, 26, 106; study of, 9, 10, 32, 52 (*see
also* international politics definition,
international regimes, international
relations, paradigms, and theory)
Power, 14, 17, 40, 52, 53, 70, 94, 105, 189,
190; of human needs, 6, 8, 9, 14, 15, 44, 54,
194-196, 273, 274 (*see also* realism)
Problem solving, 15, 48, 54, 56, 107, 188-
189, 192, 199, 200, 204

Rationality, 49, 67, 75, 166, 214-215 (*see
also* theory, basic assumptions)
Reagan administration, 181, 182, 187, 227;
and U.S./UNESCO relations, 233-249
Realism: human needs, 3, 10, 32, 33, 258-
261, 266, 273, 274; power politics, 5, 10,
12, 166, 189, 195, 214-216
Recognition, 26-32, 38, 43, 44, 49
Relationships, 7, 11, 12, 14, 15, 49, 54, 198,
228-233, 251, 271
Relativity of thought, 270-272
Religion, 43
Revolution, 36, 72, 218-221 (*see also*

deviance)
Role defence, 12, 49, 50, 58

Satyagraha, 76 (*see also* Gandhism)
Security, 28, 43, 44, 49, 136; individual, 8, 26,
222; international, 209-210
Segmentation, 141, 150, 151
Self-actualization, 26, 30-32, 69
Self-emancipation, 120
Self-esteem, 26-31, 40, 79-96
Self-realization, 15, 48, 72
Self-reliance, 12, 108, 109, 119, 158, 159
Self-sufficiency, 30, 73
Social: boundaries, 113, 114, 231, 232 (*see
also* environment); change, 4, 7, 9, 13, 15,
26, 36-43, 47, 52, 55-76, 139-140, 142-143,
152-153, 164-170, 197, 230, 262, 264;
control, 7, 8, 11, 37, 38, 52, 55, 148, 195-
197; process, 12, 13, 43, 44, 46, 54;
science, 4, 10, 12, 13, 15, 41, 42, 61; space,
11, 12, 14, 40, 140-141, 151, 152, 271;
work, 47, 48
Socialism, 46, 61, 86, 146
Socialization, 14, 37, 38, 48, 52, 53, 55, 141,
159
Society, 38, 43, 46, 47, 48, 50, 52, 55, 64, 68,
69, 131; definition, 166; structural change,
196-198 (*see also* world society)
Sociobiology, 50, 51, 55
State, 64, 70, 71, 96; and society, 164-178;
definition, 165; system ideology, 104-108,
112-114, 122-123, 166, 189-192, 213-216,
227, 233, 274
Structural violence, 47, 215, 224
Survival, 8, 28, 32, 38, 83
Systems of action, 10, 54, 171

Technology, 71, 73, 74
Theory: basic assumptions, 3-5, 12-17, 36,
41-44, 55, 104-107, 124, 139-155, 193,
199, 249, 260, 265, 271; building, 3-6, 11-
17, 44-45, 51, 123, 142-144, 151-155, 259-
260, 269-273; international relations, 12-
14, 17, 20, 104-107, 121-125, 151, 189,
225-232, 249, 260, 270-273; power, 8, 189;
social control, 7, 36 (*see also* paradigm)
Third World, 5, 114, 115, 118, 147

United States foreign policy: and Congress,
179; and human needs, 161-186, 162; and
Vietnam, 163, 177, 178; cold war
consensus, 163, 173-176, 186; competing
explanations of, 171-172, 178-182, 182,
186; in UNESCO, 233-253; national
security state, 175-179; post-Vietnam, 177-
181; role of the president, 162, 175, 179;
since World War II, 171-181
United Nations, 158, 190, 191, 206, 216; and

The theme of this book is the power of individual human needs as a source of behavior in international relations. Applying to the study of international relations a concept that has been used in other disciplines to understand human nature, the authors establish that all politics, including global politics, are inextricably tied to processes and outcomes related to the satisfaction or deprivation of human needs. Understanding the dynamics of these needs can therefore contribute to an understanding of the dynamics of world society.

The book begins with a general overview of the human needs approach and its relevance for understanding international relations. Subsequent chapters in the first part discuss the concept of human needs in the context of individual and social behavior. The second part applies the needs approach to the following areas: local individual and community involvement in world affairs, international development, the evolution of foreign policy, conflict resolution, the behavior of international governmental organizations, and international regimes. The final part of the book provides a critical review and evaluation of needs theory, weighing both its weaknesses and potential for contributing to an understanding of world society.

Roger A. Coate is an associate professor of political science in the Department of Government and International Studies at the University of South Carolina. His work focuses on the theory and practice of international organization. He is author of *Global Issue Regimes* (1982) and *Unilaterism, Ideology, and U.S. Foreign Policy: The United States In and Out of UNESCO* (1988).

Jerel A. Rosati is an associate professor of political science in the Department of Government and International Studies at the University of South Carolina. His work focuses on the theory and practice of foreign policy, with an emphasis on political psychology and U.S. foreign policy. During 1986-1987 he was the chair of the International Studies Association's foreign policy analysis section. He is the author of *The Carter Administration's Quest for Global Community: Beliefs and Their Impact on Behavior* (1987).